THE GARAGE

THE GARAGE

Automobility and
Building Innovation
in America's Early
Auto Age

John A. Jakle
and
Keith A. Sculle

The University of Tennessee Press   Knoxville

Copyright © 2013 by The University of Tennessee Press / Knoxville.
All Rights Reserved. Manufactured in the United States of America.
First Edition.

Library of Congress Cataloging-in-Publication Data

Jakle, John A.
The garage: automobility and building innovation in America's early auto age / John A. Jakle and Keith A. Sculle.
    pages cm
Includes bibliographical references and index.
ISBN 978-1-57233-958-3 (pbk.) — ISBN 1-57233-958-6 (pbk.)
   1. Garages—United States—History—20th century.
   2. Service stations—United States—History—20th century.
   3. Architecture—United States—History—20th century.
   I. Sculle, Keith A.
   II. Title.

TL153.J269 2013
728'.98—dc23
2013001468

TO OUR PARENTS:
John D. and Irene A. Jakle
and Flory A. and Helene T. Sculle

CONTENTS

Acknowledgments   ix
Prologue   xi

1. Why the Garage?   1
2. Garage Layout, 1900–1920s   25
3. Garage Layout, 1930–1950s   53
4. Dealerships: Selling and Servicing Automobiles   77
5. The Domestic Garage   117
6. Commercial Garage Evolution through Specialization and Departmentalization   141
7. A Landscape Legacy?   189

Epilogue   213
Notes   225
Index   255

ACKNOWLEDGMENTS

The garage in America's early auto age is a topic long overdue for treatment in book form. Herein we offer an introductory overview of what has remained too long not only a neglected topic but also one very broad in scope. We have many people to thank for helping us bring focus to what follows. Specific people include: in Alaska, Nancy DeWitt of the Fountainhead Antique Auto Museum in Fairbanks; in Arkansas, Francis Kuykendall of South Arkansas Community College in El Dorado and Ralph Wilcox of the Arkansas Historic Preservation Program in Little Rock; in California, Steven Finacom of the Berkeley Historical Society in Berkeley; in Illinois, Fred Delap of the Edgar County Historical Society in Paris, Floyd R. Mansberger of Fever River Research in Springfield, and Thomas Knous in Petersburg; in Indiana, Pete Wagoner; in Iowa, Gary D. Craver of Centerville and Jeff Carr and Barry N. Bennett of the Iowa State Historic Preservation Office in Des Moines; in New Mexico, Kaisa Barthuli, National Park Service, Route 66 Corridor Preservation Program; in New York, Kathleen LaFrank of the New York Historic Preservation Office of Waterford and Greta Slate, the town historian of Alexandria Bay; in Tennessee, Yolanda Reid, Robertson County historian, and Claudette Stager and Dan Brown of the Tennessee Historical Commission in Nashville. Numerous staff members both at the Illinois State Library and the Abraham Lincoln Presidential Library in Springfield and at the General Library at the University of Illinois at Urbana-Champaign in Urbana were exceedingly helpful.

Also deserving thanks are those in numerous communities across the United States apprehended mainly by chance as we stopped to inspect old garage buildings. Too many to list here, selected individuals are noted in the endnotes where specific garages are discussed in the text.

The University of Tennessee Press deserves acknowledgment, this being our third book brought to publication through their offices. Especial thanks go to Kerry Webb, acquisitions editor, who led us through the various stages of review on this manuscript. Being especially broad and heretofore little developed either in the academic or popular writing, our topic at first proved difficult to define, let alone research. It was the UT Press's current director, Scot Danforth, who initially supported our work with the Press on topics related to the history of Roadside America. Special thanks also go to Gene Adair, manuscript editor, and to Thomas Wells, editorial assistant. And we must not forget to thank the various outside readers for their critical remarks that brought important final focus to the manuscript.

PROLOGUE

The Garage. Go to any dictionary and you will find a short and to-the-point definition. Here is what the *American Heritage Dictionary* says: "1. A building or indoor space in which to park or keep a motor vehicle. 2. A commercial establishment where cars are repaired, serviced or parked."[1] The word derives from the French verb *garer,* meaning "to shelter or dock," a usage associated initially with boating. But in the United States the term *garage* was quickly and solely associated with motoring, specifically the storage and servicing of cars and trucks. In this book, we offer a brief history of the garage as a building form in America's evolving auto age. We emphasize the repair or service garage, a commercial venue often, but by no means necessarily, linked with automobile sales. We also treat domestic or private residential garages but mainly as they once related to their commercial cousins.

The commercial garage quickly came to the fore in the business districts of towns and cities everywhere in the United States; their quick spread was obviously tied to the rapid increase in car and truck ownership nationwide. However, unlike cars and trucks and unlike what has come to be called "Roadside America" (dominated initially by businesses such as gasoline stations, motels, and fast-food restaurants), little has been written about the ubiquitous commercial garage. Historians have recently explored such topics as garage labor–management relationships and the relationships between garage mechanics and their customers.[2] Yet the garage as a building form has received scant attention from popular writers.[3] And it has attracted very little academic scholarship. Perhaps its once substantial commonality sustains disinterest? Certainly, that is true of the domestic garage located behind, attached to, or integrated into American houses. Could anything be more common today? But whereas garages in residential areas remain an essential part of life in America, early repair and sales garages, the emphasis of this book, do not. Many are no longer extant, and those that survive do so mainly to house different functions. For whatever reason, the traditional commercial garage as a once historically significant building type has fallen far below the nation's radar.

As authors, we have dealt briefly with commercial garages in previous books, starting with *The Gas Station in America,* where we acknowledged repair garages as predating filling stations as places where gasoline was retailed.[4] We dealt with commercial parking garages in *Lots of Parking: Land Use in a Car Culture,* a book about parking and its impact on urban development in the United States.[5] We briefly treated automobile dealerships in *Motoring: The Highway Experience in America,* a book about car ownership and car use in the United States early in the twentieth century.[6] But none of these explorations produced a complete story. The very early commercial garages, we strongly feel, especially deserve fuller treatment.

Physical diversity certainly characterized early-twentieth-century repair and service garages. Nonetheless, as with any purpose-built construction oriented to a relatively narrow range of activities, profound similarities existed from garage to garage, so much so that a distinctive building type can be said to have emerged forcefully on the American scene. Garages (whether one story or two, whether entered from the front, from behind, and/or along one or more of its sides, or whether located at a street corner or at mid-block) were easily identifiable for what they were. Those identifying characteristics were replicated over and over again in garage buildings built between roughly 1900 and World War II. After the war, profound changes emerged that greatly altered the look of garages, especially those built by auto dealers. Thus, in the following pages, we take the garage story only through the early 1960s.

Of course, relatively small single-story garages were most numerous. Often very plain with little or no architectural decoration, the typical garage usually sported a large entryway out front, a large entrance that gave access to a repair floor behind an office, and/or sales space just inside. The Wyatt garage in Camden, Indiana, is fully representative (fig. PR.1). Constructed in 1913 just east of Camden's business district, the building (after its purchase by Olpha Wyatt) was intended to house a car dealership for Chalmers automobiles; for most of its life, however, it functioned instead as a tire store but one that also sold gasoline, oil, batteries, and assorted car accessories in addition to offering vehicle lubrica-

PROLOGUE

tion and light engine repair. The business, known as the Camden Auto Company, closed in 1980.

Most garages had load-bearing masonry walls (of brick or cinder block usually) or were framed in wood with brick veneer. Some were veneered with stucco. Buildings were usually rectangular in shape with one narrow end facing a street. Usually they were positioned flush with an adjacent sidewalk. Most garages covered parts of or all of several building lots when located in business districts. Arched or flat roofs, supported by either wooden or metal trusses, were usually hidden behind parapets, building walls that were topped off even with or slightly higher than the roofline. More than any other feature, however, it was the truss-supported roof that fully gave garages their overall distinctive look. It was the supporting roof truss that enabled the spanning of large, unencumbered interior spaces so necessary not only for repairing motor vehicles but also for maneuvering them. Most garage trusses, whether of wood or of metal, were prefabricated in a distant factory and shipped to a construction site to be assembled. Pictured here is a truss-supported roof in a garage totally prefabricated, the building being supported by a metal frame filled in with industrial casement windows to complete wall surfaces (fig. PR.2).

Figure PR.1. Restored Wyatt garage, Camden, Indiana, 2010. Authors' photograph.

Figure PR.2. Roof trusses, former garage, Trenton, Illinois, 2010. Authors' photograph.

The differences from garage to garage were many. An important variation was the incised corner, an indentation that sheltered a service drive with gasoline pumps. Figure PR.3 depicts the former 638 Garage in Springfield, Tennessee. Unlike most garages, this structure was not built all at once. The original section on the right was erected around 1900 as a hardware store. To house a growing tire business, a covered service drive was added in 1920, and a large service floor built across the rear. Located at one corner of Springfield's courthouse square, the 638 Garage (named for its original telephone number) became the town's principal auto service center despite the fact that the business never sold cars. The building also housed WSIX, one of Tennessee's early radio stations, established specifically to advertise tires. The call letters stood for "Where Service Is Excellent." The station was eventually moved to Nashville to become one of Tennessee's major radio voices.

Such garage buildings rapidly put a stamp on commercial landscapes. And the reason is not hard to discern. In the early twentieth century, the automobile quickly became a central fixture in American life, as it remains today. The earliest garages helped adapt motor vehicles to traditional small-town main streets and, of course, big-city downtowns, landscapes originally created on the basis

Figure PR.3. The former 638 Garage, Springfield, Tennessee, 2012. Authors' photograph.

of pedestrian and horse-drawn transport as well as railroading. Garages helped incorporate automobiles into established urban fabrics. Automobility vastly extended the individual's geographical range, accelerating one's getting places and greatly enhancing one's sense of well-being accordingly. The car wrought pride of ownership and brought social standing. America's built environments would never be the same. Garages helped sustain all of this.

Very quickly the nation became car dependent. Cities and towns were turned inside out and, of course, vastly expanded spatially through suburban growth. The commercial strip—with roadsides pioneered by gas stations, motels, and fast food restaurants, and then matured through auto dealerships, shopping centers, big box stores, shopping malls, and the like (all in large parking lot surrounds)—came to provide basic infrastructure for urban growth. Older parts of towns and cities were remade in the new suburban image, one fully auto oriented. Old garages were soon redundant, becoming obsolete seemingly as quickly as they had come to the fore. Today, as a fixture of America's built environment, residual garages are very much a dying breed.

We focus on traditional repair and service garages. We treat them as a distinctive building form but also as a distinctive kind of place where form did, in fact, largely follow function. We treat domestic garages but, again, mainly in relationship to storing and even servicing cars very early in the auto age. Storing one's car at home came readily to the fore after 1900 but mainly among the very wealthy, who early on dominated automobile ownership and use. Chauffeurs were employed not only to drive cars but also to do light repair work, first in converted stable houses and eventually in purpose-built domestic garages. But most automobilists found it more practical to store cars in commercial garages at some distance from their homes and to have them serviced there as well. Residential garages, certainly those built after 1910 for America's middling classes, were almost exclusively for convenient car storage.

In chapter 1, we position the commercial garage as an important part of early automobility, exploring its roots in such institutions as blacksmith, carriage, wagon, and bicycle shops as well as machine shops and livery stables. In chapters 2 and 3, we consider changing garage form and layout. We consider as well garage siting and location, including the rise of "automobile rows" in cities. Our emphasis is decidedly on the commonplace, what definitely characterized the nation's small towns and smaller cities. However, we also treat important garage variants, especially the larger garages mainly unique to the nation's largest cities. Auto dealerships, including both sales and service floors, are treated in chapter 4. Initially, cars were sold from factory and factory-branch locations in big cities, although the selling of cars quickly became an adjunct of commercial car storage. Automakers quickly developed dealer networks spanning large portions of the country and, for the largest car manufacturers, spanning the nation as a whole.

The domestic garage is our emphasis in chapter 5, including the maintenance role played by professional chauffeurs in the earliest years of motoring. In chapter 6, we consider evolving car maintenance and repair requirements and how, in general, they impacted garage work through increased specialization and departmentalization, with individual garages focusing more and more on single product lines or single-service activities—tires, batteries, body work, accessory sales, and the like. In chapter 7, we consider changing business practices over time. By 1960, garage work, especially at auto dealerships, was more than ever dominated by the auto manufacturers through franchise agreements. Management practices were increasingly dictated from afar. Thus was the local garage much less the lucrative frontier for small-scale entrepreneurship. Importantly, encouragement toward larger scales of operation brought an end to the popularity of the traditional repair or service garage building. Mainly in the nation's smaller car markets where car ownership and thus car sales were largely stable did the traditional garage remain commonplace. We conclude with a brief epilogue to sharpen focus on the traditional garage building as a residual feature in the contemporary urban landscape.

Entrepreneurship is a consideration throughout our story, but ours is not a business history, nor for that matter is it a history of garage management or of garage labor practices. We are concerned with garage operations primarily as they impacted the use of space and, through space usage, building form. How were motor vehicle repair and service functions housed? What did the garage once symbolize in landscape? To what extent was the garage a distinctive kind of place (at least one defined at the scale of the retail store)? Such questions serve logically to promote our principal objective: establishing the heritage value of residual garages in today's built environments. Our purpose is to foster recognition of the traditional garage as a threatened built-environmental resource worth managing wisely for the future. Our purpose is to excite interest in a landscape feature of historical importance, but one largely overlooked not only by popular and academic writers but, most important, by historic preservationists. It is time to put the garage firmly onto America's radar screen.

1

WHY THE GARAGE?

We begin with a cartoon. It comes from the trade journal *Motor Age* in 1923 (fig. 1.1). Titled "Sunday Afternoon in Gasville," it celebrates automobility's impact (both actual and potential) on the American scene.[1] Hyperbole abounds, but so also does a basic truth: the motorcar had already transfigured the American built environment in fundamental ways. Depicted is a traditional urban landscape evolved in the railroad age; in fact, trains shown at a distance move slowly through it. Buildings line sidewalks and streets, the city very much organized for pedestrians. Indeed, pedestrians abound. But clearly motorcars have proliferated. And, central to the artist's message, so also has auto-oriented retailing.

Traditional business buildings, many of them substantially modified to accommodate automobiles, contain both new and used car dealers, parts and accessory suppliers, tire dealers, battery dealers, and the like. There is a gas station pictured, the only place fully auto oriented—that is, with a driveway and off-street parking. But central to the illustration is another distinctive kind of building: the garage. Flush with sidewalk and street, it sports a large entryway and contains space for maneuvering cars fully under its roof. It is what tended to predate the gas station as "filling station," the predominant place across America where gasoline was once sold. And so also it was the predominant location for storing, servicing, and repairing cars. Early automobility, as depicted here, was not totally without problems. Several car accidents are pictured. There was congestion. Implied is a lack of space to park both on and off the streets. Horses can still be seen, some of them pulling broken-down automobiles in for repair. For our purposes, however, the cartoon places the traditional commercial repair or service garage front and center—a basic landscape fixture in American business districts of the early twentieth century.

Figure 1.1. Cartoon. From *Motor Age* 43 (Apr. 26, 1923): 25.

Automobility's impacts were largely unanticipated. At first the automobile was a toy, a sporting enthusiasm for the affluent classes. It was a very expensive thing to buy, to maintain, to run, and to store. Early motorcars required technical expertise that chauffeurs first brought to the fore; these were technicians only the wealthy could afford. Yet, a new kind of commercial enterprise was aborning.

The garage business evolved out of blacksmithing, carriage and wagon repair, bicycle repair, and machine shop operations—that is, wherever mechanical expertise was at hand. "A great many people are deterred from buying machines because of the lack of repair shops able to do good, responsible work," opined the editors of *Scientific American* in 1902. Perhaps, they suggested, the nation's nascent automobile clubs might organize repair shop networks just as the League of American Wheelmen was attempting to do?[2] Auto clubs did react, but mainly it was the commercial garage pure and simple that came to the fore.

At one such shop in St. Louis, as was reported in the *Horseless Age* in 1904, there were twenty-three cars awaiting repair. They symbolized just how fragile early automobiles really were and thus how frequently they needed repair. All had been involved in a cross-country endurance run from Buffalo, New York, some of them arriving in St. Louis on railroad flat cars. "Five cars experienced ignition troubles, eight had tire troubles, three were delayed by [the] breaking of driving chains, three cars were ditched as a result of skids on bad roads, one car had lubrication trouble, and one was delayed as a result of the motor overheating," the article noted. Along the way, broken axles, broken springs, and flat tires had plagued all the participants.[3] For long-distance travel, such problems were only exaggerated by the nation's poor rural roads, on which cars could be literally shaken apart. Reworking the lyrics of a popular patriotic song, one humorist lamented the costs of such damage:

> My auto 'tis of thee,
> Short cut to poverty,
> Of thee I chant.
> I blew a pile of dough
> On you two years ago,
> Now you refuse to go,
> Or won't or can't.[4]

Until more reliable cars and improved roads appeared, the horse lingered. But the motorcar was clearly in the ascendency. In 1910, two ads appeared in the *Horseless Age* to tell the story:

> Wanted to Exchange. Handsome matched, standard bred, gentlemen's road team, with rubber tired buggy, pole, shafts, single and double harness; all in first-class condition; cost over $1,000.00. Will exchange for a Stanley Locomobile.
>
> For Sale. Stanley Locomobile No. 2, Stanhope Model. Cost $750. In perfect condition. Has been run less than 100 miles, making professional calls. Price $725.[5]

The latter ad was entered by a physician hoping to upgrade to a new and better car. In 1900, there were some 8,000 automobiles registered in the United States, some 458,000 in 1910, and more than 8.1 million in 1920.[6] In 1910, there were some 3.1 million horses "not on farms" in the United States, but only 1.7 million remained in 1920.[7]

In 1918, journalist C. W. Nash in the *Blacksmith and Wheelwright* (soon to become the *Blacksmith and Motor Shop*) wrote: "During the past ten years it has been plainly evident that the days of the horse are numbered. Day by day man has been placing more and more dependence upon his swifter mechanical beast of burden. Gasoline is cheaper than oats and hay."[8] The bottom line was that blacksmiths and wagon and carriage makers needed to adapt their businesses to the growing automobile trade. There was a hefty demand for their skills. Nash continued:

> People buy cars now because they need them; because it will make them more efficient members of society; because it will save time and money. The man without a car cannot successfully compete with the man who operates an automobile. The function of the automobile to-day is an economic one, pure and simple. It is a vital part of our daily life. It has speeded up transit; it has brought thousands of miles of good roads; its has become a necessity.[9]

The Rise of the Garage

Those editing journals oriented to the building trades were hardly silent regarding the automobile's commercial prospects. "The Need for More Garages," read a headline in *National Builder* in 1921. There were over 7.5 million automobiles "in service" in the United States in 1919, the article asserted, with the total expected to climb to 12 million in 1921. Regarding domestic garages, the editors proclaimed, "It will be necessary to add two garages to every three in existence in 1919." But their main advice concerned commercial properties which still tended to be "makeshifts" that were "not suited to the purpose for which they are used." And that, of course, meant new buildings and not just the renovation of old ones:

> The design of the public garage has within a few years, progressed from the remodeled livery stable or store building stage, to its present status of a distinct type of building, in the design of which recognition must be given to the specific character of the problem. This applies to the appearance as well as the planning and construction.[10]

"For housing the automobile, special buildings must be provided. It is not enough to erect a huge shed," another *National Builder* article in 1921 argued. "An automobile cannot be led around like a horse, and so must have the space laid out for proper turning as well as storage. There must be provision for caring and repairing the car, as well as replenishing the necessary air, water, oil and gasoline."[11] Such needs had long been anticipated. As early as 1908, the editors of the *Horseless Age,* although recognizing that the garage business had lagged, predicted a rapid expansion commensurate with growing automobile sales. Local repair shops would proliferate where "repairs beyond the skill of the owner can be promptly made and where supplies can be obtained without delay." They would likely be conducted "as general automobile establishments." Most would carry one or more lines of motorcars and would, besides, conduct a repair, supply, and storage business: "It is to be expected that the majority of these garages will endeavor to get along with a minimum of equipment, yet it is to be noted that where new buildings are specially erected for the purpose the design generally provides for numerous modern features, such as cement floors, vulcanizing plants, battery charging equipment, etc."[12] Already such garages were widespread, especially in the Midwest and West.

Of course, car sales (and truck sales also) were brisk in America's big cities in the years before World War I. "Consider how our cities reflect the influence of the motor car," observed journalist C. W. Nash. "Suburban towns have sprung up miles from the business centers, their inhabitants depending almost entirely on automobiles." But it was in the prosperous farm belts with their thriving small towns that auto ownership grew most rapidly. The American farmer was breaking loose the bindings of rural isolation: "He can drive to town in the evening after his day's work is done. When he returns home at night there is no horse to unhitch; he merely runs his car into his garage and it is there in the morning. He covers more territory, sees how other successful men are conducting their affairs, and runs his farm as a business man runs his establishment." But above all, Nash wrote, the automobile has "lent to farm life by banishing loneliness."[13]

As *Automotive Industries* reported, about 55 percent of all the motor vehicles in use in 1926 were registered in towns of less than 10,000 population. As for garages, the four largest automobile manufacturers of low-priced cars had more than 70 percent of their dealers in such places. In 1926, some 57 percent of all car sales had been in small towns as opposed to only 8 percent in cities of more than 500,000 population.[14] Car ownership was also much higher in California than in other states, but the map of auto registrations showed that it was very much the nation's corn belt and southern wheat belt states that led the way (fig. 1.2).[15] And

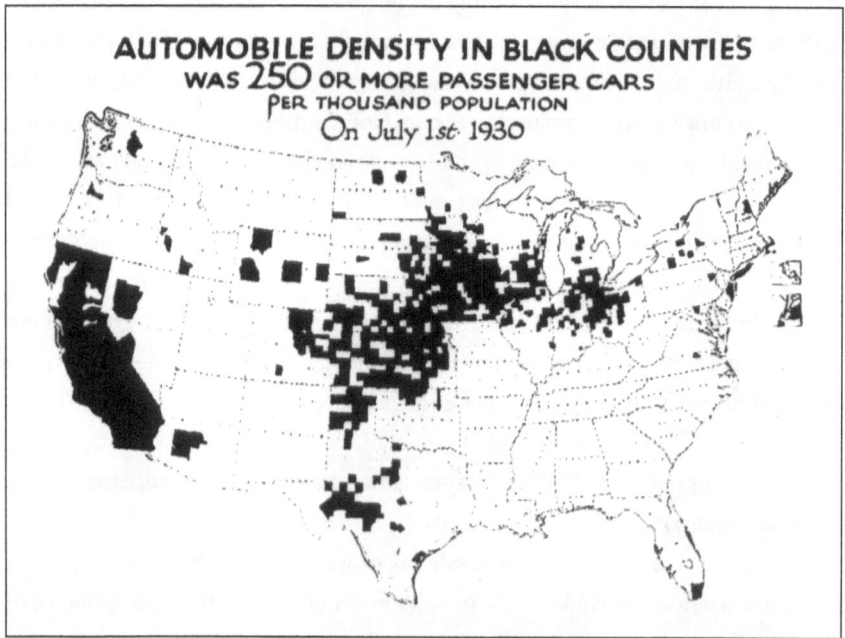

Figure 1.2. Counties with 250 or more passenger cars, July 1, 1930. From *Automobile Topics* 101 (Jan. 10, 1931): 824.

it was in the Middle West, it might be surmised, that commercial garages most proliferated. The "champion motor car commonwealth," reported W. E. Williams in 1911, was not New York or even New Jersey. It was most likely Kansas. Pawnee County, with some 9,000 inhabitants, for example, led the nation in car registrations with one car per 30 persons. Accordingly, Kansas City, Missouri, was the third largest distributing center for motor vehicles in the nation.[16]

In 1915, however, statistics on the number of garages from state to state actually gave New York the lead (1,661), with Pennsylvania second (1,138) and Illinois third (1,166). In total, there were 17,353 garages nationally. Kansas was well down the list with only 565. When dealers, repair shops, supply stores, and charging stations were added in, New York (with 2,596) again led, followed by Illinois (1,881), Michigan (1,175), Pennsylvania (1,727), and Iowa (1,646). California (1,594) came in eighth (table 1.1).[17] Unfortunately, business definitions varied from one survey to another, as well as from decade to decade in U.S. Census Bureau reporting. In 1927, *Automotive Abstracts* reported 51,715 "public garages" nationally. This figure contrasted with the 51,276 car dealers, the 23,842 truck dealers, and the 83,758 service stations and repair shops also enumerated. Much double counting was involved since a large majority of the garages in the United States were, in fact, all three. In addition, "accessory and supply stores" were reported to number 66,584.[18] Irrespective of the definitions used, it was clear that the garage had indeed become most significant numerically—by whatever name.

In 1917, *Automobile Topics* had reported an estimated 25,500 garages in the United States along with 13,500 "repair shops," 12,000 vulcanizers, 2,550 automobile supply houses, and 282 "jobbers." The average capital invested per proprietor was estimated to be $4,000. The number of employees per shop averaged five. Wages paid overall were estimated at some $184 million. Car dealers were said to number some 27,000. Along with the car manufacturers and the makers of auto parts and accessories, the automobile business already tallied up as the nation's third largest industry.[19]

In 1928, the *Accessory and Garage Journal* estimated that some 4 million people were employed in automotive industries outside automobile manufacturing and sales itself: 300,000 in parts and accessory factories; 95,000 in tire factories; 160,000 selling accessories, tires, and parts; 125,000 working in garages; and 300,000 working in other repair shops. "The average purchases of parts, supplies, replacement tires, gas, oils and service labor had jumped from $219 per car in 1926 to

Dealers, Garages, Supply, Repair and Charging Stations in the United States, etc.

States	Dealers	Garages	Repair Shops	Supply Dealers	Charging Stations	Total
Alabama	89	75	22	12	12	155
Arizona	64	56	7	7	5	97
Arkansas	80	68	14	3	5	126
California	895	1,027	96	69	101	1,594
Colorado	188	243	20	10	24	335
Connecticut	280	213	54	21	23	506
Delaware	44	50	5	2	3	68
District of Columbia	46	46	20	12	6	111
Florida	151	149	16	2	12	235
Georgia	179	201	25	9	14	227
Idaho	69	61	1	1	5	95
Illinois	1,254	1,166	93	52	144	1,881
Indiana	646	597	68	19	67	1,007
Iowa	1,334	1,077	84	19	84	1,646
Kansas	564	565	40	12	37	934
Kentucky	169	135	7	3	14	217
Louisiana	76	55	7	3	12	104
Maine	184	196	16	4	12	299
Maryland	153	160	23	10	12	251
Massachusetts	597	704	110	62	80	1,175
Michigan	540	582	46	38	53	905
Minnesota	926	625	34	27	24	1,161
Mississippi	66	59	10	3	7	102
Missouri	618	449	100	36	40	925
Montana	157	124	13	4	9	211
Nebraska	548	430	30	11	28	705
Nevada	33	34	6	1	2	59
New Hampshire	127	152	15	3	13	213
New Jersey	432	714	48	34	53	936
New Mexico	57	49	1	1	2	82
New York	1,314	1,661	196	156	138	2,596
North Carolina	151	144	14	3	10	216
North Dakota	313	214	14	1	9	413
Ohio	979	839	92	58	110	1,479
Oklahoma	210	178	14	12	9	314
Oregon	159	165	11	17	14	253
Pennsylvania	1,062	1,138	73	110	105	1,727
Rhode Island	80	114	12	38	8	208
South Carolina	83	89	4	8	3	134
South Dakota	318	213	2	17	10	400
Tennessee	124	95	11	16	8	188
Texas	457	367	33	55	45	713
Utah	49	37	3	9	5	76
Vermont	120	112	3	13	3	181
Virginia	160	119	10	14	10	218
Washington	251	227	21	34	20	289
West Virginia	133	97	3	7	16	168
Wisconsin	683	558	15	52	50	887
Wyoming	41	33	None	6	4	59
West Indies	13	10	None	1	None	15
Canada	524	430	26	29	68	691
Mexico	9	9	None	None	2	12
Hawaii	4	5	None	None	3	5
Total	17,903	17,016	1,787	947	1,553	27,702

Table 1.1. From "2,070,903 Cars in United States," *Automobile* 33 (Aug. 12, 1915): 272.

$229 in 1927," the *Journal* reported. "Of this amount $41 was for parts and supplies, $40 for tires, $101 for gas and oil and $47 for service labor. The staggering total of $5,317,000,000 had been spent for the above!"[20] This total, however, included sales at gasoline stations as well as sales at garages and accessory stores. In 1930, the number employed in auto manufacturing stood at approximately 325,000, and those in car sales at 300,000.[21]

In 1929, the U.S. Bureau of the Census reported "garages and repair shops" as numbering 60,627 nationwide. Additionally, there were 8,142 tire stores; 7,762 accessory stores with tires and batteries; 6,409 battery, ignition, and brake repair shops; 3,379 body, fender, and paint shops; and 728 radiator shops. New car dealers numbered 40,797, while used car dealers numbered 3,097. Or course, there was once again much overlap in how businesses were categorized. "Filling stations" were tabulated in three categories: those selling only gas and oil (52,727), those additionally selling tires and accessories (25,775), and those selling (presumably in addition) "other merchandise" (42,011). However, when all retailing within the so-called auto group was added up, including "parking stations," auto dealers, and auto supply houses, the total number of business establishments said to be "automobile-focused" numbered 257,685. Involved were some 242,800 proprietors, employing some 625,333 persons full time and 57,644 part time.[22]

The 1930 U.S. Census of Population additionally enumerated retail chains. For new car dealers there were 166 chains with 1,290 stores; for used car dealers 6 chains with 33 stores; and for accessory, tire, and battery dealers 126 chains with 2,048 stores. Filling-station chains numbered 804 with 30,038 stores. In contrast, repair garage chains numbered 18 with 113 stores.[23] The numbers are not surprising. The rise of the gas station figured prominently in chain store development. The garage figured hardly at all. Indeed, the gas station's rise had diverted auto-oriented retail trade from traditional garages and was continuing to do so very rapidly.

Nonetheless, in 1950, there were still some 71,199 "independent auto repair shops" in the United States, many of them, we suspect, still housed in traditional garage buildings. There was, in other words, one repair shop for every 678 motor vehicles registered in the United States. At the same time, there were 46,251 car and truck dealers in the nation, one for every 1,044 motor vehicles registered.[24] One out of every five retail dollars spent in the United States in 1950 went for automotive products and services, according to *Automotive Abstracts*. Involved, it reported, were 60,147 general repair garages. Other totals included top and body repair shops (10,425); radiator repair shops (2,844); paint shops (2,567); tire repair stores (1955); battery and ignition shops (1,890); wheel, axle, and spring repair shops (1,197); glass shops (1,079); and brake repair shops (751).[25] Interestingly, small-town America continued to claim a large share of this auto-oriented retail activity. Regarding new car sales, some 36 percent of all dealers as late as 1947 were in places with less than ten thousand people. They accounted for 65 percent of all motor vehicle sales.[26]

Beginnings

As we noted, the word "garage" derives from the French verb *garer*, meaning "to shelter." Many words descriptive of early motoring, including the word *automobile* itself, were adopted from the French, a reminder that motoring was something that matured initially in Europe and not in the United States. In North America, the term *garage* was first applied to buildings specifically built to house or store cars. Not until the second decade of the twentieth century were automobiles commonly stored overnight at one's residence. Only the rich could afford to do so in the earliest years of motoring. In the era of open motorcars, when motoring was primarily a warm-weather activity, cars in northern climes were stored mainly in commercial garages, usually up on blocks during winter months. Automobile repair and sales quickly became adjuncts of garage storage. Accordingly, the term *garage* became an umbrella word for buildings that housed repair and sales activities as well as parking functions. With the coming of enclosed cars after 1920, many storage garages were converted exclusively to automobile repair and sales. Many began specializing in tire, battery, or accessory sales. Therein lay much of the difficulty observed in statistical reporting. The term *garage* came to be applied to a wide range of automobile-oriented activities.

Confusion was also introduced through the diversity of garage origins. Garages, like every other kind of business, had their commercial precedents. In the auto trade, precedents were tied mainly to the use of horses: blacksmith shops, carriage and wagon shops, and livery stables. But the garage business logically attracted skilled mechanics from other lines of work. Indeed, whole machine shops were reoriented to automobile repair, especially those that had specialized previously in gasoline engine work. Many carriage makers turned to fabricating and/or repairing car bodies or car tops, being expert at metal bending or fabricating with wood and canvas. Bicycle shops were very important, since many of the earliest automobiles were little more than light "quadri-cycles," and thus very much bicycle-like. Above all, however, it was car storage that led the way.

STORAGE GARAGES

Cars could be stored at home, and many affluent automobilists did exactly that, converting stable houses or building new structures, in many instances complete with repair floors and quarters for a live-in chauffeur. But use of commercial storage facilities located in or near a city's downtown or along or near a small town's main street was necessarily more common among the less well-to-do.[27] There, cars could be readily refueled (or, in the case of electric vehicles, batteries recharged), with the hazard of fire greatly reduced in contrast with home garaging. There, cars could be repaired as well as winterized, the putting up on blocks a means of safeguarding fragile tires. Early automobiles needed constant maintenance and repair, requiring skills well beyond that of most car owners. True, the chauffeur or professional driver was one answer. The chauffeur was a servant who could not only drive but also do car repairs or oversee a car's repair by others.

The commercial garage quickly became the focus of everything automotive beyond car manufacture itself, although in some instances, garage mechanics additionally performed final assembly work using "car kits" delivered by manufacturers. Early advertisements, such as the one pictured here, testified to what garage owners thought their services should be (fig. 1.3). A 1900 news item in the *Horseless Age* further illustrates this development:

> Homan & Schulz erected a two-story and basement building at 2642 Broadway, New York, for the sale, storage and repair of automobiles. The building is being put up especially for the purpose, and will contain vaults for gasoline, electrical appliances for charging batteries, complete machine shop, salesroom, lockers, ladies room, etc. The storage room will have a capacity for 75 carriages.[28]

Typically, storage rooms involved large barn-like interiors, with roofs supported by wooden or metal trusses (fig. 1.4). In 1920, big-city garages had become quite large, Cleveland's Euclid Square Garage, for example, claiming storage capacity for some 2,500 automobiles (fig. 1.5).

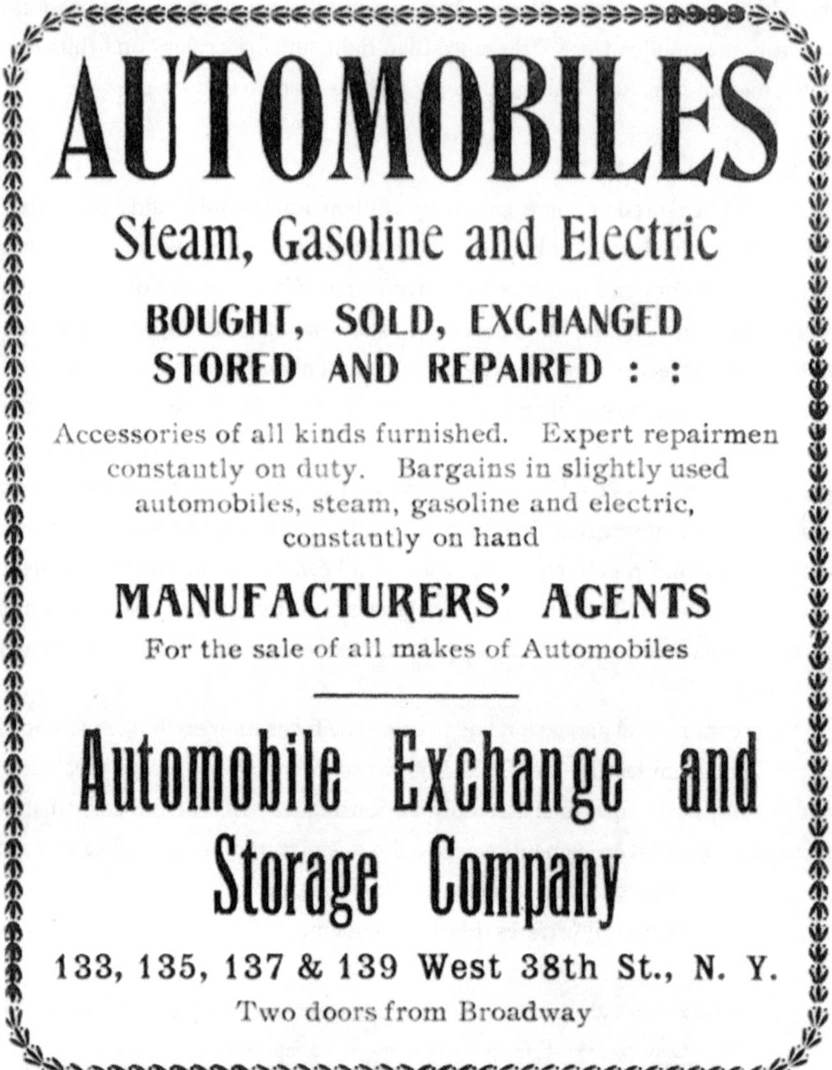

AUTOMOBILES

Steam, Gasoline and Electric

BOUGHT, SOLD, EXCHANGED STORED AND REPAIRED : :

Accessories of all kinds furnished. Expert repairmen constantly on duty. Bargains in slightly used automobiles, steam, gasoline and electric, constantly on hand

MANUFACTURERS' AGENTS
For the sale of all makes of Automobiles

Automobile Exchange and Storage Company

133, 135, 137 & 139 West 38th St., N. Y.

Two doors from Broadway

Figure 1.3. Advertisement for the Automobile Exchange and Storage Company. From *Horseless Age* 7 (Mar. 27, 1901): 5.

The rise after 1910 of mass automobility involved less expensive but, nonetheless, better engineered and constructed cars. It fostered the popularity of domestic garages. At-home car storage at last became practical. Commercial storage garages, accordingly, turned more and more to daily commuter parking and, of course, car servicing. By the late 1920s, their advertisements were emphasizing light maintenance. "Park you car here by hour, by day, night, week,

Figure 1.4. Interior view of the Tudor Garage, Chicago, Illinois. From "Big Buildings Bureau," *National Builder* 59 (Mar. 1917): 51.

month or Season," read a 1927 ad for Detroit's Grand Circus Garage. Amenities and services, as listed in the ad, included double ramps, roomy car spaces, passenger elevators, waiting room, rest rooms, battery recharging, "oiling and doping," gasoline sales, tire repair, car washing, and vacuum cleaning.[29]

Big-city automobile clubs reoriented their garages similarly; some, like service and repair garages in general, sold one or more brands of gasoline.[30] This was evident, for instance, in signs advertising the garage of the Hoosier Motor Club, which were systematically placed along Indiana highways outward from Indianapolis (fig. 1.6). Trade journals encouraged garage proprietors to sell gasoline and related products as a matter of survival. "Look it squarely in the face," advised one. "Suppose, as is liable to happen, that some oil company decided to open gasoline stations like Childs restaurants, or United Cigars all over town, where would the garage man 'get off'?"[31] That, of course, is exactly what happened: chains of gas stations evolved to substantially syphon off the gasoline trade, thus leaving many a garage proprietor very much in the lurch.

So also did storage garages foster car sales, but at first rarely by the garage management itself. Early on, it was common for sales agents, sometimes

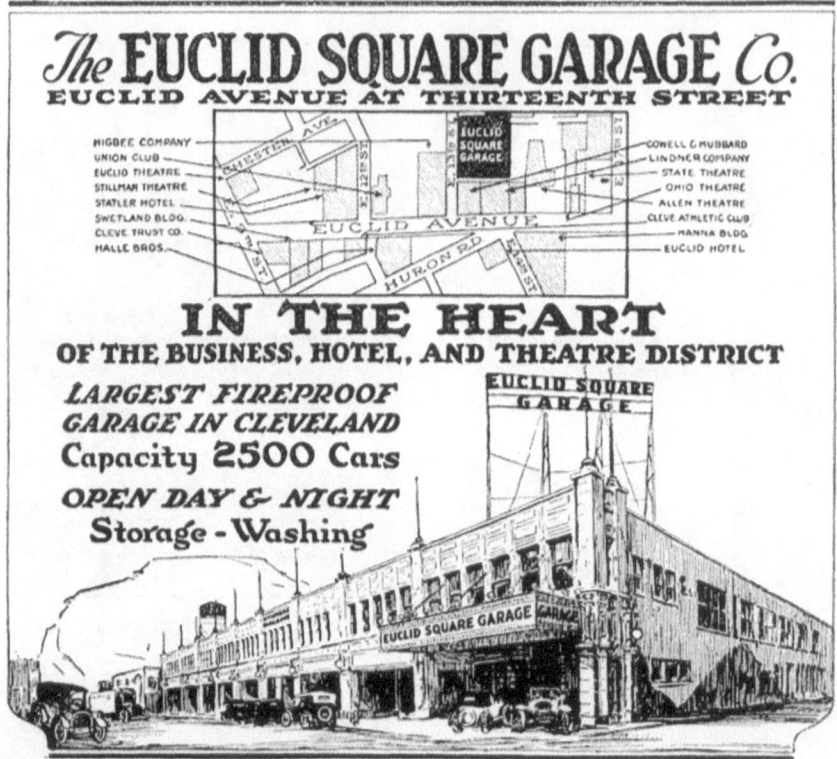

Figure 1.5. Advertisement for the Euclid Square Garage Company. From *Ohio Motorist* 12 (Oct. 1920): 46.

representing several automobile manufacturers, to rent space in a garage from which to conduct business. As most manufacturers distributed their vehicles through factory branches in large cities, a sales agent in a small town or city, for example, might interest customers with a demonstrator vehicle housed locally, make a sale, and then take responsibility for local delivery. Rented garage space would be used for final tune-up (and, of course, final touch-up) and used as well to make necessary adjustments once the customer took ownership. For new car owners, it was at the garage that driving lessons began.

Thus, at the very beginning, car repair and car sales were variously combined in what remained primarily storage garages. After 1910, however, following the lead of the Ford Motor Company and General Motors, most manufacturers had come to require of their dealers self-standing sales and service buildings, facilities exclusively dedicated to that company's name plates. The choice of which make of car to sell and the question of whether or not that brand would thrive—

Figure 1.6. "Hoosier Motor Club's Road Markers," *Hoosier Motorist* 5 (Jan. 1917): 25.

and thus make a required garage investment worthwhile—were something every would-be car dealer faced. The fact is that the vast majority of the car companies failed and most only after a few years of operation. In 1919, 230 companies assembled automobiles in the United States. By the end of 1921, there were 88, and by the end of 1924 only 59.[32] Gone was the Chalmers brand along with names like Winton and Stanley, firms whose products once led the industry. Many newly built dealer garages quickly became independent repair garages.

Livery Stables

Storage garages were much like livery stables. Indeed, former horse-era livery barns and stables were readily reoriented to the automobile business, especially in smaller cities and towns where the term "auto livery" became quite popular (fig. 1.7). As the *Horseless Age* reported as early as 1899:

> A number of enterprising livery stable keepers in different parts of the country are preparing to take charge of automobiles by the week or month. They have installed electric plants for charging batteries, secured the services of mechanics competent to care for and repair the different classes of vehicles, and are already finding customers. That they will find more and more customers as the industry progresses goes without saying, and it is the early bird that catches the worm. Later they will feel a demand for expert motormen, just as they now do for coachmen.[33]

In the horse era, livery stables rented horses to traveling salesmen who arrived in a city or a town by train. They also stored the horse, equipment, and vehicle of the town doctor, and of the town grocer. Many such functions would continue into the auto age.

Figure 1.7. Auto livery in Larned, Kansas. From "The Kansas Farmer's Motor Cars," *Motor* 32 (June 1911): 37.

By 1920, converted livery stables had become quite passé, except in the smallest of places and especially in the less-developed sections of the country. As one journalist observed:

> So many of the Southern service stations are old livery barns and present anything but an inviting appearance. The light is bad and much of the repair work is carried on right in the entrance, where

> most of the light comes through a big door. The result is cars are parked in front of the building, and the mechanics have to walk back and forth from cars to building for tools and parts, losing much time, to say nothing of the way in which the sidewalk, door jambs, etc., are besmeared with grease and dirt.

Dirt floors tended to prevail, the reporter said. Accumulated signs festooned walls inside and out. Workbenches were crudely made and cluttered. Parts were poorly stored. Telephones were missing.[34] No wonder the petroleum companies wanted more control over how their gasoline brands were sold.

BLACKSMITHS

As horses declined in number, blacksmiths, especially those whose principal enterprise was horse-shoeing, necessarily looked for new business in the automotive field.[35] The transition was a natural one, although not necessarily easily accomplished. "The motor vehicle is but the development of the horse-drawn carriage in mechanical form," opined the editors of the *Blacksmith and Wheelwright* in 1910. Skills that applied to one were potentially transferable to the other, but new and heavier tools (especially power tools) were usually necessary, not to mention new knowledge, especially in regard to electrical, steam, and internal-combustion gasoline engines. Right from the first automobile's appearance in a locality, blacksmiths would regularly be called upon to repair broken springs, straighten bent axles, and perform repairs the average automobile repairman was not capable of doing "because of lack of knowledge concerning metals."[36]

Invariably, the transition to full-scale auto repair was incremental, usually starting with metal bending or forging. Often the transition was out of pure necessity. "I do all kinds of work," wrote Elmer Roberts, an Indiana shop operator in the *American Blacksmith*, "such as general blacksmithing work, wood work, automobile work, tinning and, in fact, anything that comes along and I find that is something that can keep a man busy."[37] Indeed, blacksmiths generally found that auto repair work was something that first just "came along." As another shop owner reported: "We were pushed into automobile work by our customers. At first we repaired springs, straightened out axles, attached fenders, ironed bodies for tops, installed tire holders, shock absorbers, fuel tanks, etc., work that was sent to us by repair shops." Successfully contracting to do bodywork on police cars and fire trucks for town government, he had hired a mechanic and then several assistants. And thus eventually he outgrew his space, leading to a new one-story brick building containing a repair shop, office, and storage space for oil, gasoline, and grease. A gasoline pump was installed out front at the curb.[38]

Similar stories were told all across the country as trade journal cartoons testified (fig. 1.8). Transition to auto repair is fully evidenced by the receipt for services rendered by blacksmith John Teufel in an Illinois small town in 1923 (fig. 1.9). And a verse originally printed in the *Chicago Post* read:

Figure 1.8. Cartoon. From *American Blacksmith* 15 (Dec. 1915): 54.

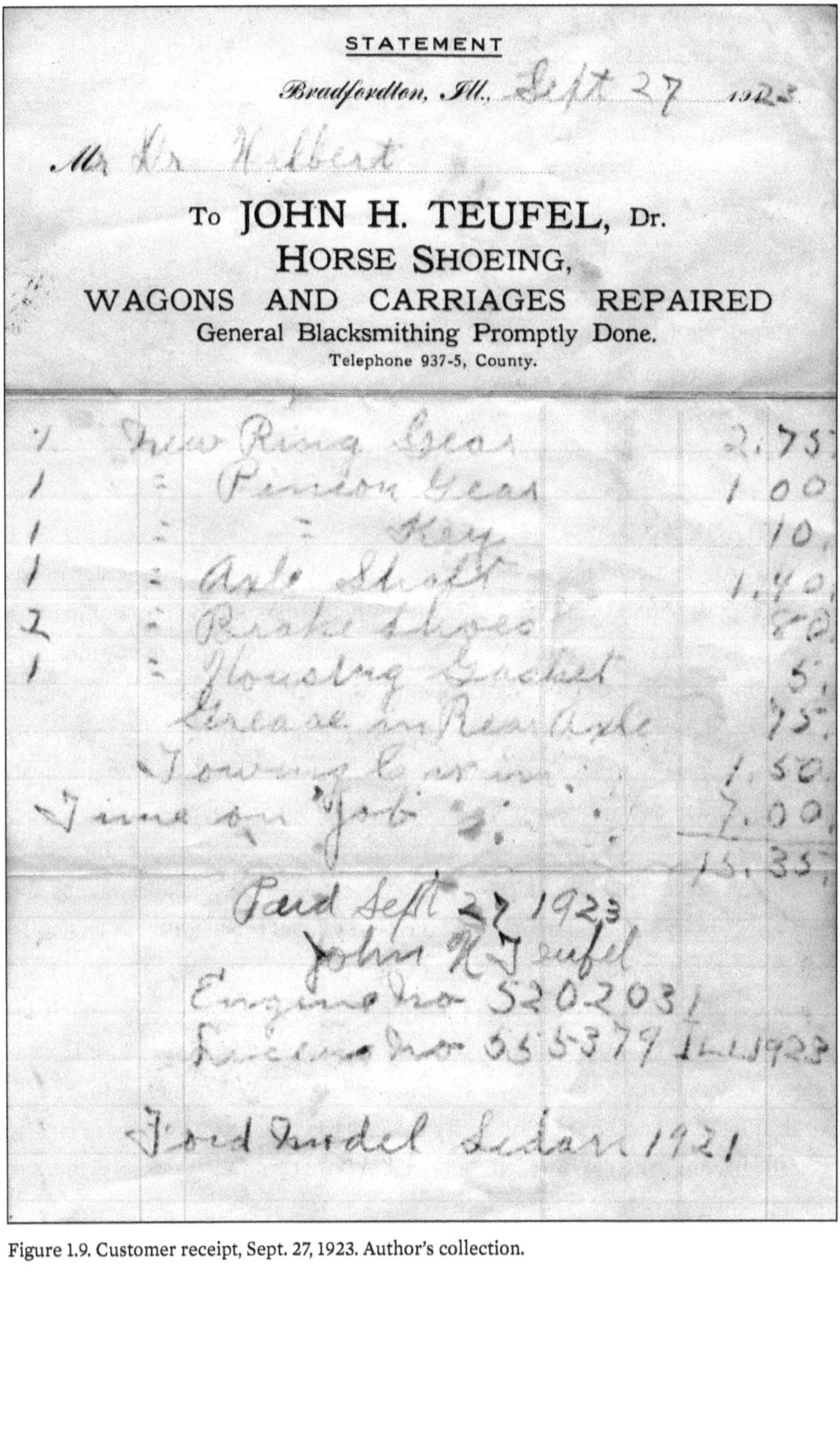

STATEMENT

Bradfordton, Ill., Sept 27 1923

Mr Dr Hilbert

To **JOHN H. TEUFEL**, Dr.
HORSE SHOEING,
WAGONS AND CARRIAGES REPAIRED
General Blacksmithing Promptly Done.
Telephone 937-5, County.

Qty	Item	Amount
1	New Ring Gear	2.75
1	" Pinion Gear	1.00
1	" " Key	.10
1	" Axle Shaft	1.40
2	" Brake Shoes	.80
1	" Housing Gasket	.05
	Grease in Rear Axle	.75
	Towing Car in	1.50
	Time on Job	7.00
		15.35

Paid Sept 27 1923
John H Teufel
Engine No 520203/
License No 555379 Ill 1923

Ford Model Sedan 1921

Figure 1.9. Customer receipt, Sept. 27, 1923. Author's collection.

Under a costly canopy
The village blacksmith sits;
Before him is a touring car
Broken to little bits,
And owner, and the chauffeur too,
Have almost lost their wits.
The village blacksmith smiles with glee.
As he lights his fat cigar,
He tells his helpers what to do
To straighten up the car,
And the owner, and the chauffeur too,
Stand humbly where they are.[39]

Carriage and Wagon Shops

Local wagon and carriage shops supplied most of the nation's vehicular needs up through the final decades of the nineteenth century, but then big companies, like the Studebaker Corporation of South Bend, Indiana, began to dominate the national market, franchising the handling of their vehicles to local wagon and carriage dealers. The Studebaker Brothers were originally blacksmiths. By 1900, from locality to locality, there were numerous carriage and wagon dealers whose business was mainly to sell the vehicles of Studebaker and the other large manufacturers. Carriage and wagon shops quickly fell under the grip of the automobile's rapid rise. In 1904, there were 4,982 firms making wagons and carriages, but by 1921, that figure had fallen to 897, and to 88 in 1929.[40] That such decline was inevitable could, of course, be denied. "Wagon makers say it's a Fad," headlined one article in *The Hub,* a trade journal for the horse-drawn vehicle industry, as late as 1910. Joy Riders and the great number of fatalities caused by automobiles would surely rejuvenate the carriage and wagon business.[41] Indeed, in rural America, considerable animosity toward "sky-hooting" motorists (largely wealthy urbanites) still remained. But even in farm country, as statistics proved, automobile ownership was soaring.

Editors of *The Hub* were not totally unsympathetic to motoring, and, indeed, they were already encouraging wagon and carriage makers to make the transition into one or another automotive field. "The carriage builders, being associated with vehicles, their style and their form of construction are especially well fitted to handle the self-propelled vehicle," they wrote.[42] Perhaps it would not be engine repair, or even heavy bodywork, that would entice them. Perhaps it would be automobile "trimming." One journalist advised, "There is one branch of the automobile business which falls rightfully to the lot of the concern which has been specializing in buggy and carriage trimming, and that is the repair of tops and curtains and upholstery." Let the mechanic handle the grinding of valves, the cleaning of cylinders, or the replacement of brake drums. Let the carriage trimmer replace broken side curtains, damaged convertible tops, or torn upholstery.[43] Wagon and carriage makers might manufacture trailers to be pulled behind automobiles and trucks.[44]

More important, perhaps, wagon and carriage dealers were hotly sought after as auto dealers. In 1909, the American Motor Car Manufacturer's Association announced that would it again extend special invitations to carriage dealers to attend the New York City Auto Show: "It was proved last year that carriage dealers throughout the country are well situated to act as automobile agents."[45] If one found it difficult to fight them, then one could join them.

Machine Shops

Machine shops came in all varieties and in all sizes. Perhaps it was inappropriate to think of them, as with the garage business, as a single category of enterprise unto themselves. Machine shops were organized around power tools, whether for cutting and turning wood or for cutting, bending, or forging metal (fig. 1.10). The Rutland Machine and Automobile Company of Rutland, Vermont, was located some two blocks from the parent Rutland Carriage Company (fig. 1.11). It occupied two former industrial buildings adjacent to one another—a small frame structure and a larger brick building. On the first floor of the brick structure, and to the right of the main door, were a large office and an even larger stock room for both automobile and bicycle accessories, the bicycle shop being next door. Beyond and to the left of the main entry was space reserved for car storage. The second floor was equipped for tire repair and battery charging, containing, as it did, "machine tools, a pit, a steam vulcanizer for tires, and a mercury arc rectifier for charging storage batteries."[46] On the third floor was a paint shop. Floors in the main building were serviced by elevator. The company sold Franklin and Reo motorcars.

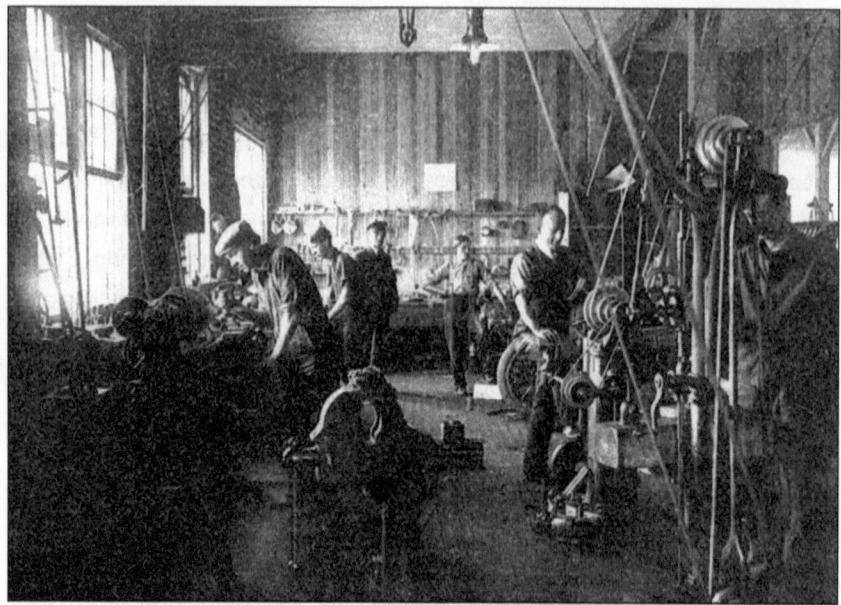

Figure 1.10. Machine shop of the Gray Auto Company, Denver, Colorado. From "Denver Garages," *Horseless Age* 17 (May 30, 1906): 803.

BICYCLE SHOPS

The coming of the automobile both aided and abetted the bicycle business. From bicycle sales of some 1.1 million in 1899, demand steadily fell off as motorcars came to the fore. In 1919, 479,000 bicycles were being produced, but by 1929, that number had fallen to 308,000.[47] What sustained the industry, of course, was the continued popularity of the bicycle for sport and recreation. Many automobile manufacturers got their start in the bicycle business, among them Albert Pope, the nation's largest bicycle maker, who founded the League of American Wheelmen in the 1880s. The league was, in the nineteenth century, the nation's most active lobby group for rural highway improvement. So also had John and Horace Dodge made bicycles in their Detroit machine shop before producing engines and auto parts for Ransom Olds and then Henry Ford. John N. Willys owned a chain of bicycle stores before turning to the manufacture of spark plugs and motorcars in Toledo.[48]

Bicycle manufacturing brought numerous innovations to the automotive field, including use of tubular steel frames, chain-and-sprocket drive mechanisms, and metal rims and steel spokes on pneumatic tire mounts. From bicycle

Figure 1.11. Rutland Machine and Automobile Company, Rutland, Vermont. From "Some Vermont Garages," *Horseless Age* 25 (Feb. 2, 1910): 199.

manufacturing came electric welding, gear cutting, and drop-forging technologies.[49] Much early experimenting with motorized vehicles took place in bicycle shops, including, for example, the perfection of the early motorcycle. However, all was not progress. The *Horseless Age* editorialized in 1900: "The primary object of the bicycle mechanic who undertakes to construct a motor carriage seems to be to build the lightest machine that will hang together until it is sold.... Such flimsy toys are a detriment to the industry."[50]

For the typical bicycle shop, any commercial storefront would do. Indeed, from a distance, the typical shop differed little in appearance from any other retail store, lined up as they were mainly in city downtown business districts or along small-town main streets shoulder to shoulder in business blocks. Thus, the bicycle shop made little contribution to what Americans would come to consider a garage, mainly because of its small size, as the handling of bicycles did not require an undue amount of space. However, it is important to note that, like carriage and wagon dealers, bicycle shop proprietors were also vigorously recruited by automobile manufacturers and their wholesalers to become auto dealers.

* * *

Like every other business formed in the early twentieth century, automobile sales and service had nineteenth-century precedents, precursors largely having to do with horse-drawn transport but also with bicycling. Much of it was ad hoc, with individual entrepreneurs reacting to market opportunities predicated on past business experience, whether shoeing horses, repairing wagons, turning wood, or cutting metal. Automobiles, however, made novel demands on work spaces. Space had to be large enough to handle turning vehicles that were mechanically powered and thus moving at relatively high speeds. Doors had to be wide. Somehow mechanics had to be able to get under cars by tilting them, lifting them, or crawling into pits beneath them. Lifts for heavy components like engine blocks were needed. Work floors were needed to accommodate large shop equipment such as electrically powered presses, lathes, and drills. Stationary steam engines were common well into the age of electric motors. And they demanded space. The sale of automobiles made its own special demands—well-lit display floors, for example. Contractors and even architects were quickly called to design special-purpose buildings fully appropriate to the automobile business. Any building might be utilized when garages were first established. But demand quickly arose nationwide for distinctive prototype structures: buildings that not only functioned as commercial garages but fully looked like them as well.

Unfortunately, we will never know exactly how many garages there were at any one time early in the twentieth century. Trade journal statistics were, as we have said, never totally reliable, many of these numbers being little better than estimates. Bureau of the Census reportage was little better, given the varying business definitions used from census to census, and from one kind of census to another. What we can be sure of, however, is that something Americans called a garage (and, as often as not, something actually signed as a "garage" across its front facade) was vital to automobility's rapid rise. Associated with car storage initially, the idea rapidly took on car repair and car sales implications. The garage idea evolved out of what had come before. But it was also a new kind of place born very much out of necessity. Owning and operating an automobile made demands that motorists typically could not and would not handle themselves. Their needs had to be met commercially. Of course, the garage was something that would change constantly in response to rapidly improving automobile technology.

2

GARAGE LAYOUT AND LOCATION, 1900–1920S

Few of the very earliest garages were purpose-built as new structures. Car storage and repair functions were housed in preexisting buildings where previous business activities were either displaced or added to, whether a livery stable, carriage or wagon shop, or blacksmith shop. With the automobile's space demands, larger buildings that had formerly housed industrial, wholesale, and even retail activities were modified for garage use. Where car repair was not an issue, traditional storefronts sufficed as sales floors, although by 1910 most car dealers found themselves by necessity either in the repair business or closely associated with a repair shop. Of course, before 1910 many (if not most) car dealers operated out of storage garages, leasing space as independent businesses.

In general, the earliest garage operations fit easily into existing urban fabrics, thus reinforcing traditional downtown and Main Street business districts. Certainly building conversion often occurred, but when a totally new structure was erected, it was as often as not sited on a side street at the edge of a business district or along a back alley. With time, this would change. After 1910, the building of new garages became the order of the day. Increasingly, such structures replaced buildings in locations that were highly visible and accessible to the public—that is, along a town or city's main thoroughfare. They helped pioneer the rise of commercial strips along major streets leading into and out of downtowns. New garages were oriented increasingly to peripheral highways.

Garages in Converted Buildings

We begin this chapter with a 1910 photograph of the Early Motor Car Company of Columbus, Ohio (fig. 2.1). How appropriate the name is for our purposes. The firm, which sold an array of automobiles (Babcock Electric, Rambler, Patterson, Whiting, Warren-Detroit, and Parry brands), occupied what had previously been a small department store. The large show windows were retained and used to display tires and accessories, although cars for sale on the sales floor were also quite visible from the sidewalk outside. The basement was converted to a repair shop and washing floor. As was typical of early dealerships, the firm only serviced the cars that it sold, with the company holding exclusive territorial rights to sell and service cars across a dozen or so counties of central Ohio. Gasoline was stored in tanks at the rear of the building, drawn by hand pump into small containers and then poured into auto gas tanks. A battery-charging station for electric vehicles was also located in the basement.[1] Many such storefront garages remained well into the 1920s, as, for example, W. H. Wood's Franklin dealership in West Chester, Pennsylvania, pictured in an advertising postcard (fig. 2.2).

Figure 2.1. The Early Motor Car Company salesroom, Columbus, Ohio, 1910. From "Department Store Remodeled as Automobile Salesroom," *Horseless Age* 25 (May 4, 1910): 668.

Full-scale repair garages, especially those associated with car storage, required large buildings. Brock's Garage in Trenton, New Jersey, occupied what had previously been a small factory (fig. 2.3). The first floor was used for "live storage" (cars regularly coming in and out on a daily or weekly basis). The second floor was used for car repairs, battery recharging, and "dead storage," especially long-term parking in the winter months. As the *Horseless Age* described it:

The work bench is 100 feet in length. It is located under windows on the south side of the building which give a strong light. Two endless chain blocks on iron girders, extending the entire length of the repair department, provide easy means for heavy lifting. The lathes, drill presses, saws, shapers, grinders and other machinery as well as the elevator are operated by electric motor.[2]

Purpose-Built Garages

When located in traditional business districts, the earliest purpose-built garages tended to be multiple-story structures; the number of stories constructed and the size of the overall footprint were a function of the scale of business anticipated, itself a function of town or city size. In small cities, two-story structures

Figure 2.2. W. H. Wood's Franklin dealership, West Chester, Pennsylvania, circa 1910. From authors' postcard collection.

occupying one or two building lots tended to suffice. In big cities, taller garages were the rule, some filling entire city blocks. Given the relatively large investments required, some architectural styling was usually deemed desirable, even if they were only decorative motifs suggested by material-supplier plan books. Particularly aggressive in this regard were brick manufacturers and the manufacturers of decorative terra cotta. The facade of the Old Post Road Garage in

Figure 2.3. Brock's Garage, Trenton, New Jersey. From "The Garage Situation in Trenton, NJ," *Horseless Age* 27 (May 3, 1911): 758.

Tarrytown, New York, was sheathed in brick with stone and trimmed with terra cotta lettering and decorative pieces (fig. 2.4). And yet, the building's description in the *Horseless Age* made no mention of architectural styling. Rather, it was the novel support system employed: the contractor's use of reinforced concrete in floors and supporting columns.[3] Slowly, however, trade journal reportage came to respect what competent architects could accomplish. The new garage and showroom of the Zell Motor Car Company in Baltimore was described as follows: "Tapestry brick with tooled concrete columns and trimmings compose the front. The roof projects over the third floor line in front, and its large, semicircular green tile covering adds a dash of color to the structure."[4]

But even architectural journals (as opposed to garage trade journals) tended to report more on structure than on decorative styling. In the largest big-city garages, as with factories and mills, roof supports definitely needed the careful attention of an architectural engineer. Where use of metal or wooden trusses was deemed inadequate, builders turned increasingly to reinforced concrete, a building technology widely innovated in industrial buildings after 1900. In large

Figure 2.4. The Old Post Road Garage, Tarrytown, New York, 1907. From *Horseless Age* 24 (Nov. 3, 1907): 507.

multiple-story garages, floors were usually supported by I-beams embedded in concrete or by concrete spans reinforced with iron bars. As well as providing strong floor and roof support, poured concrete walls were thought to be fireproof. The Willys-Overland Company's facility in Kansas City, Missouri, one of the company's regional branch facilities, was an example (fig. 2.5). Occupying a large corner lot, the building's sidewalk-facing walls were additionally sheathed with "dull glazed buff terra-cotta," although a very large proportion of each facade was given over to plate-glass show windows at street level. Supported by a rigid reinforced-concrete frame, the building was sheathed only in brick on its back sides. The rigid frame (as opposed to a pin-connected frame) was reported to be not only safe but also very economical: "It is well suited for girder bridges, power houses, machine shops, train sheds, [and] churches."[5]

Garage layout was divided into front and back regions, especially in dealer buildings where car sales combined with car repair. Just as facades invited decoration, so also did showroom interiors. Backs of buildings that were little seen from street-side could be left utilitarian. In organization and equipage, repair

Figure 2.5. Willys-Overland Company, Kansas City, Missouri. From George Volney Rhines, "Sales and Service Buildings for an Automobile Manufacturer," *American Architect* 113 (Mar. 20, 1918): 362.

floors tended to be strictly utilitarian, irrespective of the materials used. In 1918, the most pretentious, as well as the "most artistic," new garage in Pittsburgh was reported to be that of the McGurdy-May Pierce-Arrow dealership. The building's exterior walls were of light-colored pressed brick faced with white terra cotta, the windows set in indented-arch surrounds that gave the structure something of the look of a bank building. But it was the inside that impressed the most. "The big showroom on the first floor is a wonder to visiting motorists," gushed one journalist. "You tread upon a rubber interlocking tile floor.... The big plate glass windows, mezzanine gallery and sumptuous furniture, and the tasty decorations, make this showroom the finest auto parlor in the State."[6] The sales floor, with its oriental rugs, tables, and chairs, as well as its stylish cars, sported potted plants and a stuffed elk head on one wall (fig. 2.6). Such décor contrasted sharply with the repair floor and machine shop located on the building's second floor (fig. 2.7).

Figure 2.6. Showroom, McCurdy-May Company, Pittsburgh, Pennsylvania, 1913. From "McCurdy-May Salesroom and Garage, Pittsburgh, Pa.," *Horseless Age* 31 (May 7, 1913): 798.

The Traditional Single-Story Garage

Relatively few of the new purpose-built commercial garages in America's small towns, and even in the nation's smaller cities for that matter, were overly large. Most were of but a single story and capped by arched or flat roofs supported by prefabricated wooden and metal trusses—the traditional garage form emphasized in our prologue. But increasingly this was true even of the nation's largest cities, where standardized plans and prefabricated materials became ever more important. Wrote one journalist:

> There is one type of garage in New York City which can make money, and that is a one story building covering a large ground area. There are a number of these, particularly in the uptown district. They are more or less temporary buildings—that is, erected on property leased for five or ten years, plots of ground which the owner is holding as a real estate speculation.

Such buildings were relatively cheap to build, cheap to equip, and, importantly, cheap to heat in the winter.[7] The majority of the garages in Los Angeles were single-story structures. "Land is not expensive enough . . . to force the garage owners to go to the inconvenience of installing and operating costly elevators for more than one story," one writer observed.[8]

Very modest in size, few single-story garages displayed novel engineering or styling initiative. This was especially true of garages that sold and serviced trucks (fig. 2.8). Truck buyers, it was argued, were hard-nosed business people interested only in profit margins based on utility. They would not be much impressed by a building's amenity frills.[9] But car buyers would prove to be something else again. And slowly but surely architectural styling did come to the fore, if only minimally on the front facades of buildings of all sizes—much of it, like the roof trusses and other standardized building elements, prefabricated and purchased out of order books.

Again, most single-story garages were constructed with brick, cinder block, or hollow tile walls and with roofs supported by wooden and metal trusses—in other words, the most affordable materials available. And they were constructed quickly. Cheap materials and expedient building practices were certainly evident

Figure 2.7. Repair floor and machine shop, McGurdy-May Company, Pittsburgh, Pennsylvania, 1913. From "McCurdy-May Salesroom and Garage, Pittsburgh, Pa.," *Horseless Age* 31 (May 7, 1913): 798.

in the decades-old garage photographed after Southern California's destructive March 10, 1933, earthquake (fig. 2.9). "The men and firms in Long Beach directly engaged in the sales and maintenance of the automotive industry are at this writing struggling up through the debris of their ruined plants, sorting out tools, equipment and stock and getting ready to carry on their jobs of keeping cars and

Figure 2.8. City Hall Garage, Paterson, New Jersey, 1920. From "Make Utility the Keynote of Your Truck Sales," *Motor World* 63 (June 30, 1920): 11.

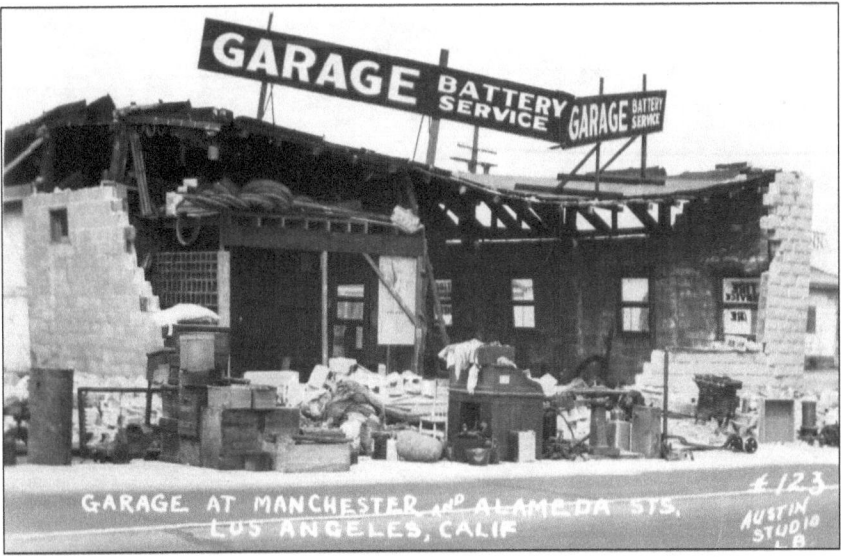

Figure 2.9. Postcard view of Los Angeles garage following earthquake, 1933. From authors' postcard collection.

trucks in running order," wrote one journalist. But positive spin could still prevail: "Everywhere you can see evidence of the old American spirit to carry on."[10]

Standardized Layouts

Very quickly, floor arrangements in new garages, especially those of the single-story variety, became remarkably standardized, their functions organized from garage to garage in more or less the same manner. Trade journals led the way by publishing descriptions of recently constructed buildings and, more important, publishing plans for future buildings. Figure 2.10 is a diagram that typified garage construction by 1920. In this example, the garage service entrance was to one side. Driving into the garage, the motorist passed windows with accessories displayed. On an adjacent wall, a state road map was posted. Behind the accessory store, but also opening onto the service floor at the rear of the building, was the parts and accessories stockroom. A pedestrian entrance opened directly from the sidewalk onto the sales floor. Out in front at the curb were a gasoline pump and an air hose in combination. Also prominent out front was an electric sign projected out over the sidewalk, one large enough to attract the attention of the passing motorist. This particular diagram, and the article it complemented, promoted a garage design that was thought to be especially attractive to tourists

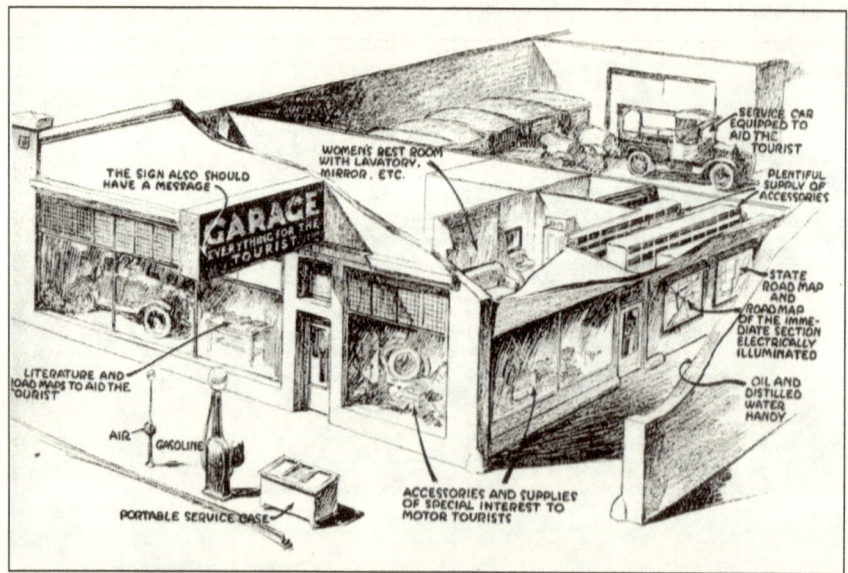

Figure 2.10. Cutaway view of ideal garage layout. From "Get Ready for the Touring Season," *Motor Age* 35 (May 15, 1919): 7.

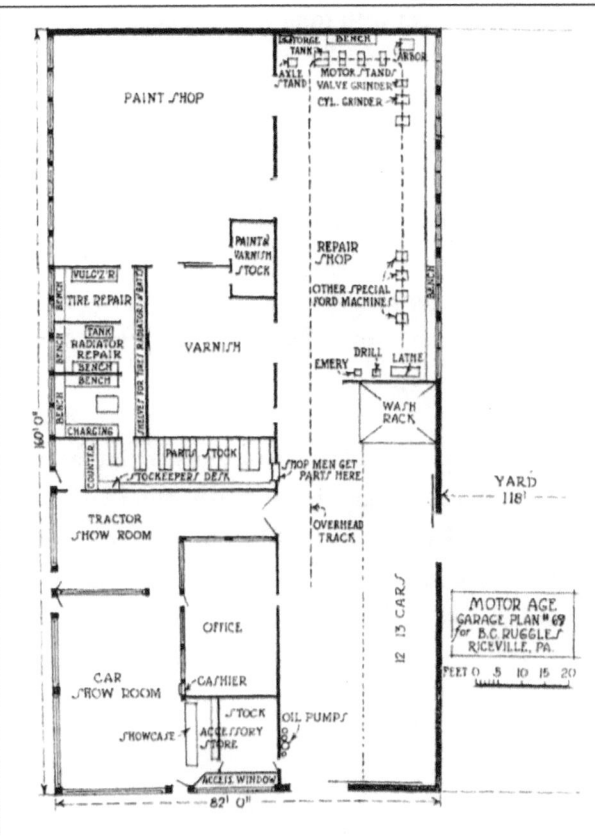

Figure 2.11. Floor plan for proposed garage. From "No. 69, Space More Than Ample," *Motor Age* 35 (June 19, 1919): 27.

and others transients.[11] The look of a place, it was understood, was what attracted (or repulsed) strangers, not to mention new customers from within a locality.

Figure 2.11 is a diagram of a 1919 plan for a new Ford garage proposed for Riceville, Pennsylvania. The gas pump outside, serviced by an underground tank, was supplemented inside the main entry by pumps that dispensed lubricating oil into tin containers; the oil would then be poured into auto crankcases. (Oil in quart cans would not be popularized for another decade.) Intended for a small town, the garage plan included showrooms for both cars and tractors, each to be served by an office with a cashier's window. The stock room was to be fronted by a showcase and a counter facing out onto the automobile sales floor. Besides a repair shop, the rear of the building would contain paint, varnish, and tire repair shops, with small storage rooms partitioned off of each. Also, a wash rack was intended for the rear of the building.[12]

Perhaps more common were garages with front entrances centered rather than set to one side (fig. 2.12). Although popular for a while in the 1920s, interior sales floors for selling used cars, as included in this latter diagram, did not last. Created by *Motor World*'s "Department of Better Business Buildings," the layout here also includes a greasing pit where the proverbial "grease monkey" lubricated cars. Other popular layouts included additional side (and/or rear) exits facing onto side streets (or back alleys). Cars could then be moved in and out of garages in a "flow-through" manner. Turning cars in cramped garage space was a universal problem, one also solved very early on by the use of turntables.

Programming Space

By the 1920s, scientific management was the order of the day in literally every field of enterprise. "It is a good thing to get far enough away from routine, occasionally, to study our own business and check up on ourselves," is how the editors of the magazine *Motor World* (whose subtitle was "for Dealers, Jobbers and Garagemen") put it, not wanting, perhaps, to sound too demanding. So they also provided a cartoon (fig. 2.13). Most of the journalism produced was little more than com-

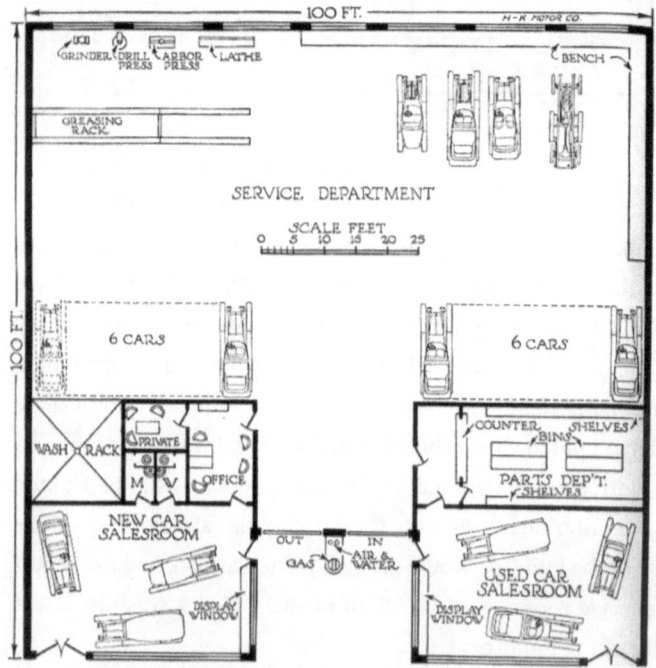

Figure 2.12. Floor plan for proposed garage. From "Center Drive Features Dealer Building," *Motor World* 75 (May 30, 1923): 32.

monsensical. "Scientific construction," it was said, was all about "fitting buildings to business." The first question was how large a building to build. The second was how to arrange it. But both required careful attention. The building had an important bearing not merely on function or utility but on costs, both overhead and operating expenses. If a building was too large, the rent expense (meaning lease, mortgage, tax, and other obligations related to real estate) could be excessive, and if it was too small, it might necessitate a reduction in a firm's volume of business and thus reduce its capacity to compete. Or, the latter might simply lead to shop congestion and an increase in accidents or even a reduction in service quality.[13]

It was necessary to "departmentalize" one's business, especially if the garage was large.[14] Of course, front and back regions needed to be fully separated, which meant that sales and service floors needed not only to be kept apart but out of view of one another. Women customers, it was said, were especially put off when "blue collar" mechanics from a repair shop intruded into a "sales parlor," the realm of "white collar" salesmen (fig. 2.14). But it was also a matter of management control, keeping lines of authority straight by defining clear geographic boundaries between different kinds of activities.[15]

Figure 2.13. Cartoon, "Ever Do This?" From *Motor World* 71 (June 7, 1923): title page illustration.

Figure 2.14. Cartoon promoting garage "departmentalization." From B. M. Ikert, "Departments Essential to Transportation Store," *Motor Age* 46 (Dec. 4, 1924): 9.

Large-scale automotive retailing logically divided three ways, each division with its own space and territorial implications. Journalist Tom Wilder called them (1) the executive group (office, car display, accessory store, customer amenities, etc.); (2) the shop group (the work floor, parts stockroom, battery room, tire room, tool room, machine shop, mechanics lounge, etc.); and (3) the garage itself, which, to Wilder at least, still implied, in part, car storage. Building layout could accommodate these divisions variously, but simplicity (meaning ease of complementarity) was critical (fig. 2.15).[16] Whereas trade journal writers fussed over such details as to how workbenches might be organized and how tire repair and wheel alignment equipment might to be related, academics, writing mainly out of business schools, sought greater sophistication, advocating, for example, time and motion studies tied to performance tests and new inventorying procedures tied to modern accounting.[17] Underlying it all was a quest for efficiency, thus to enhance productivity and reduce costs—labor costs particularly. In all

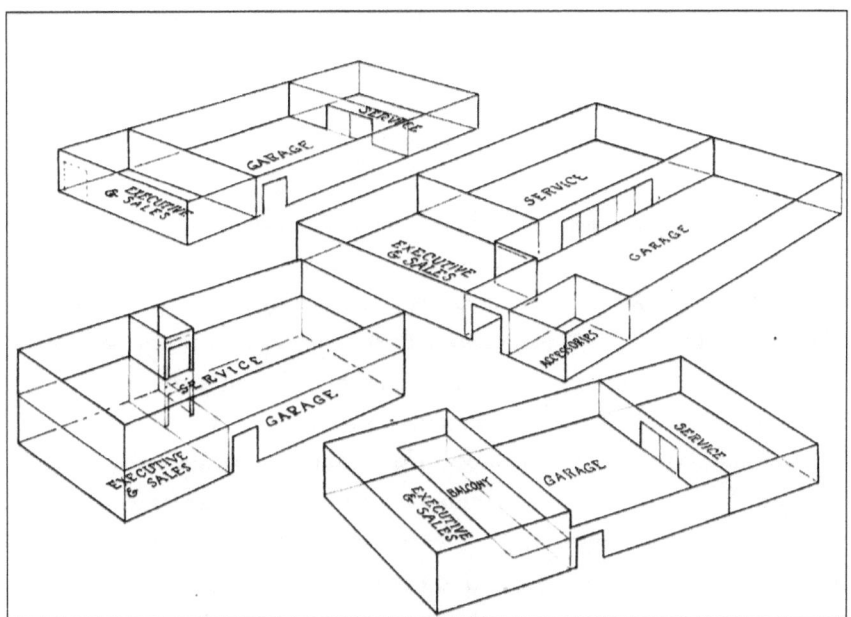

Figure 2.15. Programing space in garage planning. From Tom Wilder, "Laying Out the Dealer Building for Economy and Efficiency," *Motor Age* 41 (July 20, 1922): 10.

this there was nothing new that had not been or was not being applied to commerce and industry generally. Always at issue was suitability.

A sales floor was certainly analogous to selling floors elsewhere. They needed to be attractive, if not suggestive. They needed to variously predisposition customer spending, reinforcing that both during and after a sale. The repair floor was more analogous to a factory floor. Indeed, by the 1920s, a large proportion of the mechanics at work in garages, especially those of car dealerships, were "factory trained." As service and repair required more interior space, it should not be surprising that even the most refined businesses selling the most refined motorcars were said to operate from "garages."

Thus it was that industrial design came to dominate programming decisions as to what garage buildings ought to be like. Like factories, garages were invariably rectangular structures; of particular concern was the flow in and out. Garages were to be fit organically into whatever site was available, but most building lots, being rectangular, lent themselves readily to rectangular structures. Power distribution, at first largely mechanical through belts and pulleys from large electric motors (and even steam engines) and then by wires connecting small electric motors, was logically accomplished in linear arrays, again supportive of rectilinear work spaces in buildings.

As in industrial buildings of all kinds, standardized fixtures, from window casements to roof trusses, further wrought standardized building form. Charles Evans Fowler in 1929 outlined the ideals that underlay industrial architecture. They were: (1) the blended dichotomy of organic and standardized plans, forms, and construction, as dictated by actual rather than implied functionalism; (2) a regularity of form and articulation imposed by programmatic needs for light and ventilation and relieved by the expression of various internal functions; (3) a reliance of framed construction, both traditional methods of building and innovative and best-practice techniques (and either the accentuation of structural elements or their concealment with engineered curtain walls); and (4) an emphasis on rationalized simplicity in design respecting the inherent qualities of the materials used.[18] Garage architecture, as a kind of industrial expression, followed right along. Largely undecorated structures (save, perhaps, for showroom facades) with a "no fuss quality" were the result.

Henry Ford was, of course, at the forefront of factory planning and thus factory-floor organization. And it is, perhaps, appropriate that his name has been co-opted in describing work that seemingly pits workers against machines on such floors. "Fordism" replaced expensive skilled labor with inexpensive unskilled labor. Work on moving car-assembly lines in Detroit and other cities was largely reduced to machine tending. Auto plant workers came to perform mainly single, highly rationalized, but also exceedingly monotonous tasks.

Car repair was never reduced to such complete efficiency.[19] Nonetheless, a kind of Fordism, what sociologist David Gartman calls a "Fordism of visual aesthetics," did to a degree set in. Ford's factories not only produced cars in highly rationalized ways but also produced highly standardized cars, especially during the era of the Model T. Standardization and, importantly, the appearance of standardization became a virtue. Promoted was a machine aesthetic: a new "visual order" that rejected elite traditions in valuing how things appeared. As Gartman elaborates:

The objects that increasingly dominated the vision of Americans in the 1920s announced loudly that they were tailored for use, not ostentation. Products were designed not for the aesthetic contemplation of the elite, but for the efficient use of the masses.... The visual order of Fordist instrumentalism was not confined to consumer goods but also spilled over into the built environment. The emerging economy of mass production and mass consumption demanded new spaces—new factories to product commodities, new stores to sell commodities, new homes to consume commodities, and new roads to drive the quintessential commodity of Fordism, the automobile.[20]

After 1920, new garages, even in the smallest towns, were increasingly built with factories in mind. Enabled universally were open and largely unobstructed spaces ideal for moving cars around and ideal for relating complementary repair activities. And they lent themselves to logical lines of flow, whether it was the moving of materials from stockroom to repair floor or the cars themselves from entry to repair to exit. Transparency and continuity of space enabled managers to survey work more effectively and thereby to enforce the quantity and the quality of work.

As with basic building materials, fixtures in garages were increasingly standardized, as they were also purchased out of order catalogs. Lighting, for example, improved with stronger lamps and larger luminaires evenly distributed (fig. 2.16). So also were heating and ventilation improved, the latter especially worrisome to garage workers because of carbon monoxide in car exhaust. New innovations were announced and their benefits widely promoted in speeches delivered at conventions and, perhaps more important, in trade journal articles.[21] And they were aggressively sold by manufacturer sales representatives, whose advertising sustained the journals.

Standardized cars with carefully machined, interchangeable parts greatly cut down on the effort and time required to make most car repairs. No longer were broken parts machined to be reused so much as merely replaced, something facilitated by the supportive growth of parts wholesalers, who maintained large warehouses and ran fast delivery trucks to supply garage needs, especially in the nation's cities. And increasingly the tools used to repair cars were standardized, with the largest car manufacturers, for example, requiring their dealers to use only the tools they had specially engineered for use on their vehicles. The look of

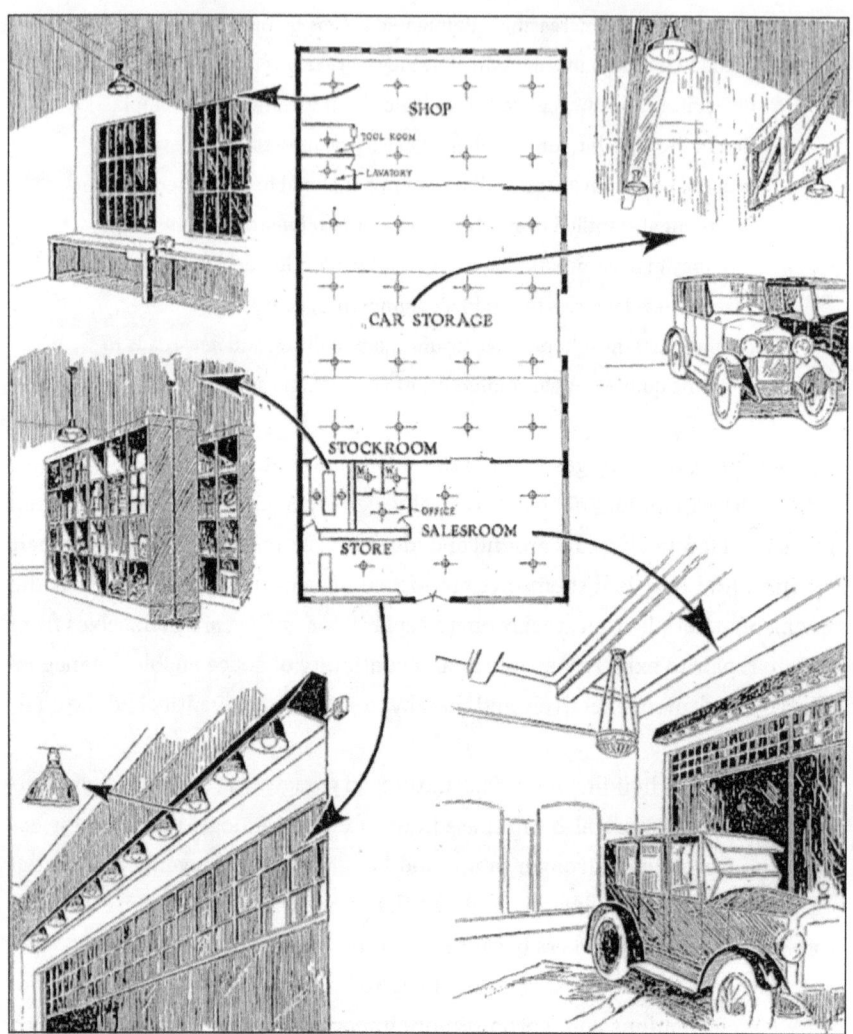

Figure 2.16. "How to Effectively Light the Dealer Building." From Donald D. Blanchard, "Good Lighting is Good Salesmanship," *Motor World* 65 (May 14, 1922): 17.

new garages, including that of the signs attached, ideally needed to communicate the new modernism within.

Curb Appeal

Unfortunately, what applied to new buildings did not necessarily apply to old ones, and the bulk of the garages a motorist might encounter in a town or city through the 1920s usually dated from preceding decades, many of them festooned with garish signs accumulated over the years. Facades were often left unpainted or otherwise ill maintained. This was particularly unsettling to motorists traveling from afar whose only basis for judging the quality of a garage lay mainly in how it looked. Too often, a motorist, hoping for one thing, found something else altogether (fig. 2.17). Even new garages could, if proprietors neglected their appearance, be off-putting. In the *Horseless Age,* a series of cartoons appeared in 1917 to illustrate the point, two of which are reproduced here (figs. 2.18 and 2.19). It was not just a matter of being modern but also one of constant upkeep and careful application of signage. The old-fashioned garage, "which found its inception in a tumble-down barn or some other derelict habitation, is rapidly becoming a thing of the past," suggested the *Ohio Motorist* in 1921. Its demise was "not due to absence of work, but rather because of the fact that the car owner has come to associate the quality of work rendered with the type of place in which it is produced."[22]

It was worrisome that so many garage owners associated messiness with utility, or, at the very least, accepted degrees of slovenliness as an adjunct to the naturally dirty work of repairing cars. Accordingly, the nation's petroleum companies, realizing that garage appearance was largely beyond their control and thus potentially hurtful to the branded gasoline trade, began vertical integration into retailing, replacing independent garages as gasoline outlets with company-controlled gasoline stations.

Like the new filling stations, garages needed to give the impression of "up-to-dateness." And that involved the coordination of all aspects of the business, the careful packaging of places to make their services and products predictable in the most positive of ways: "Electric signs, fresh coats of paint, completely modern entrances, new and unsoiled claim checks, fresh looking equipment, plenty of light throughout the entire establishment, cash registers, systemized methods of handling cars, etc."[23] That is generally what the petroleum companies

Figure 2.17. Cartoons: setting customer expectations. From Bill Strong, "To Get Transient Trade You Must Go After It," *Motor Age* 35 (May 1, 1919): 28.

accomplished with their new gasoline station chains, bringing to the fore what has come to be termed "place-product-packaging."[24]

Site and Situation

Location also reflected the worth of a garage in a motorist's eyes. Location was not just a matter of convenience for motorists but also a matter of how a garage related to other businesses and, more important, to other land uses in its immediate vicinity. Most early commercial garages, being located in former livery stables and other commercial buildings once oriented to horse-drawn vehicular use, were in downtown areas. In cities both large and small, horse-oriented facilities tended to cluster either at the margins of a business district, especially in warehouse or factory zones, or along lesser streets and back alleys well within business districts. Each cluster provided a full range of services, from livery, sale, and feed barns to blacksmith shops and carriage and harness shops. Taken to-

Figure 2.18. Cartoon, "Service 'as Is'—Sometimes at Least." From *Horseless Age* 39 (Mar. 15, 1917): 24.

gether, they provided mutual reinforcement such that nowhere in most business districts were customers far removed from any one service or product required for horse or carriage. In Champaign, Illinois, a city of some forty thousand people, four such clusters serviced downtown in the early decades of the twentieth century, one of which evolved into city's first "automobile row."[25]

In 1911, the *Horseless Age* reported on the garage situation in Philadelphia: "There are a great many buildings about the older part of the city which were formerly used as stables, which have been turned into garages; these are makeshift garages, of course, but garages nevertheless." Additionally, some automaker branch salesrooms with garage facilities had been erected, but no "modern city garage building" had yet to be started downtown, although the first purpose-built garage, the American Garage and Machine Shop, had, indeed, just opened behind the Bellevue-Stratford Hotel, the city's leading hostelry. Instead, "credible" garages were appearing along avenues out toward the city's suburbs.[26] *Scientific*

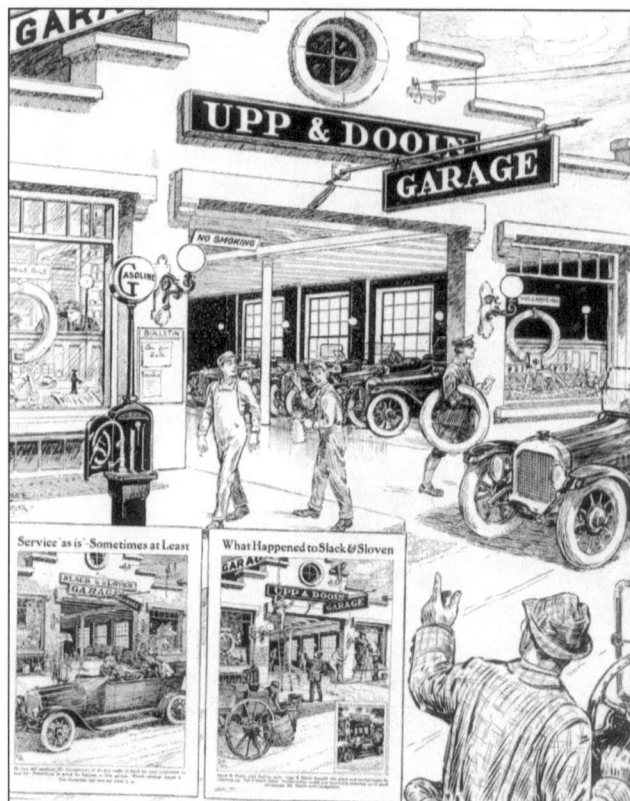

Figure 2.19. Cartoon, "Upp and Dooin On the Job." From *Horseless Age* 39 (Apr. 15, 1917): 16.

American reported as early as 1902 that in the nation's largest cities "nearly all the automobile stores are located on thoroughfares convenient to fashionable patronage."[27]

In Buffalo, New York, in 1909, most garages were, it was reported, "located in the residential sections, the average distance from the business centre being one and three-tenth miles."[28] Those residential areas were rapidly being intruded upon by all kinds of commercial land uses. However, new garages and then new gas stations tended to be the commercial pioneers in displacing housing. In Buffalo, the highest density of early garages was just north and northeast of downtown, an area oriented to the axis of Delaware Avenue, traditionally Buffalo's highest-value residential boulevard (fig. 2.20). There, garages and gas stations along all major streets intercepted affluent motorists commuting into the city's downtown.

With increased automobile use in small towns (and especially after the arrival of a named or numbered highway capable of bringing large numbers of tran-

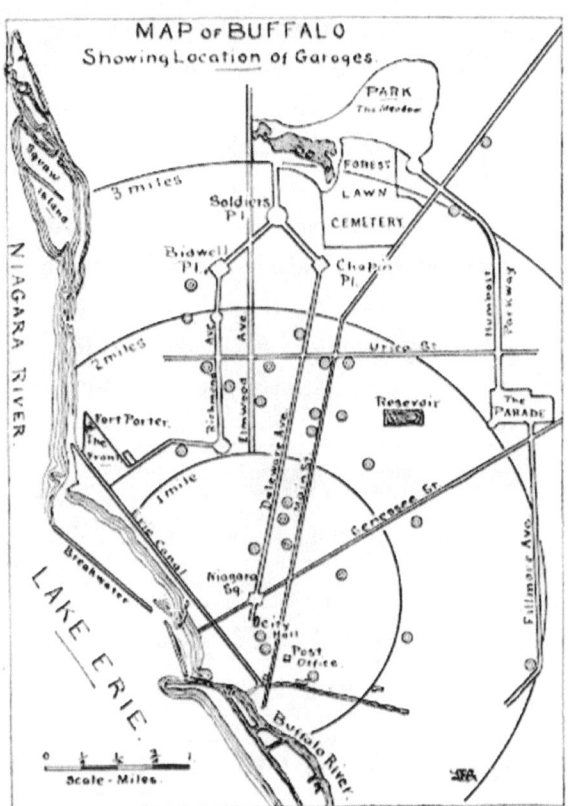

Figure 2.20. Garage locations, Buffalo, New York, 1909. From "The Garage Situation in Buffalo, NY," *Horseless Age* 23 (Apr. 21, 1909): 524.

sients through a town), garages became more common on Main Street itself or, as the case might be, around a courthouse square (fig. 2.21). As often as not the widest street and often the only street paved or hard-surfaced for any distance, Main Street was the logical candidate for highway marking and thus heavy use, this despite the fact that the big houses of a community's well-to-do usually lined it, at least on one side of downtown. Large corner lots made especially ideal properties for new purpose-built garages (fig. 2.22). Again, garages, along with gas stations, became the leading pioneers of land-use change. Corner locations were, of course, readily visible from two streets and not just one. Thus, they were valued for their ease of access in small towns as well as in cities (fig. 2.23).

Automobile Rows

"Automobile rows" came to characterize the nation's largest cities: Euclid Avenue in Cleveland, North Capitol Street in Indianapolis, South Grand Avenue in Kansas City, or West Farnam Street in Omaha. An automobile row, unlike the horse-oriented businesses before, tended not to be a business cluster so much as a business array, something linearly distributed along a single thoroughfare. Chicago's "auto row" (originally called "gasoline row") stretched for over two miles along Michigan Avenue south of the city's downtown. According to the editors of *The Automobile,* the automobile had done much for the area "which was formerly the residential district of the very elite, when that elite consisted of stock yard magnates, wheat emperors, real estate monarchs and railroad kings." But when the well-to-do began to abandon the area in the 1890s, mansions were converted to boarding houses, and retail, warehousing, and light industrial ac-

Figure 2.21. Blue Book advertisements. Smith's Garage and the Hotel Dixie clearly complemented one another in the town center of Shelbyville, Tennessee. From *Official Automobile Bluebook,* vol. 6 (Chicago: Automobile Blue Book Publishing Co., 1921), 483.

tivities began to intrude, making the area "frayed at the elbows." The automobile showrooms and garages then moved in. One hundred twelve different brands of automobile were sold in Chicago in 1910, the majority of them on "The Row." Especially noticeable were the factory branches opened by various auto manufacturers. From its building, the Locomobile Company of America, by way of example, serviced a sales territory extending from Ohio to Colorado. In total, an estimated fifteen thousand automobiles were being sold each year in Chicago, and another ninety-five hundred cars to sales territories beyond.[29] "If one will imagine a street almost twice as wide as Fifth Avenue, smoothly paved and maintained to the minute, flat as a billiard table in its longitudinal lines, symmetrically curved to the gutters in its cross section, as straight as an arrow from end to end, he will have an idea of the geographical setting of Chicago's automobile sales district," wrote one admiring New York journalist.[30]

New York City's "Automobile Row" stretched up Broadway from Forty-seventh Street on the south to Seventy-sixth Street on the north, although most of the seventy-odd salesroom/garages were bunched between Fifty-first and Sixty-third Streets. There "it would be impossible to throw half a brick without damage to some well known make of automobile," another journalist wrote. Some thirty-three thousand automobiles were sold each year in Manhattan, he estimated, of which some twenty-seven thousand were to city residents. Broadway (as well as major cross streets back a block or so) also sported automobile accessory stores and other auto-related businesses, including storage and independent repair garages.[31] The automobile rows of New York City, Chicago, and lesser cities such as Kansas City were very much dominated by the large branch offices of the larger auto makers or their designated regional wholesale agents.

* * *

From 1900 through the 1920s, a distinctive and thus readily identifiable place of business evolved in towns and cities across the United States. It was the garage,

Figure 2.22. Thomson and Britton Garage, Alexandria Bay, New York, circa 1920. From authors' postcard collection.

Figure 2.23. The importance of corner locations. From "The Value of a Corner," *Motor Age* 39 (Jan. 6, 1921): 7.

typically a rectangular structure either multistory, especially in large cities, but usually one story almost everywhere else. If it was a dealership, it usually sported large plate-glass windows, if only across the front at ground level, with an automobile sales floor visible within. Across the back of the building or in the basement or on upper floors were located car repair, parts storage, and other related functions. For the most part, they were fully utilitarian structures reflective of both their mode of construction and their purpose. Front facades might have a modicum of decoration but seldom true architectural elegance. Larger garages were often constructed of reinforced concrete, but masonry and wood-framed structures with masonry veneer, as with smaller buildings, were not uncommon. Smaller garages might be of wood frame but were usually veneered with masonry. Almost always, roofs were supported by prefabricated wooden or metal truss work.

Most garages faced directly onto streets, with motorists entering through large doors out front or sometimes off of back alleys or side streets. Inside they were logically organized. If engaged in automobile sales, salesrooms were invariably up front and, indeed, located with corner windows showing on two streets if possible. Ideally, salesmen greeted customers at the door, showed them the cars displayed indoors on the sales floor before showing them the vehicles parked outside in storage lots. Sent off on test drives, customers, if convinced to buy, had their purchases finalized usually in small offices partitioned immediately off of showroom floors. There then followed a trip out to meet the service manager in the repair shop.

If only a repair garage, the office was usually to one side of the front entrance, sometimes coupled with a storeroom selling accessories. Nonetheless, the customer typically had the feeling of driving directly onto a repair floor. If it was a multistory garage, tire repair, bodywork, painting, and other specialized activities were usually on an upper floor. In the purpose-built garage, layout smoothly predisposed customer behavior, if not additionally bringing order to the repair work itself. The garage did not just involve the builder's use of new materials and new methods of construction but also garage management's newly rethought use of space. Taken altogether, new garages in the 1920s spoke of a new modernity, with speed and convenience fully implicit. The customer drove in. A shop manager ascertained customer need and eventually assigned the car to a mechanic, who drove it off to an assigned work space. Customers lingered in an adjacent waiting room or returned later to find their cars finished. A quick stop at a cashier's window and then he or she was off. The experience was very much the same everywhere, part of the automobile's contribution to standardizing life.

3

GARAGE LAYOUT AND LOCATION, 1930–1950s

The stock market crash in 1929, followed by the Great Depression, shook American confidence. Gone was the unbridled enthusiasm that, encouraged by laissez-faire attitudes regarding investment and wealth, had produced an economic bubble after World War I. Thus, the Roosevelt Administration took unprecedented peacetime initiatives to restart the faltering economy by variously subsidizing investment in the built environment, especially in public infrastructure, including highway repair and new highway construction. But private enterprise also benefitted—for example, through low-cost loans that enabled retailers to upgrade storefronts, thus to generate incentive for consumers to spend money. In city downtowns and along small-town main streets, merchants were encouraged to revamp traditional storefronts using new materials (especially structural glass) and new decorative motifs dubbed "modern," including "streamline modern." Desirable were storefronts fully opened up to inside view from sidewalks and streets, thus to give passing motorists, as well as pedestrians, a better look at store interiors. Whole facades made sign-like, with large lettering integrated into highly simplified decorative motifs, were desirable as well.[1] Garages were not exempt.

The purpose-built garage, brought to full maturation by the mid-1920s, had already been challenged by an important new player in the automobile-servicing field: the gas station. Garages, it would turn out, were not an end result but only a transitional feature in petroleum retailing. With garages, facades were flush with lot lines, and buildings tended to fill entire building lots. As with traditional storefronts, they were directly oriented to sidewalks (pedestrian spaces) rather than to streets (vehicular spaces). Automobile convenience lay mainly in garage entrances being close to streets and garage interiors being relatively spacious—building interiors made into extensions of street space.

By location, garages were convenient to most other kinds of business activities in tightly packed traditional business districts, including work destinations for commuters and shopping destinations for shoppers. They were close to hotels that serviced transients. What the new gas stations tended to do was to move car refueling well beyond central business districts to outlying locations, thus intercepting motorists before they reached downtowns and, of course, with facilities that were fully automobile convenient. They sported open driveways with ease of entrance and exit. Often they had sizeable parking areas. Pumping gas was fast. And the smaller overhead of small-building upkeep, coupled with the larger-scale pumping of gasoline, meant that gas was usually cheaper than at garages. What remained was for the lowly filling station to take on at least limited car maintenance and repair functions—to further co-opt the garage. In other words, gas stations would add service bays. And garage owners would have to respond.

The Gas Station

Previously, we have detailed the rise of the gas station in America, and so here we restrict ourselves to mere outline in telling the story.[2] Gasoline was initially sold in tin cans, marketed in a wide variety of places, including hardware stores, drug stores, and, of course, livery stables, blacksmith shops, and other horse-related commercial establishments reoriented to motorist needs. Gasoline itself was delivered by tank wagon not only to retailers but also to residential garages to be stored in tanks or barrels, hand-pumped into tins, and hand-poured into automobile gas tanks. By 1910, curbside pumps had appeared, especially out in front of garages, thus removing refueling from inside work floors. The first off-street filling stations (complete with driveways, small office buildings, and gravity-feed gasoline tanks with hoses) appeared in about 1908, many of them started by wholesale jobbers in conjunction with gasoline storage yards. Almost immediately the gas station became a common sight at the edges of city and small-town business districts, an important commercial pioneer, as we have said, in previously residential areas. Pictured from a trade journal is an early gas station in Detroit (fig. 3.1) "In most cities of this country," the accompanying narrative read, "the needs of the motorists are supplied by public garages. Here he buys his gasoline while his machine is being overhauled and cleaned." But here was something new: "In Detroit, stations for the exclusive sale of gasoline have been established on the principal boulevards and highways of travel. These stations supply the needs of the passing autoists, and are patronized to a surprising extent."[3] Of course, many early gas station proprietors also carried a few tires and a handful of accessories, some servicing electric vehicles with battery-recharging facilities.

The nation's petroleum companies quickly came to embrace the idea. Some were forced to do so. When Buffalo, New York, outlawed curbside pumps because of their perceived fire hazard, the Standard Oil Company of New York established an architectural department to design off-street gas station facilities.[4] Additionally, the company had found gasoline sales especially problematic at garages. Garages, being independently owned and oriented more to car storage, car sales, and, of course, car repair, gave gasoline sales relatively little emphasis; they offered it mainly as a customer convenience. Gasoline was initially sold as a

Figure 3.1. An early service station, Detroit, Michigan. From "A Modern Gasoline Station," *Horseless Age* 34 (Nov. 18, 1914): 744.

cheap, largely generic product, and that meant very small profit margins for garage owners. Brands of lubricating oil, on the other hand, were more vigorously marketed, with brand promotion exciting decent profits and thus more interest among garage proprietors. However, once branded gasoline also came to the fore, interest changed. Garages began to sport distinctively decorated gas pumps out front, usually selling the brands of several producers. Point-of-purchase signs became quite common, all designed to create and sustain brand consciousness and brand loyalty. Thus a sense of disorder often prevailed, as curbsides were crowded with competing pumps and building facades were festooned with competing signs.

It was a function of independent ownership. Garages were beyond the direct control of the petroleum companies regarding the look of individual properties. As journalist V. B. Guthrie observed as late as 1926, independent dealers offer "as many as five—as far as noticed—brands of gasoline and even more brands of lubricating oils, any or most all of the following: limited or complete lines of automobile accessories, tires, tire repair service, batteries and battery service, varying degrees of garage repair work, washing, polishing, top dressing." Thus did garage merchandising tend to give "a carnival appearance."[5] The solution to the problem was to put dealers under restrictive contracts, making them, for example, responsible to but a single company for the products they sold. It was better still for a corporation to own properties, leasing them to proprietors and, through those lease agreements, forcing them to abide by the edicts of place-product-packaging.

Place-product-packaging could be most readily accomplished with chains of new, look-alike gasoline stations. Every petroleum company wishing to vertically integrate forward into retailing necessarily established an architectural department and charged it with designing gas stations that would carry some kind of distinctive look, thus giving a company something of a personality at the retail level. For the Jenny Manufacturing Company, an early gasoline refiner in New England, various "colonial" architectural motifs predominated, rooting the company symbolically in its marketing region (fig. 3.2). (Such building motifs, called "blend-in" architecture in the gasoline trade, also smoothed gas station intrusion into previously residential areas, especially gentry neighborhoods such as along Delaware Avenue in Buffalo.) Yet there was much standardization, as various building types came to the fore to be widely shared across the petroleum industry. Design departments, accordingly, worked largely at producing what might be termed "difference in sameness," distinctive looks that would set each gasoline brand apart but would not disguise stations for their purpose and functionality.

A serious problem for independent gasoline dealers, whether of the garage or gas station variety, was weak financing. Another reason for the petroleum companies to discourage gasoline sales at garages was the inability of marginal businesses to pay their bills or to pay them in a timely fashion. "Poor Garage Credit Starts Big Station Plan," announced the *National Petroleum News* in 1913: "To get away, presumably, from the bad credit conditions prevailing in the auto garage trade and to make sure of maintaining gallonage, etc., a string of auto filling stations are being installed in Ohio and large Middle West cities, the eventual ownership or control of which is credited to the Standard Oil Company." Stations would sell only Standard Oil (later Sohio) products, leading the way with "Red Crown Gasoline."[6]

Most of the new gas stations were small, inexpensive, and purely functional. "The successful aim has been to put stations where the public needs service; to make them as efficient as possible; as good looking as possible, and yet . . . hold their expenses down to barely what is necessary to accomplish their important service," concluded Warren C. Platt, the longtime editor of the *National Petroleum*

Figure 3.2. Manchester, New Hampshire, gasoline station, circa 1925. From authors' postcard collection.

News. "These stations," he thought, would become "the biggest and most important means of advertising the oil industry to the public." They would communicate corporate individuality through color schemes, signs, and logos.⁷ And indeed, each company did assert something of a distinct persona, orchestrating how its stations not only offered superior products but superior service. Also, the term "filling station" dropped out in favor of the term "service station" (fig. 3.3).

Incrementally, the big petroleum corporations diverted the gasoline trade to company-owned or leased stations. In Los Angeles in 1926, companies like the Standard Oil Company of California (today's Chevron), the Union Oil Company (its retail brand now controlled by Conoco/Phillips), and Richfield (now part of BP) operated 482 of city's 1,290 gasoline outlets. Company stations, however, did tend to be bigger and thus sold more gas. Some were very big. One unnamed company was said to operate "deluxe" stations, selling as much as 700 gallons of gasoline a day as opposed to the city average of only 250 gallons. Large stations handled tires but also wiper blades, soaps and polishes, fan belts, and other auto accessories. Stations large and small sold candy and soft drinks; a peanut machine was hardly unusual.

The Super Service Station

The 1920s saw the arrival of the "super service station," mostly corporate-owned or corporate-leased stores that were very much enlarged in size, with much wider service and product lines. It was nothing short of a further assault on the independent garage trade, one designed to take away not only gasoline sales but also a wide array of car maintenance and repair functions, including lubrication, tire repair, light engine work, and car washing—a variety of services sometimes called "TBA" sales (tires, batteries, and accessories). In 1929, the typical motorist drove some one thousand to fifteen hundred miles, spending an estimated $230 to operate and maintain a vehicle. The year before, reported one journalist, there were "more piston rings, pistons, piston pins, valves, real axle gears, [and] brake band materials sold than ever before." In 1929, there would likely be "more jobs of carbon removing, body washing, hose replacement, radiator cleaning, auto-electric replacement and battery repair" than previously. The petroleum companies, through their dealers, wanted a larger piece of that pie.⁸

And why not? Why should motorists have to go to more than one location to obtain the services and products required for normal car use? Super service stations could do most of it as a "one-stop" service center.⁹ Various labels emerged.

Figure 3.3. Frontispiece advertisement on Gulf Refining Company road map, circa 1930. © by Chevron U.S.A. Inc. and used with permission.

On the West Coast, where the super service station idea originated, the phrase "complete service center" was preferred. "By complete service station is meant an establishment where a man can purchase oil, gas, grease, and accessories, have washing or lubricating jobs done, and his battery charged or replaced, as well as, in most instances, obtain mechanical attention," the editors of *Motor Age* explained.[10] Not even the largest stations, however, were equipped to handle engine overhauls or do bodywork. That could be left to the repair garages. But regarding most other repairs and services, why not a kind of "auto department store"?[11]

Usually spread out over a large corner lot, some super service stations filled an entire block. The idea of a separate station house was sustained. It contained not only a central office, but also merchandise displays and sometimes storage space for the sundry accessories sold. In California, a large canopy usually extended off one or two sides of the building, thus shading pump islands from the sun. Auto-repair facilities, on the other hand, were usually located in service bays elbowing one another across the back of a property or down one or both sides of a lot. The Pure Oil Company station pictured on a 1934 roadmap was typical (fig. 3.4). In California, the Richfield Company completed twenty-eight look-alike super service stations in 1928 alone.[12] Union Oil and Standard Oil of California (later Chevron) followed suit. Street frontages varied up to several hundred feet in width. Parcels could vary upwards to two or three acres in size. However, lot depth was usually shallow, the idea being to keep buildings and their products and services within clear view of passing motorists. In addition to car servicing and repair, many stations, especially those in or near big-city downtowns, operated parking lots. Some incorporated lunch counters, and at least one was said to include a beauty shop as a draw to women shopping downtown.[13]

In areas of the country with severe winters, compact stations under a single roof, with fully enclosed work bays, tended to be the rule. Canopies were rare in northern states. The Pure Oil Company, headquartered in Chicago, enlarged their stock-in-trade station type, one designed as an "English Cottage," by adding similarly styled service bays.[14] The station in downtown Evanston, a Chicago suburb, occupied a lot measuring 200 feet by 125 feet, the station complex pushed up against one lot line. An underground parking garage held some 125 cars (fig. 3.5). The oil companies were not alone in promoting the super service station idea. So did various department store chains, including Sears, Roebuck &

Figure 3.4. Frontispiece advertisement on Pure Oil Company road map, 1934. From authors' road map collection.

Company and Montgomery Ward. And so did various tire manufacturers, prime among them the Goodyear Tire and Rubber Company and the Firestone Tire and Rubber Company

Garage Interests Respond

Many garage proprietors responded to the threat of super service stations by remodeling existing garages or by building new garages specially configured to better accommodate gasoline sales. The latter were usually street-corner buildings with one corner cut away to accommodate a driveway (fig. 3.6). As often as not, the roof of the garage was extended over this space not only to provide the pumps protection from sun or inclement weather but also to respect building rooflines and overall plan. The strategy moved gasoline pumps away from streets and onto protected concrete aprons immediately accessible to car showrooms and accessory sales counters. Perhaps most of these new garages were built initially to accommodate car dealers. The repair floor, relegated as usual to the back of the building, was often entered through a side entrance. Another strategy was to dedicate a building's entire front to gasoline, oil, and accessory sales, something recommended for small garages without car sales. It was what garage

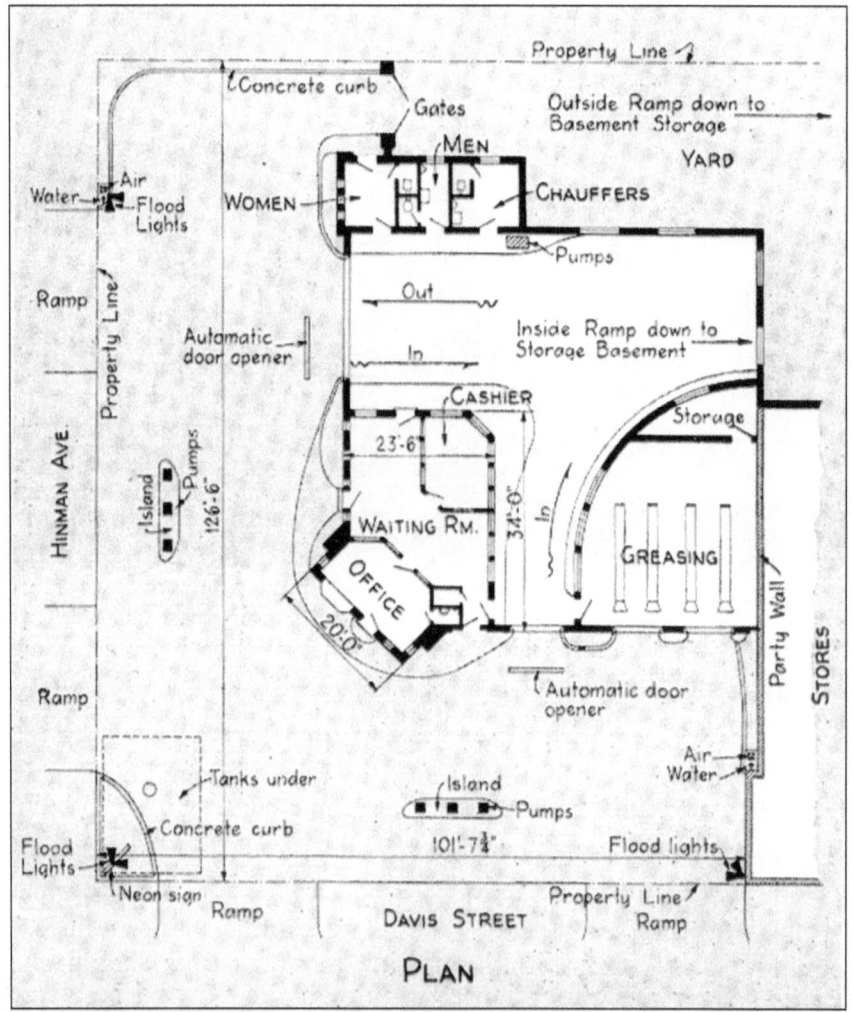

Figure 3.5. Super service station layout, Pure Oil Company, Evanston, Illinois. From "'Best' in Service Stations," *American Builder* 58 (May 1936): 72. Courtesy of Simmons-Boardman Corp.

proprietors had traditionally done with curbside pumps, except now the pumps tended to be placed back from the curb across a narrow driveway space, sometimes covered with a large canopy.

These buildings were prac'tical at the centers of blocks as well as at intersections. One such garage in Peoria, Illinois, advertised itself as "a super service station under one roof," its owner claiming it to have "the first adaptation of the California type station to the wintry climate of the Great Lakes region."[15] The building's busy opening day was duly reported: "It was a day of service demonstrations. One colored washer in the automobile laundry turned out nine cars, thoroughly cleaned. The young men in the tire repair department took off a customer's tire, vulcanized the tube and had him on his way in 12 minutes. Receipts in the greasing and crank case department were $112 for the day."[16]

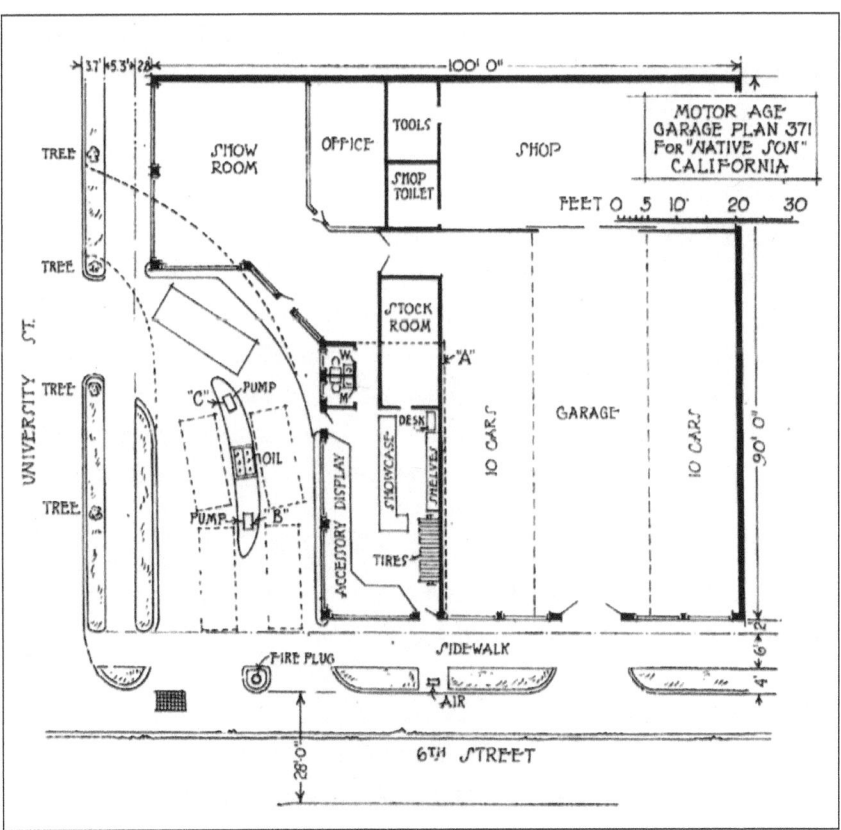

Figure 3.6. Idealized garage with super service station implications. From "An Advantageous Location for Filling Station," *Motor Age* 41 (Jan. 26, 1922): 39.

Car dealers necessarily took notice of gas station successes. Traditionally limited to repair work on cars sold, dealers were encouraged into general car maintenance by the automakers. As summarized in *Automotive Abstracts*: "More and more car dealers are looking for the major part of their shop profits from maintenance operations instead of from emergency repair work. The rapid rise of the independent super services led them to take this stand. They are installing their own super service stations."[17] The Ford Motor Company moved most aggressively, adopting a program of "neighborhood stations" in large cities in the mid-1930s. In Detroit, Hi-Speed Gas (later Pure Oil) and Ford Automobiles were marketed together in new buildings, most of them located out along the major thoroughfares that radiated from the city's center. Buildings were veneered in white glazed brick and sported tall clock towers, making for a distinctive architectural signature.[18]

In 1933, *Business Week* shared with its readers the following statistic: servicing the nation's 24 million automobiles cost car owners some $500 million, $319 million of it going for replacement parts. Profits were split about evenly between garages (both automobile dealer operated and fully independent garages) and gas stations. Independent garages, therefore, were still very much alive. "The independents have graduated from the back alley to Main St. They owe their start to the neglect of the service end by the regular dealers during the fat years. They owe their growth of recent years to the aggressive activities of parts makers," the report concluded.[19] The economic depression had softened new car sales. Owners were running up the mileage on their old cars; others were replacing them with newly purchased used cars. Thus did the car maintenance and repair business, supported by parts suppliers, assume a more central position in the auto industry. Car dealers necessarily took note. "Car dealers throughout the country," noted the *National Petroleum News*, "are re-equipping their shops so as to render chassis lubrication, transmission and differential cleaning, crankcase service and other types of operations, which are common to the Super Service Gasoline Station."[20]

Thinking Modern in the 1930s

The super service station was meant to appear spacious, thereby suggesting convenience of access and efficiency of function. Bigness, of course, was something at which Americans marveled. Many stations were deliberately styled to suggest the exotic, not only to attract customer attention but also to offer something unusual in what otherwise might loom as the mere mundane servicing of one's car. Architectural styling entered forcefully. In Los Angeles, for example, several large super service stations were styled as mosques, one said to be "Tunisian" and another "Byzantine"; both were topped by domes and provided with minarets, the stucco on the latter colored a brilliant indigo blue on which silver stars were painted.[21] Of course, in the 1920s, many were the gas stations, small and large, that were configured as windmills, tepees, lighthouses, and the like. Yet rarely did such stations sustain the patronage for which the owners wished, mainly because highly standardized gas station buildings had come to dominate gasoline marketing that was now fully dependent on place-product-packaging. Readily identifiable as links in corporate chains, standardized buildings resonated well with customers. Exotica did not.

Enthusiasm for super service stations led to overbuilding. Raising a temple to gasoline retailing required careful market assessment. Too many dealers made the mistake of building on too large a scale with overly ornate buildings, warned C. L. Buehl in the *Accessory and Garage Journal*: "A substantial structure that is modestly pleasing in appearance, efficient, usable, and easy of access is far more essential, desirable, and usually more profitable than those with lots of unnecessary 'frills' and 'whatnots' that in no way assist in rendering quick and helpful service to your patrons, nor are they in many cases even artistic." As he advised, "Let the other fellows build the monuments."[22] In building and leasing stations, the petroleum corporations very much preferred a minimalist approach. Preferred eventually were scaled-down gas station prototypes replicated over and over again, sometimes in high densities, especially in the nation's large cities. These stations quickly made the super service stations latter-day dinosaurs. Architectural minimalism came to prevail.

Starting in the mid-1930s, corporate design departments produced modestly sized, box-like buildings for gasoline sales and light repair work, buildings that minimized interior space while maximizing functionality. The new building type not only reduced construction costs through use of materials such as cinder block but also reduced maintenance costs, being veneered with durable porcelain-enamel sheeting that shone brightly day and night and was easy to clean. Most embraced modern styling that echoed what architects were calling "international style." Enter the "oblong box": rectangular gas station buildings left largely undecorated save for corporate logos and complementary lettering (fig. 3.7). Offices were located in one corner where a small TBA line was displayed. There were usually two work bays, one for lubricating and the other for washing cars. Restrooms were provided: the men's room was entered from inside the office; the women's room was placed around the corner on the outside. Gas pumps were located in front.

Architectural styling on gas stations also underwent a substantial shift when federal subsidies were offered to retailers (and, more specifically, the owners of retail buildings) during the Roosevelt Administration's New Deal. By introducing new modernistic styling, architects saw themselves as offering customers new enticement to buy and consume and, at the same time, escape the commonplace. Industrial design, a new profession, came to the fore, energized by such practitioners as Raymond Loewy and Norman Bel Geddes. Their studios applied "streamlining" to everything from home appliances to railroad locomotives. Actual streamlining worked to reduce wind drag on airplane fuselages. It was Fordism wrought in visual terms, although in the automobile field it was actually Alfred Sloan of General Motors, who, in vigorously promoting annual model changes, fostered streamline styling. So also did Walter Chrysler, with his company introducing exaggerated "Airflow" designs. Loewy and Bel Geddes both designed gas stations for various petroleum companies.[23]

The garage industry was not totally immune from the new fashion: the facades of buildings, in at least small numbers, were remodeled to the streamlined look (fig. 3.8). "It is necessary to be modern today to attract the new buyer, or to

Figure 3.7. Frontispiece advertisement on Standard Oil of Indiana road map, circa 1950. From authors' road map collection.

hold the present owner," the editors of *Automobile Topics* advised auto dealers in 1938. Modern buildings and, more important, buildings that looked modern, they said, were a prime requisite. Nonetheless, even traditional buildings, if well maintained, were perfectly acceptable. Indeed, automobile-related retailing in general, led perhaps by gasoline retailing, scored high marks in "appearance surveys" conducted by the Federal Housing Administration. Assessed in twenty-three cities across the United States in 1936, gas stations, automotive supply stores, tire and battery stores, new car salesrooms, and used car lots ranked, as a group, third behind apparel and jewelry stores among sixteen retail classifications. Over 50 percent of the 944 automotive stores surveyed were rated "good" as to general exterior and interior impressions. Signs, entrances, and display windows, however, were only appraised as "fair." "We doubt," the editors of *Motor* observed in reporting the figures, "if the trade would have made as good a showing five years ago. Modernization has made long strides recently and is still under way."[24]

Postwar Modernism

World War II interrupted storefront modernization. And with the economic boom that followed the war, it was not remodeling so much as new construction that came to dominate, at least with automobile-related commerce. The traditional garages of the early twentieth century were proving increasingly outmoded. In small towns, old garages might survive. In the cities, however, traditional

Figure 3.8. Ford dealer with new facade veneered with Libbey-Owens-Ford "Vitrolite." From "The New Materials for 'Face-Lifting,'" *Automobile Topics* 131 (Aug. 8, 1938): 49.

garage buildings were increasingly given over to different uses as new garages were built. Out along major city thoroughfares, old garage buildings came to be favored by plumbers, electricians, and building contractors, among others, who sought not only inexpensive work and storage space but also covered parking for trucks and other vehicles. Of course, many old garages were demolished for parking lots, as parking became a predominant land use around and within most city business districts by 1960.

It was the car dealership that tended to sustain the construction of new garage buildings or at least buildings that replicated most of the traditional garage functions in formats highly reminiscent of earlier decades.[25] Many auto dealers had closed up shop during the war, although in January 1946 there were still some 32,400 car and truck dealers operating, along with some 42,000 independent auto repair shops. By December of that year, the number had grown to an estimated 35, 000 and 46,000 respectively.[26] With an end to the war-induced material shortages, construction boomed.[27] New buildings needed not just to be new but to look new. Such has always been the case with the start of every new building era. It was, for example, the case after the construction hiatus of World War I.

America's glass manufacturers had long promoted the "visual" storefront, one created out of large plate glass windows enabling potential customers both on sidewalks and in cars fully unobstructed views of sales floors. Now the designers applied the idea with vigor to the new postwar car agencies (fig. 3.9). Large sheets of tempered plate glass set in metal frames stretched from floor to ceiling

Figure 3.9. Idealized auto dealership with "visual front." From *Planning Automobile Dealer Properties* (Detroit: Service Section, General Motors Corp., 1948), 66.

and usually the entire length of building's facade. Sales areas remained much the same but tended to be, especially in big-city dealerships, much larger than they were previously.

At many new dealership buildings, garage work floors, still essentially located to the rear of sales floors, were no longer entered from the front but from the side, entryways being much larger and better signed than previously (fig. 3.10). Through the 1950s, however, it also became quite common to place dealer sales floors and repair floors side by side, with the entrances to both facing front (fig. 3.11). Especially in small towns, gasoline pump islands were continued in front driveways. The new construction after World War II required very large investments, not tens of thousands of dollars as in the 1930s but millions of dollars. Accordingly, new buildings were increasingly designed by architects—a way of protecting, if not attracting, investment capital. As the 1950s unfolded, greater variety (and, it might be said, greater imagination) came to building design, especially where building massing and signage were carefully integrated. Typical garage layout tended to be more sophisticated, particularly when an array of specialized repair services was offered (fig. 3.12). No single building type any longer prevailed.

Site and Situation

After World War II, central-city automobile rows began a steady decline. Manufacturers, much reduced in number, had before the war begun to reorganize car distribution, closing branch offices and cancelling contracts with regional wholesalers. As described in the next chapter, the landmark buildings housing factory branches had dominated automobile rows of large metropolitan centers. But, beginning in the Great Depression years, branch profits and the ground rents charged for real estate in downtown areas slipped out of conjunction, making much traditional branch marketing no longer profitable. This was also true for independent repair garages. By 1940, much of the demand for repair services—in big cities, at least—was located very much in the suburbs. A substantial portion of every city's downtown building stock, including its garages, was demolished for parking lots, something that almost totally wiped out small repair garages previously scattered along back alleys and marginal side streets.[28]

The depression had put most of the nation's smaller auto manufacturers out of business, thus putting their dealers out of business as well. Automobile

Figure 3.10. Welcoming garage entry as idealized for a Dodge dealer. From advertisement, *Dodge News* 23 (June 1958): back cover. Courtesy of Chrysler Group LLC. Dodge is a registered trademark of Chrysler Group LLC.

nameplates had been disappearing rapidly ever since World War I. By 1934, only eight firms were reasonably profitable (General Motors, Ford, Chrysler, Hudson, Nash, Packard, Studebaker, and Willys-Overland); the others (including Huppmobile, Graham-Paige, and Auburn-Cord) were just holding on.[29] When new car production halted in 1943, remaining car dealers survived on maintenance and repair work and selling used cars. Many ceased operating. In big cities especially, many commuters, faced with steep gas prices, gas-rationing restrictions, and no prospect of replacing their cars any time soon, put their vehicles in storage for the war's duration, resorting thus to mass transit.

When in 1946 car production began once again, automakers sought to renew and expand prewar dealer networks. New big-city dealerships were invariably located along major streets out toward the suburbs or well within the suburbs. Desirable, of course, were locations where show windows (and signs also) could be positioned close to traffic now moving generally at faster speeds (fig. 3.13). Show windows worked best when placed directly in motorists' lines of sight. Accordingly, indented showroom facades, where windows appeared to be thrust out toward a street, became faddish (fig. 3.14). It was best to locate dealerships on important commuter thoroughfares and especially on the out-bound sides of

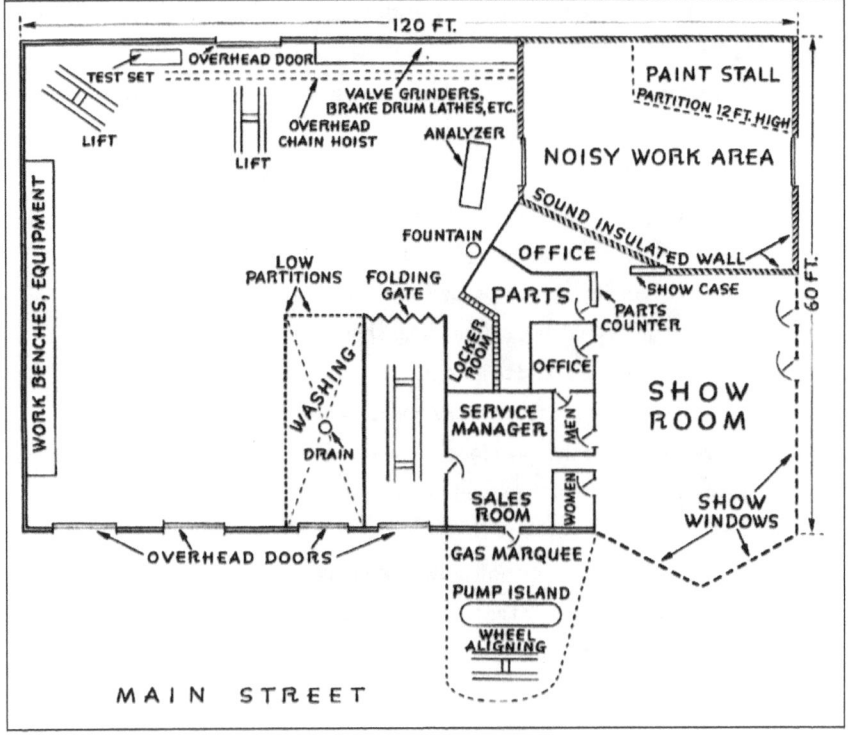

Figure 3.11. Idealized dealership layout. From "Small Pacific Coast Shop Features Silence," *Chilton's Motor Age* 69 (Aug. 1950): 59.

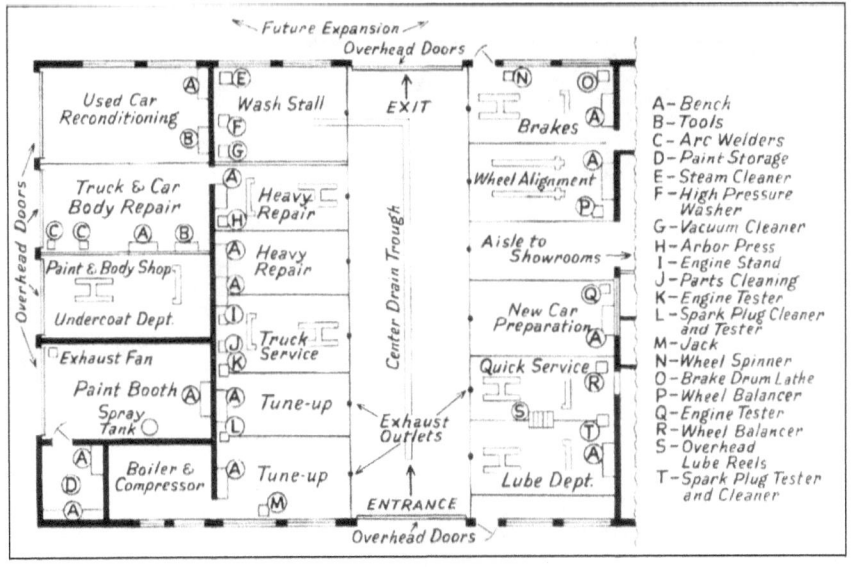

Figure 3.12. Idealized repair shop layout. From *Chilton's Motor Age* 80 (Dec. 1960): 24.

streets. Commuters were more readily enticed to stop and shop for cars when homeward bound from work.

Even before the war, Pontiac dealers, for example, were advised the following:

> 1—Corners are preferred to inside plots. They are lighter, and the dealer gets a "shot'" at people on two streets.
>
> 2—Wider and shallower plots provide more "advertising" space and more room for maneuvering than narrow and deep ones.
>
> 3—Odd shaped lots and buildings should be avoided as they waste space and are hard to lay out.
>
> 4—Location should be near some form of transportation to the business center of the town for convenience for those customers who leave and call for their cars; and to make it easier for buyers to reach the salesroom.
>
> 5—The trouble with downtown locations is parking. The location should be so selected as to have at least one street available for that purpose, or should be planned with a concrete apron for parking and gasoline sales.[30]

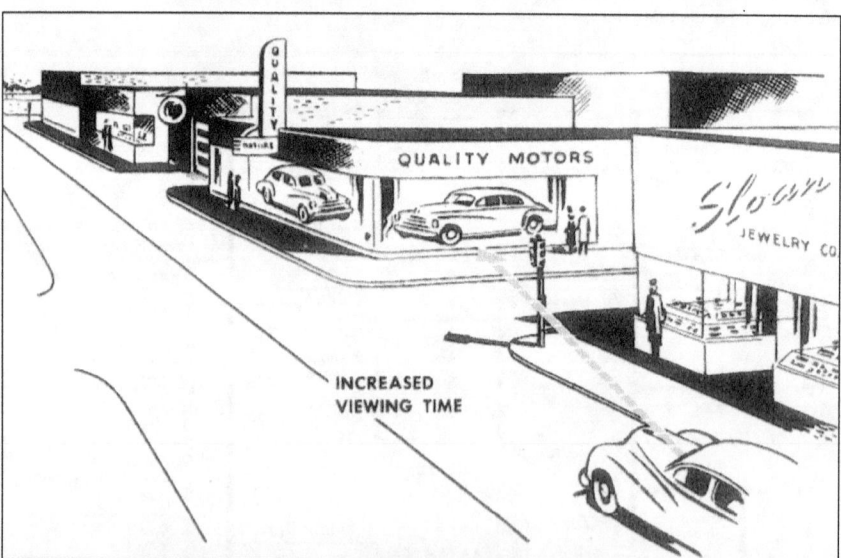

Figure 3.13. Diagram illustrating desirable street-front dealer location. From *Planning Automobile Dealer Properties* (Detroit: Service Section, General Motors Corp., 1948): 6.

GARAGE LAYOUT, 1930–1950S

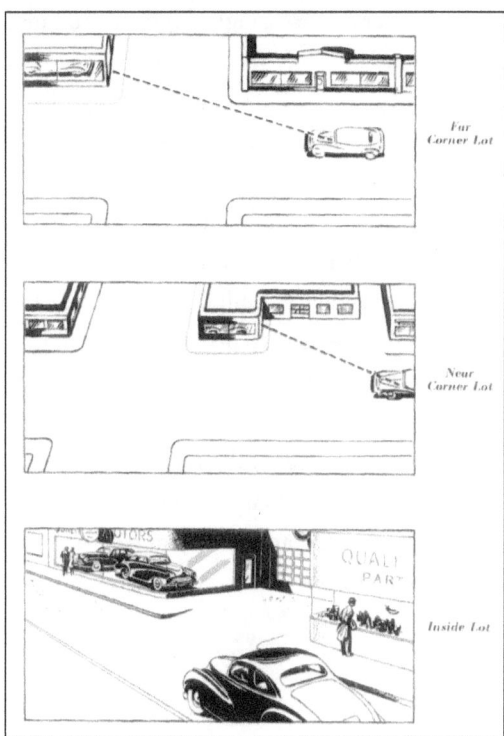

Figure 3.14. Diagram illustrating desirable facade treatments vis-à-vis lot location. From *Planning Automobile Dealer Properties* (Detroit: Service Section, General Motors Corp., 1948), 7.

A diagram made site preferences clear when it came to locating at street intersections (fig. 3.15).

By the end of the 1950s, however, advice began to change once again. Now a dealership on a very large lot with one or more buildings sprawling across it could be pushed well back from a street. It was the complex as a whole that would attract attention (fig. 3.16). A very large curbside sign, multiple wide driveways, and an expansive front lot for displaying new cars (and sometimes used cars also) had become the order of the day by 1960. Many dealerships located in auto parks, where several dealers complemented one another to provide what once again could be termed "one stop" shopping.

* * *

Nothing ever stays the same in America. And why should commercial garages have been any different, especially tied as they were to a rapidly evolving automobile technology and increasingly sophisticated marketing strategies? As time went on, some tasks simply required more space but others less. In general, car size grew through the 1950s, making many older repair garages truly congested. Crowded, poorly lit, and poorly ventilated work bays made many older garages fully obsolete. Crowded sales floors were no longer attractive. Sales floors not only needed to be comfortably arranged with elbow room to display cars, but they also needed to be clearly visible from streets beyond. For several decades after 1930, most newly built dealer facilities embraced modernism's invitation to rationalize space use—to program space in highly standardized and thus highly predictable ways. Such programing was based first and foremost on customer convenience and satisfaction. Satisfied customers were those whose predispositions to patronize were fully reinforced.

The traditional repair garage flourished when linked to car sales. As the auto makers encouraged and then required their dealers to expand into routine car maintenance in the 1930s, independent repair garages lost business, prompting

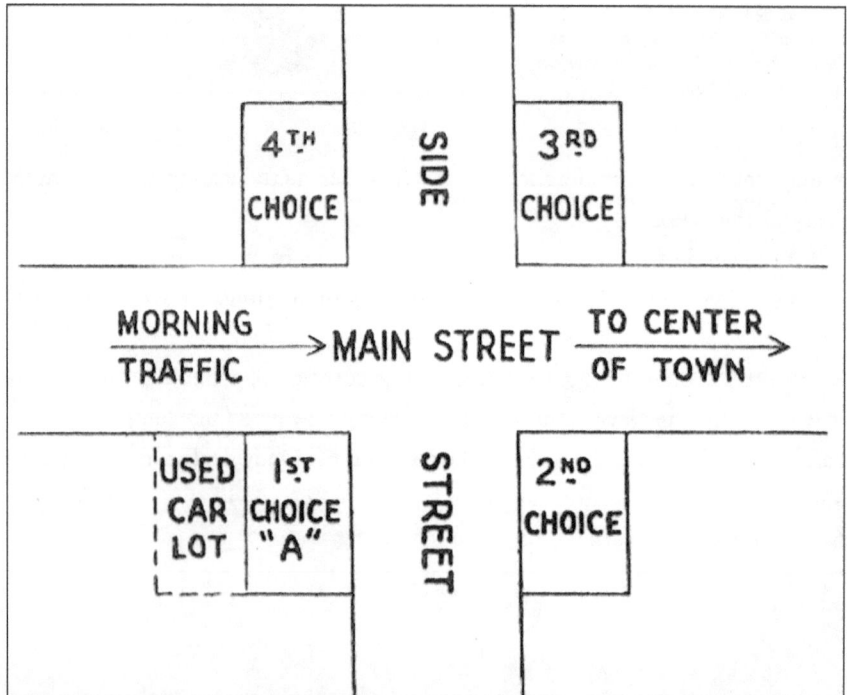

Figure 3.15. Locational preferences at city intersections along commercial strips. From "Planning to Move?" *Automobile Topics* 132 (Dec. 12, 1938): 278.

many of them to specialize by emphasizing a given service or product line: tire sales and repair, spring and shock absorber replacement, battery sales and recharging, or bodywork, for example. Refurbished garages from earlier decades were thus given extended life. The question in the 1950s was really not: "What *should* a garage be?" Rather, it was: "What *could* a garage be?" And aging garage buildings, for their part, could be almost anything. The traditional garage as it evolved through the 1920s did not have to remain a car repair or car sales facility. As buildings, they made ready conversion to artisan shops—indeed, into any kind of business that involved manipulating and sheltering materials on at least a modest scale. Surviving older garages were generally large, reasonably well built, and, for the most part, located in towns at the center and in cities out along major thoroughfares away from the center. Although given to other uses, the traditional garage, nonetheless, remained readily identifiable as having previously been a garage building.

Figure 3.16. Advertising postcard for Beaver, Pennsylvania, auto dealer, circa 1960. From authors' postcard collection.

4

DEALERSHIPS: SELLING AND SERVICING AUTOMOBILES

Garages to maintain cars by the schedules and standards of their manufacturers and repair them with parts and by the manuals of those manufacturers are routine today. A century ago, on the other hand, maintenance and repair followed many different courses, of which car dealers offered but one choice. Even the term *garage*, in conjunction with a dealership, had a different meaning, often referring to the dealers' showroom plus the enclosure for repair and maintenance. Again, the garage's multivalence through time reemerges, and so, to trace it into one of its primary streams fully demands attention to selling. The importance of sales in its own right can be simply summarized for the consumer by the riveting fact that up to one-third of a car's cost was attributable to the various aspects of sales, including service and repair obligations.[1]

At the start of the auto age, cars were sold off of factory floors, and commercial garages were irrelevant. But perhaps more important were sales made at car shows, a venue that persisted even after the auto dealers established factory branches and contracted with wholesale distributors, encouraging them in the supplying of retailers from locality to locality. It was the dealer garage, of course, that eventually became critical to auto sales. Buyers needed assurance that most cars bought would be readily serviced at a location close to home.

Automobile Contests and Shows

Founders of the automobile industry initially sponsored speed competitions and reliability contests between 1900 and 1916. These waned after 1920 because the automobile had been proven to the public, no longer needing spectacular public demonstrations of speed and durability.[2]

For simply exposing the public to the available brands, sales in various cities retained adjacent displays concentrating on their products' various features as a key means for spurring sales. The bicycle magazine *Referee,* in 1896, first promoted the idea of a show, and a Daimler automobile was shown in New York City at the Sportsmen's Exhibit in Madison Square Garden. In 1900, automobile shows expanded into multidealer events through the auspices of the National Association of Automobile Manufacturers in cooperation with the Automobile Club of America. These groups collaborated to produce the first nationally promoted automobile show in 1900 at Madison Square Garden—an event that exploded onto the sales scene (fig. 4.1).[3] By 1905, the annual show in New York City ranked as the foremost industrial show in the nation, but shows remained centered in that big city and Chicago until 1909, when Atlanta hosted its own automobile show.[4] Promoters were turning up in scattered smaller towns by that time too; the publicity strategy had fired imaginations. On the national tier, the New York show in 1920 had 307 exhibitors, of which only 81 were car manufacturers.[5]

County fairs, by 1900, were a common location for automobile shows in small cities.[6] In 1909, the first show in Terre Haute, Indiana, exuded excitement and showed off the allies it had rallied to the auto industry. Clothiers featured the specialized coats, gloves, and headwear tailored for automobilists, and the 104-page Sunday issue of the local newspaper on February 28 claimed to be "the largest paper hitherto published in the state." Hoping to spawn the "swell social event" the automobile show had in Chicago, the newspaper expected Terre Haute's show would "surpass any previous similar society event."[7]

Figure 4.1. Detroit Automobile Show, 1903. From *Horseless Age* 11 (Feb. 18, 1903): 276.

References to a few automobile shows help give a sense of what they were like on site. New York's 1905 show opened with "no pompous official ceremonies," in the words of one reporter, but for fifteen minutes the crowd that had waited for the gates to be opened streamed through without interruption when permitted entrance. Absent any "showy decorations" the hall was "rather sombre" until lighted in the evening. Manufacturer exhibits fascinated an "observant crowd" watching engine parts in motion beside each car chassis. The reporter's detailed description of each display suggests that the audience perhaps was as much gaining an introduction to new models as it was still learning what parts there were to a car.[8] Over a decade later, in the 1916 show in Seattle, autos and displays certainly were at center stage, but also attendant were a tea room, orchestra concerts, and soloists—features that helped the show bolster the city's reputation.[9] The pageantry that characterized these shows endured through the early automobile era.[10]

Selling at the Start—Factory and Distributorship Sales

Car sales by 1910 moved well beyond car shows. It did not take much to sell vehicles in the first fifteen to twenty years of the automotive industry, a period that a practiced businessman and teacher of marketing at the time, Harry Tipper, ideally termed the "virgin market."[11] So simple were the early settings that they included storage garages where local dealers rented office space for sales without retaining an inventory for display. "In all new and rapidly growing businesses there is a great flux and change among individual concerns, whether in the manufacturing or the distribution end," Tipper generalized in 1922. "This is particularly true of all the elements involved in the distribution and sale of automotive products."[12] The following discussion of the virgin market and its subsequent development does not lay out a smooth and rational plan but reflects the exploratory, sometimes sporadic and questionable decisions made by frenetic and self-certain entrepreneurs in a fledging industry lured by huge potential profits and threatened with commensurately disastrous losses. Or, in Tipper's choice words, "the distribution of the product was carried out along the lines of the least resistance and in response partly to the pressure from the potential market outside the manufacturer's establishment, and only partly from the manufacturer's conceptions as to the advisability."[13]

In retrospect, it is clear that demand outstripped supply and that most consumers were at the high end of the income scale. Essentially, dealerships lacked winnowing economic reason. Always weak vis-a-vis manufacturers, dealers were especially so in the virgin market. Curtis Publishing Company's *Saturday Evening Post* carried roughly 60 percent of the nation's magazine advertising for automobiles; and, curious as to why all magazines were not carrying more, since it was the most important way to reach a national audience at the time, Curtis systematically analyzed auto dealers in 1914. It concluded that dealers of the time performed poorly because of their backgrounds: they consisted of family or friends of the wealthy put into business because it seemed like refined work requiring little exertion, people who had failed in other work, and bicycle repairman who at least knew just enough of automobiles to service the chassis and transmission.[14]

Manufacturers, however, lacked sufficient wealth to produce their automobiles *and* launch their own dealerships. Historian Donald Finlay Davis asserts that production was never funded on a shoestring; rather, help came from the investment capital of the upper- and middle-class social groups in Detroit, where the automobile industry was quickly centered. Cars were expensive to make, and distributors essentially put up the funds that the manufacturers lacked. Investors intervened to become independent agents (also called distributors), a mode long lost to current memory in the auto industry and, curiously, to most historians. In the early years, most sales were made in factories or by regional distributors who created sales agencies. Past the founding years, when dealers were each manufacturer's agent, distributors bought cars at wholesale prices from manufacturers and sold them to dealers in the area. The distributors were in truth individual businesses. In no way were they in business as agents, although the term "agency" found its way into use because of casual, vernacular speech. From the fledgling manufacturers' viewpoint, these distributors brilliantly anted up—the gambling metaphor is not inappropriate—most of the capital necessary for production and bore the cost of storage and sales themselves. They paid cash on the manufacturers' delivery, thus freeing the manufacturers to concentrate only on the production aspect of their fledgling business. A few independent local dealers did obtain cars directly from the manufacturer. Customers of the time were capable of paying cash.[15] There just were no strong inducements for the elaborate system of franchise dealerships that developed later.

Factory branches became a common component of sales in the virgin market in a roundabout way. By 1915, the Ford Motor Company, in a move characteristic of its unchallenged supremacy in the industry's early days, established a nationwide system of twenty-four branch plants whose assembly lines produced half of Ford's products. This system had reciprocal benefits, spurring not only availability but also helping keep costs low with consequent high consumer demand. Furthermore, since parts were shipped for assembly at those twenty-four locations, it kept down the possibility of cars fully built for delivery being damaged through transport on freight cars. Regional distributorships augmented the local economy, put local labor to work, and paid local taxes, making them very welcome businesses. And they brought with them the incipient garage industry, for Ford equipped each assembly plant with the capacity to overhaul and rebuild their products. At least one lesser manufacturer quickly followed suit as an expedient: the Elgin Six advertised how dealers and owners in the territory that spanned from Cleveland to Oshkosh, Wisconsin, had a comparatively short drive to the plant in Elgin, Illinois, to buy and leave with their automobiles at a time when the demand for railroad cars during World War I held up delivery otherwise.[16]

Factory branches obviously made sense in various ways to a wide range of manufacturers, big and small, such as Ford and the Elgin Six. Sales, however, entered branches obliquely. Consumers had always wanted to see and drive the products for which they were shopping, but it was an insightful revelation for manufacturers at the time. Roy Chapin, the president of the Hudson Motor Car Company, understood but took the uncommon step of explaining the challenge. In an interview in 1910, he stated succinctly that automakers were not in the "mail-order business." The products were too expensive; the consumer "wants to see the vehicle. He doesn't want to buy it by mail." Sales consequently became a studied component of the automobile industry, not something done casually.[17]

When showrooms were combined with storage, repair, and maintenance, the factory branch took full form. It went without any entrepreneur saying so that a single location for production and sales saved the money required of separate locations. Numerous descriptions of these separate functions housed in one architecturally refined building filled many articles in the industry's trade magazines from the late 1910s to the mid-1920s. They also stood as something of a boast by the companies, themselves symbols of consumption, but especially by their managers. It required far more capital to hire factory branch managers than Hudson possessed, Chapin acknowledged.[18]

Most were multistory buildings. G. G. C. Peckham, a "driving force" such as Chapin had in mind, was linked in an *Ohio Motorist* article about the New Ohio

Buick Building in Dayton, a majestic five-story building. The ground floor was occupied by retail car sales and a branch of Goodyear Tire and Rubber Company. A ladies' room on the mezzanine, "furnished in wicker and a dainty cretonne," exemplified its implied social grace. The used car department and general offices occupied the second floor. Repair was handled on the third floor. On the fourth floor, cars were prepared for delivery, and on the fifth floor they were stored.[19]

In a 1911 article, the *Horseless Age* fixed on a factory branch in Portland, Oregon, recently constructed by the White Motor Car Company (fig. 4.2). The first floor included "live storage," which was parking for a few hours or overnight, complete with lockers for those who parked there. A custodian was always present. A chauffeurs' clubroom was made available while the occupants waited on the completion of work. Car washing and lubricating oil equipment also occupied the first floor. The second floor housed salesrooms, a supply department, showrooms, general and private offices, and ladies' parlors and waiting rooms. On the third floor, cars were stored. Repair, rebuilding, and painting were done on the fourth floor.[20]

Investors publicly scouted for opportunities to invest wisely in the new and expanding car market. The trade magazines carried advertisements by those wishing to come into the trade and also advised investors what to consider. For

Figure 4.2. White Motor Car Company, Portland, Oregon. From "The New Automobile Center, Social Hall Avenue, Salt Lake City," *Horseless Age* 27 (May 3, 1911): 755.

example, in an 1898 issue of the *Horseless Age,* one classified stated, "A gentleman well known in New York City, and with the highest credentials, desires to actively represent a prominent manufacturer of motor vehicles. Would invest."[21] Anyone seeking to become a dealer or to change lines or add a new line of cars, the *Horseless Age* forewarned, confronted the fact that one must pick from what manufacturers were open, presumably not just the ones they preferred. (It should be remembered that many early dealers dealt in several manufacturers' brands.) They ideally must also pick a class of car appealing to the local market and their own sympathies. "No more readily can a man whose tastes and habits have always been simple and economical make a success of selling $5000 cars," the magazine cautioned, "when he feels in his heart that the cheaper car would be just as satisfactory and has no sympathy with the scale of living with which such cars are associated." Furthermore, the product's general performance record, not its mechanical features, had to be taken into consideration. High on the list were the "stability of the manufacturer" and its reputation for fair treatment of its dealers; to be avoided especially were manufacturers who required dealers to take cars regardless of consumer demand or who were lax in delivering their product when it had been sold. Not only the resale value of the cars but also the capacity to retain older dealers was crucial.[22]

In Seattle and Spokane, Washington, the Eldridge Buick Company exemplified one of the first highly successful distributorships. Begun in 1920, it could, within six years, reasonably boast of sales via sixty-nine dealers: Eldridge's range included the entire state of Washington, northern Idaho (fig. 4.3), and four dealers in Alaska. These provided for almost all of a Buick owner's needs in the area: oil and grease service, washing and polishing, bodywork, tire repairs, and all required shop work. As the regional central authority on Buicks, Eldridge gave its dealers a wide array of services, including information helpful for used car sales, means to expedite the sales of less popular vehicles, and a complete inventory of parts and accessories that were sent rapidly upon demand to the far-flung dealerships.[23]

The new trade's jargon highlighted two terms, "service" and "station." "All distributors and dealers, as well as independent repair stations, whether they realize it or not," a garage manual in 1928 lectured, "are vitally interested in the service problem in its entirety" because they not only had to give good service to retain customers but also had to attract owners who might switch from what they drove for the type sold by the distributor doing their work.[24]

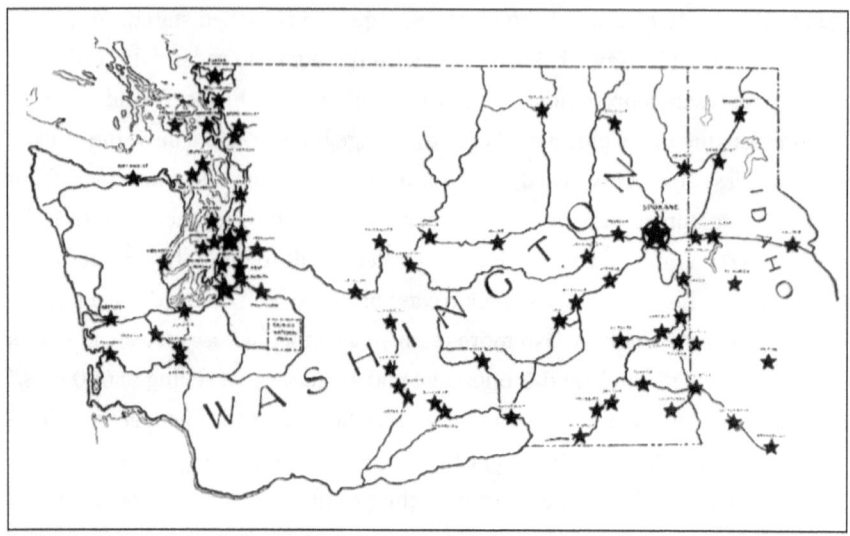

Figure 4.3. Eldridge Buick Company locations in Washington and northern Idaho. From *Motor World Wholesale* 84 (May 6, 1926): 13.

Legendary were the successful entrepreneurs who had forged their way in the days before published advice. M. L. Bridgman, first a credit manager in a dry goods business, next rose to selling Columbia bicycles, just one of the products manufactured by Col. Albert Pope, who briefly was the nation's leading bicycle and car manufacturer. Pope so valued Bridgman that he made him his personal representative. A gifted salesman, Bridgman went down in the annals of automobile fame for selling the first automobile in New York City, a Columbia electric in 1896. Twenty years later, he was celebrated in the *Ohio Motorist* for carefully planning five Willys-Overland "sales and service stations" in Cleveland, which he also readied for their openings. J. B. Melvin, distributor for the Grant automobile in Indianapolis, articulated the principle that service encompassed the totality of the relationship with the customer but focused on the repair work necessitated from time to time of any quality product. Another mogul, Don Lee, the Cadillac distributor for California, who by 1918 had expanded to fifty dealers from his lone, original "store," based his business expansion upon "an ideal of service" that invited customers to bring their cars in for free adjustment and inspection for an entire year, according to *Automobile Topics*. Lee equipped his shops to work not only on Cadillacs but also on numerous other marques. The capacity of Lee's dealerships included complete overhauling, making tops (in that era of open cars), painting, and "blacksmith" work.[25]

Ralph Temple earned a biography for his entrepreneurship in a 1922 issue of the *Hoosier Motorist*. He "was the first man in America prominently connected with the bicycle industry to enter the motor car field," the trade magazine recalled. He was also Ransom E. Olds's first dealer and himself sold one-third of the first year's output. Later, he organized the Chicago Automobile Trade Association; its Central Market Used Car Blue Book became the national standard for resale. In what was no small assertion in an emergent industry when elites purchased cars to enhance their status, Temple could claim to have personally taught several socially prominent persons how to drive before their cars were shipped to them in Europe. Fully appreciative of the infrastructure necessary for automobiles to expand their market, he publicly endorsed the Good Roads movement and its founders. Assuming the stereotypically successful businessman's optimistic demeanor, Temple ended his interview with this article of faith: "All we have to do is to do our level best, and hold our heads up high and keep smiling." He had just been appointed the general sales manager in Indiana for the Durant motorcar.[26]

Selling Matures

The mid-1920s, following the recession immediately after World War I, witnessed the galloping growth of the mass market. Distributors took on cooperatives known variously as "sub-dealers," "associate dealers," or "community dealers." Cars no longer were many miles out of reach from would-be small-town owners; these sub-dealers went into business in or very near these towns. Big cities, too, required distributors to expand to sub-dealers. *Automotive Industries* in 1924 explained that "[u]ntil the past few years the distributor or factory branch was the wholesaler of cars for a considerable territory, containing anywhere from twenty-five or fifty to three or four hundred dealers." In big cities, distributors placed a sub-dealer in each of the five to twelve "shopping centers" that automotive traffic had built upon earlier streetcar lines. That same year, *Automotive Abstracts* reported that in Cleveland, for example, the distributor's own store sold one-third of the cars, and in outlying areas "sub, associate, or community dealers" sold the remaining two thirds.[27]

The relentless pressure to sell ever more cars soon structured the character of the relationship between manufacturers and dealers that marked much of the next thirty years of auto sales. When Chrysler acquired Dodge Motors in 1928, it coveted Dodge's well-developed dealer network no less than its legendary parts manufacturing. As a model for the future, *Motor World Wholesale* touted the Nebraska Buick Company's distributorship, which oversaw dealers throughout the entirety of Nebraska, the eastern half of Iowa, and the southern part of South Dakota. The distributorship reasoned that the best way to help its dealers was to "help them sell more cars." This it did twice each year by bringing in every dealer to the central office in Lincoln for discussions about selling and service. On top of that, "block men" visited the company's territory throughout the year to help with advertising, financial problems, and aid in selling cars to particular customers if the dealer was having difficulty. This especially meant working on the terms of credit for the dealer through General Motors' financing program should a potential customer be reluctant about the terms. A customer might even receive suggestions about various possessions he could sell to raise the needed funds for the purchase. Current owners with large families would be urged to buy a good used car as a second family vehicle. The distributorship also employed advertising specialists to create "direct-by-mail" letters and newspaper advertising for dealers. For mechanical work, the central office ran a school twice a year for the dealers' mechanics, and should a mechanic be unable to repair a car, the central office dispatched its own technician to complete the work. It was reported approvingly that in each of the twelve months before the September 10, 1928, article in *Motor World Wholesale* appeared, the distributorship sold more cars than it had in the equivalent month during the year prior to that.[28] Exemplary sales-and-service strategy meant high-pressure tactics.

Distributors began to ask who benefitted from sub-dealers. *Motor World Wholesale* posed that very question in the title of an article in 1925. First, too many sub-dealers meant undue competition among themselves, driving some sub-dealers out of business and raising doubts among customers about reliability. Distributors predicated their business at the outset on sub-dealers; but, just as manufacturers had to learn, the truly beneficial nature of a mutually respectful relationship was imperative, yet not fully appreciated at first. Distributors were warned to look for many virtues in would-be dealers. What, for example, was the potential sub-dealer's standing in the community? *Automotive Industries* a year earlier warned against a sub-dealer who directed customers to come back with appraisals from a factory outlet and promising twenty-five dollars more on trade-ins. Remedy lay in sub-dealers' attendance at informational meetings and a willingness to educate themselves. Vocabulary had turned to "The Subdealer Problem," as *Automotive Industries* entitled its cautionary article.[29]

From the 1920s through the 1930s, the automobile became a well-established fact of life for every social class.[30] Ford, the premier car manufacturer through the early 1920s, understood that although the rise of the mass market was based on customers' belief in the automobile's utility and charm, they still had to be persuaded to buy it. Consumption became its own justification in the nation's new value system, and circumstances, at least at first, were on the side of the manufacturer and salesman.[31] Ford's widely based system of assembly plants, described above, in unison with its central plant at River Rouge disgorged and, in 1921, sold three-fifths of the nation's cars; this enabled the company to assume defining power over its distributors, who were required to sell no other marques.[32] (Other dealers, meanwhile, were often selling multiple lines.) Ford's practices reached an extreme in the recession that year, when the parent company called upon its dealers to accept more than the agreed-upon quotas in order to see Ford through the economic slump.[33]

Henry Ford understood the need for sales and distributor management and so hired Norval Hawkins to develop the system. It was highly centralized and worked on the principle that, each month, dealers would purchase a fixed number of cars set by Ford's office, buying them at discounts of 15 to 25 percent but selling them at Ford's set price. Any dealer who failed to meet the sales quota or sold outside their territory could be let go. However, dealers remaining in the system obtained the exclusive right to deal in Fords.[34] Other aspects helped fully define Ford's franchising system, but it was in the terms outlined above that trouble eventually brewed because in them lay Ford's ultimate power.[35]

Other manufacturers developed their own systems as franchising became universal in the 1920s. In enhancing the operation of the General Motors Corporation (GMC) after he became its chief executive in 1923, Alfred P. Sloan Jr. took a wholly different viewpoint toward dealers than that of his Ford competitor. Aware that the era of the seller's market had ended, he worked on developing respectful relationships with GMC's dealers. He drove around to dealers' meetings and also talked with them individually, improved means for regularized corporate communication with them (including hearing and settling dealer complaints), and stipulated more provisions for financial assistance and discounts.

Sloan also set a unique model for a rationally constructed sales program with the data collected each month.[36]

Still, many dealers became disgruntled through the late 1920s because of the continued pressure on sales and were further strained in the sales slump of the 1930s. In 1934, it was reported that dealers made one-half cent of profit on each dollar of sales and slightly over one cent two years later. The standard that dealers sought was an elusive 5 percent. Feeling that they had but one privilege, that of buying cars on discount, dealers complained of newly issued franchises violating the territorial integrity of extant ones, arbitrary cancellations, and pressure to take unwanted cars and meet unfair sales quotas. On behalf of the dealers, the National Automobile Dealers Association (NADA) called for a federal examination. The Federal Trade Commission investigated their claims, produced nothing of importance to remedy the problems, and finished its report in 1939, after automobile manufacturers had already undertaken their own solutions.[37] It was at this juncture that the Buick and Chevrolet dealer Morfitt in Astoria, Oregon, uttered the strident denunciation of the entire sales industry quoted at the end of this chapter.

Ford never assumed a coequal relationship with its dealers, failing to fully grasp their admitted principle that sales did not result merely from making cars available. One of Ford's traveling representatives, wanting to school a dealer about sales, obtusely referred to them as "breaking down sales resistance."[38] Historian Thomas Dicke has underlined the consequences of Ford's attitude: "when times were hard, the dealer network would be prone to resentment and defections."[39] Indeed, specialized dealerships in hard times brought with them more organized dealer relationships, such as the NADA, which was founded at the interval during World War I when the government ordered reduction of passenger car production.[40] In times of slackened sales, Ford leveraged its franchising supremacy over dealers, especially in the early years of the Great Depression, forcing them to acquire all the cars the company produced. It also increased the number of dealerships in hopes of increasing sales.[41] In 1937, faced with high failure rates among financially depleted dealers and the likely impression of Ford as an ogre, the manufacturer finally began to improve its dealer relationships, setting boundaries on Ford's and its dealers' obligations as well as ensuring certain rights for the dealers. Terms were set on the required amount of time before a dealer's termination by Ford; and the company guaranteed to repurchase all parts and cars in the dealer's inventory at the time of cancellation, to provide a proportional rebate on cars sold at reduced prices, and—most important of all—to set a ceiling on the number of cars that dealers were required to carry. Various successive changes over the years after 1937 improved the relationship. Nonetheless, fears of quick cancellation and intimidation in executing terms still hung over Ford and its dealers.[42]

One of the collateral fallouts of the manufacturer-dealer friction was conflict with independents in the repair and accessories trades. Complaints arose that dealers had to sell parts, repairs, and service in order to make decent profits. They grew to "resent the existence of almost twice as many independent repair shops as there are dealers," reported *Business Week* in 1938, because selling parts to the repair shops only detracted from the dealers' own garage work. Dealers' profits came mostly from accessories sales because automobile sales were a "loss leader," according to *The Nation* in 1940.[43]

Dealers did grow financially stronger after World War II, which marked the end of the distributorship era. Dealers had become solvent enough to no longer need distributors for selling them cars from the manufacturers at retail prices. Rumblings between manufacturers and dealers, nonetheless, resumed in the 1950s. The case of J. Ed "Brick" Travis Jr., a GMC dealer in St. Charles, Missouri (a St. Louis suburb), stirred national attention about the rising new phase of discontent among sellers. NADA, focusing on the Travis case, reported that although he had sold 25 percent more cars between November 1954 and July 1955 than during the same period a year earlier, GMC had canceled his franchise.[44]

NADA brought added pressure to bear in early 1956 by encouraging the U.S. Congress to undertake hearings later that year. The result was the Federal Automobile Dealers Franchise Act, popularly known as the Automobile Dealers' Day in Court Act, a title that discloses just what dealers hoped they had achieved after long years of oppression. Pressure did let up on dealers; yet, by the very fact that dealers depended on manufacturers for what they sold, superiority in the relationship inherently remained with the manufacturers.[45]

For consumers, the Automotive Information Disclosure Act of 1958 won some gains. With the resumption of a flush economy after World War II, dealers had set out to run their sales records as high as possible. Sales teams grilled customers in special rooms where they were offered various deals that cultural historian James Flink has charged "often skirted legality."[46] "Packing," as the corrupted arrangements were called, may have originated decades earlier when dealers believed they could recover losses on too-generous trade-in allowances by adding to new car costs through their time-payment plans.[47] Various forms of packing subsequently evolved: these included the "plain pack," which involved inflated dealer-preparation costs; the "top pack," or adding an inflated trade-in value to the new-car price; and, among many more, the "switch" (or "bait and switch," as it is perhaps more popularly known), a scheme in which an attractive advertisement was used to lure the customer to the dealership, where he or she was then offered a poorer deal on a car other than the one advertised.[48] The Automotive Information Disclosure Act of 1958, sponsored by A. S. "Mike" Monroney, a U.S. senator from Oklahoma, brought the term "sticker price" into the popular vocabulary. This was shorthand for all the prices that a dealer was required to post on a sticker attached to the driver's side window of every car; these included the manufacturer's suggested retail price, equipment in the base price, and suggested prices for other equipment and dealer preparation, also known as "dealer prep." Thus, hosts of questionable past practices were precluded, although packing could persist because dealer preparation could be set at a cost higher than the actual cost to the dealer. Buyers' skepticism remained perhaps the most common feature of new car shopping.[49]

The Service Floor

Automobiles required delivery to dealers if their buyers did not drive them away from the assembly plant. During the industry's early years, owners did commonly take that on themselves. Ford's voluminous production of two thousand cars per day in 1915 drew comparatively slight notice to the unromantic delivery component, but the automotive trade literature paid some attention to it. In practice, delivery was no less extraordinary than production. Each day's production had to be moved out of the factory, and it took a specialized workforce of three hundred people. They readied each new car by removing the outer shell of the body, wheels, fenders, and guards or bumpers and loaded them onto railroad cars (fig. 4.4). The chassis and removed parts were arrayed vertically at opposite ends of the railroad cars, each of which had special brackets to secure the cargo and prevent it from slipping in transit. Inspectors made sure that every railroad car was ready for movement.[50]

Equipment manufacturers devised provisions for other car companies. Carbo Steel Post Company in Chicago Heights, Illinois, for instance, devised a

Figure 4.4. A Ford loading dock. From *Ford Times* 8 (June 1914): 423.

deck that permitted one car to be loaded upon another without disassembling most of both cars. These decks fit comfortably within railroad cars for shipment, and some automobile dealers and warehouses found them preferable to pits like those sunken beneath the automobiles for work in garages. An ingenious inventor in Detroit, Stephen Kramer, designed a sixty-foot-long trailer that could carry four cars of standard wheelbase behind a tractor. Its other virtue was the capacity in one operation to turn into a twenty-foot alley where the back side of dealers, warehouses, and garages were commonly located.[51]

Companies filled the opportunity left open by manufacturers that, unlike Ford, lacked their own delivery equipment. *Automobile Topics* reported in 1931 that 43 percent of shipments from factories was done by trucks with specialized trailers. These were calculated to be cheaper than railroad delivery or cars driven from the factory. Off-loading a car of one type at one dealer and another type at another dealer was akin to the common practice of local trucking companies delivering merchandise to local businesses. Loading cars onto trucks was simpler than loading them onto railroad cars and required no special blocking equipment. Gasoline prices imposed fiscal limits on this type of delivery, but trucking companies with a specialty in car delivery were entering the field. No longer were enterprising individual truckers the only recourse.[52]

Financing Car Sales

How was the flow of capital necessary for car production continued when sales volume could vary so much because of competition among manufacturers and periodic fluctuations in the economy? In the virgin market, sales were in cash for the full amount and exceeded supply. One Ford dealer in a small western town probably characterized the practice of extending credit when needed to a buyer without cash in hand and then collecting it later, after the owner took possession, or threatening to repossess the car. Dealers' decisions about whether or not to extend credit to a customer were based on instinct or limited personal acquaintance. But conditions, of course, fluctuated in a growing consumer economy like that of the United States and the lack of credit through banks threatened dealers, especially during the recession at the beginning of the 1920s. Late in 1920, a vice president of American National Bank in Indianapolis tried to reassure a gathering of local Marmon automobile dealers that banks would not adopt a loan policy detrimental to their sales. Drought in the region of central Montana through North Dakota between 1916 and 1920, however, severely threatened the economy there, and bankers quickly refused financing deals for prospective car buyers except for those of unquestionable resources. The result: used cars filled dealers' lots to capacity without prospect of sale.[53] This situation typified many places nationwide, and the shortfall of supply turned to sellers pushing demand.

In response, dealers and manufacturers created a new institution to stabilize their livelihood: finance companies based within the automobile industry that precluded payments through local banks. Finance companies served not only the individual consumer but also distributors who had trouble acquiring money to obtain cars from manufacturers. With regard to building the auto industry, one historian has called this development equal in importance to assembly-line production. Had it not been for finance companies, cars might have been more expensive with far fewer sales. This approach to financing began on a small scale in 1910, with others multiplying by 1915 and the General Motors Corporation installing the first big plan in 1919. By 1921, a prominent banker, in an address to the

Automobile Club of America, reported that more than 110 corporations across the country existed as automobile or other private financial formats performing equivalent work. They operated on a system of deferred payments as opposed to the early system of complete cash payment. Nearly one-half of the cars sold depended on the structure of installments in 1921 and, within four more years, more than 75 percent of the sales. Banks came to learn that without the specialized knowledge that finance corporations acquired, they were best off staying out of the automobile finance business, at least through the early years.[54]

By the mid-1920s, members of the automobile industry were unquestionably committed to installment buying and sophisticated financial arrangements to expand their fortunes. The length of payments also extended from the original terms of one year to several years.[55] Contrary to lingering doubts among some conservative financiers, A. R. Erskine, chief executive of Studebaker, came to this conclusion in a 1922 article in *Motor Age*: "The large finance corporations, operating an organized financial plan on a national scope, offer manufacturers and dealers a necessary and efficient service. They are a desirable asset to the industry."[56] GMC's own proof lay in the fact that its credit corporation helped enable it to surpass Ford to achieve the rank of leading manufacturer.[57] To counter the opposing view that automobiles were a nonessential and foolhardy investment, the industry's entrepreneurs held that automobiles had raised the American standard of living. Of course, only food, clothing, and shelter were essential, the proponents of the car acknowledged. However, as a 1923 article in *Automotive Industries* argued, cars were like other inventions such as the telephone, the electric power system, and the railroad: they had "raised standards of living to an extent which would have been unbelievable a few years ago and they have made present industrial methods possible."[58] Automobiles, in short, came to be integral to a way of life that presumed progress. Implicit in cars was a worldview, and financing them on credit made it possible. Thus, the anthem in peroration: "The automobile has made it possible for millions of city dwellers to buy suburban or county homes. It has had a potent influence in making Americans a race of homeowners. It is doing more every year to relieve urban congestion and take the sordidness out of city life."[59]

Time payments remained a staple of the automobile industry but not without questions of how best to manage them. The National Automobile Dealers Association head and a Hupmobile distributor and dealer in Chicago warned dealers in 1925 that there were reasonable limits to the extent of time that should be granted for repayment on a loan. The year before, the association had adopted one year as the allowable limit. By 1935, it was acknowledged that dealers had become increasingly unable to finance their operations without help from outside financiers. Ford, at first reluctant to consider financing, adopted a system in 1925 that permitted an incredibly low down payment for driving off with one of their cars. It was tested first in Detroit, where a minimum of $12.40 was set and created a sensation. The Commercial Investment Trust Corporation (C.I.T.) eventually replaced Ford's financing system. By the late 1930s, banks had become so numerous in automobile financing that dealers worried about the competition. Meanwhile finance companies tried to draw dealer interest by having dealers focus on what they did best—selling cars—while leaving the complicated and multifaceted aspects such as consumer credit investigations to the specialists, the finance companies.[60]

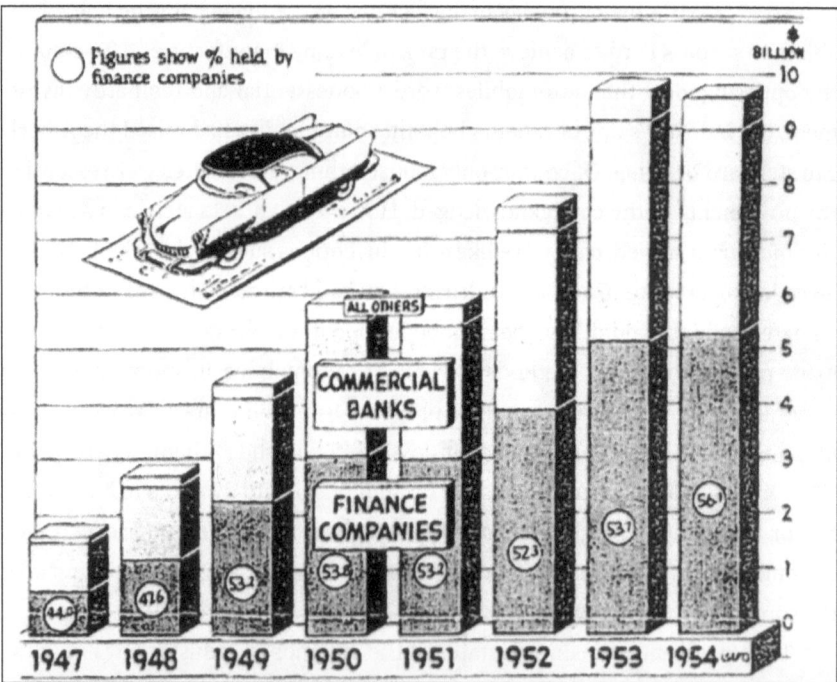

Figure 4.5. The increase of finance firms as a percentage of automobile purchases on credit. From *Automobile Topics* 56 (Mar. 1955): 4.

Even discounting the mad rush among Americans to own cars in the affluent 1950s, statisticians reported that 75 to 80 percent of cars had long been sold on installment plans just short of thirty months' duration. Sellers kept up their pressure tactics, reaching an extreme in the mid-1950s with no-down-payment plans, an unusually long repayment period of forty-eight months, and even all-expenses-paid trips overseas or to Florida (fig. 4.5). Fearful of the end to production and, consequently, new car sales on the eve of America's entry into World War II, the industry had gladly realized just how dependent Americans had become on cars. The American Automobile Association produced data showing that although 50 percent of car owners could get to work by other means, 75 percent of round trips were considered "necessary."[61]

Salesmanship

Successful salesmanship became a practiced art form if not a kind of profession (fig. 4.6). The virgin market witnessed considerable eccentricity by later standards. Salesmen catered to prospective buyers. Cars were "pleasure cars" in the dealers' vocabulary, not "passenger cars," as they later were known.[62] The First World War may have been the turning point. An author on automobile salesmanship lectured in 1917 that "pleasure car" had "a sinister meaning in war time."[63] Anecdotal evidence concerning sales suggests a far less structured and routine experience than developed in the mass market later, when customers no longer brought presumptions of social superiority and traditions of servitude to the dealership. Cars for this elite were accoutrements of pleasure.

A salesman of fifteen years in 1924, who therefore bridged the virgin and mass market, recollected his years in sales for *Motor Age* and left precious evidence otherwise missing from automobile history archives. James Parker sold cars in New York City. His first memory was of a cold winter day when a man with no overcoat or gloves came to the dealership. After looking at a car for an hour, the prospective buyer gave Parker his address and asked Parker to meet him there the next day, which Parker did. Again, the man was wearing no overcoat or gloves despite the cold. The lack of protective clothing was especially notable in an age when cars had neither windshields nor "foredoors"—that is, doors between the front seat and running board where passengers dismounted from the car. In this bitter weather, Parker honored the man's request to drive him to an address on Long Island and, when they returned, was invited into the

Figure 4.6. A staged presentation of an entrance into an actual salesroom (Maxwell-Chalmers, New York City) to demonstrate how a salesman can approach and welcome entrants, not wait for them indifferently. From *Motor World* 63, Summer Merchandising Number (Apr. 14, 1920): 17.

man's house. The man gave Parker a drink, said he liked the car, "would see me again," and let Parker out of the house. Parker despaired of ever seeing the man return—"I would have sold him as a prospect for two cents"—but soon received a certified check for five thousand dollars plus five hundred dollars for extras. He understandably lodged in Parker's memory: "A very nice fellow, very eccentric, and some years later, shot and killed by his wife, a noted South American beauty."[64] Customers simply did not become salesmen's biographical icons in the later age of the mass market. Perhaps this was attributable to the fact of a so-called "lower salaried group" that had entered the market, to use one automotive journal's vocabulary. In 1926, 3,271,015 low-priced cars were sold, compared to 13,285 in 1907. In the same period, the production of low-priced cars jumped over two hundred times while the increase in total production was nine times, due in large measure to the mass production of the comparatively inexpensive Model T Ford.[65] These new buyers were probably less likely to bring presumptions of superiority to the marketplace, where they felt they should be pampered. As they were also greater in number, personality differences among them were probably lost in the mass market.

Another of Parker's recollections indicates not only the arrogance of wealthy customers in the early market but also the way salesmen might deceive them to make a sale. Parker was "[h]aving a terrible time trying to sell a fussy old gentleman a rebuilt car," even though he knew the man had the money and desired to own the car. Thus, Parker told him, when he came in again, that the car had been sold. "Right away he was all upset. . . . He should have signed before," Parker said, describing the prospective buyer's lament. The would-be customer then asked, "Couldn't we see the purchaser and offer him a premium to release it?" Parker went away and, "after a fake phone conversation with the mythical buyer," returned to report that the car could be resold for a one-hundred-dollar profit. The deal was done and Parker later learned that the buyer was one of the biggest real estate salesmen in the area. Likely judging that the buyer himself practiced similar stunts to make a sale, Parker believed the man would not be angry if he learned the truth.[66]

Parker summarized: "Wealthy customers are often hard to handle, and must be humored."[67] But he also generalized about changes in the mass market corroborated in others' detailed reports.

Careful analysis of the dealers' local market and record keeping became de rigueur by the mid-1920s. In Oxnard, California, dealers took a census of every car owner among the town's six thousand in-town inhabitants and those of the surrounding area. Salesmen were instructed to spend three hours each day in a designated area where they made a record, not only of the owner's occupation but also of the make and model of each car. All part of the census were lodge affiliations, hobbies, and, among farmers, the crops they grew. The data was used in selling cars throughout the area. Prospective buyers were visited again to determine if they would sooner or later be in the market for a purchase. Different salesmen undertook this function in an area other than the one to which they had been assigned in the initial census so as to avoid leaving the impression that the first encounter would eventually be turned to sales in subsequent visits.[68]

W. H. Taylor, one of the Oxnard dealers, also calculated how to achieve the most productive relationship with his salesmen and buyers. He learned that salesmen worked better on salary than on commission. Commissions had led to many salesmen quitting the staff, but with salaried men, there was no reluctance to turn prospective buyers over to other salesmen. Taylor appreciated and allowed for the elusive human psychology that pervaded the realm of sales. In the case of one particular customer, numerous contacts by different salesmen had failed but ended in a sale by another salesman "because the prospect's pride refused to let him yield from a negative to an affirmative attitude, although he was really sold by the first man." Repair and service following sales were also integral to Taylor's strategy. Two free inspections (one at five hundred miles and another at one thousand miles) were offered to everyone who had purchased a car, and if the new owner could not bring his car to Taylor's garage, a "service wagon" was sent to the owner.[69]

H. H. Batcheller, the head of Chevrolet's school for salesmen in the Chicago area, represented state-of-the-art practices in large urban centers. To the Training of Salesmen Group Meeting in Cincinnati in April 1929, he explained that inductees had to be made to realize that they must be determined to make sales; car sales were "not a moving stairway on which they can ride to the heights of success." Individual buyers, unlike wholesale buyers for distributors, are not grounded in appeals to reason, Batcheller insisted. He taught salesmen not to talk too much and too fast: "Our men are instructed to pause for several seconds before taking up a new point, thus being sure the previous one has had an opportunity to make a lasting impression on the buyer's mind." Nor should they have a standard sales pitch. Finally, a demonstration of the car was imperative because buyers understood that salesmen's words could be crafted to go "after his money."[70]

An eminently successful used car salesman in Haddonfield, New Jersey, corroborated the essentially material appeal of the cars themselves and secondary reliance upon the interpersonal dynamics of sales psychology. Get the people to the location where the cars are for sale and "get the people to look at them," E. A. Burroughs emphasized. "After that," summarized the *American Garage and Auto Dealer* for Burroughs, "it is more or less a matter of personal salesmanship." (This was at the time when salesmen still made personal calls upon customers at their home or business.) Burroughs appreciated the need for personal appeals as part of his sales approach. An employee in the advertising department of several newspapers before turning to automobiles sales, Burroughs wrote his own advertisements and utilized folksy vocabulary. Examples include the following:

>FORD TOURING—Looks like Hades, but runs like the Old Boy himself: $25 cash

COUPE—One of our Antiques. Don't look so good, but—Oh, Baby! How she runs!⁷¹

James Parker, whose biography in sales was covered above, comprehended in sparing summary the things he understood from experiences of people such as Taylor in Oxnard, Batcheller in Chicago, and Burroughs in Haddonfield to signify the maturation of a "staid, quiet business." No longer could one speak respectfully, as was done originally, of "the auto game," Parker warned. Salesmen no longer offered long demonstrations to shoppers. Salesmen's expense accounts were severely reduced or nonexistent.[72] Batcheller identified the salesmen he trained as tantamount to an entire social and intellectual cadre. His students had various levels of previous education—some grade school, a few college, and many high school. Most were "not of the studious type, or have long since ceased to study." They had to be taught about automobile construction in lively and dramatic lessons and "are bored if kept inactive long."[73]

Closing a deal with the buyer became an interaction on which dealers harangued their salesmen in this ever faster and more manipulated mass market. Batcheller judged that this was the point in the sale at which salesmen were weakest.[74] *Motor World* outlined a twelve-step sales program whose final two points were to get and secure the signature on the sales contract. When the purchaser signed, the trade magazine advised, the salesman should "[c]ongratulate him on his purchase, but don't say anything that will re-open the discussion about the sale."[75] At the twelfth and final step, the salesman should walk to the door with his customers. This shepherding was judged courteous but also calculated "to prevent 'wandering' about the sales floor which might prompt the purchasers to wonder if they had bought the right model."[76]

Sales also came to mean more than the initial step of clinching a deal. It increasingly took on responsibility for the consumer's satisfaction with the sale after it was completed. In using the term "service," salesmen (at least at first) were referring to this follow-up work, not to repair and maintenance in the garage. The superintendent of one Ford dealer explained for a reporter how a salesman kept in contact for three months following the sale, labeling the program "Smiling Service." Forty-eight hours after the sale, a card introducing the program was sent to the car owner; information on auto care followed on cards sent weekly for the next five weeks. For example, the second card, sent on the fourteenth day, explained the significance of keeping the car's front end properly aligned, while the fifth card emphasized the importance of tending properly to needed repairs. The end purpose was to sell the buyer on the dealership itself, not just the car. Dealers reporting back to the manufacturer about owners' experiences resulted in some significant mechanical improvements, too. Chrysler, for example, knew that six- and eight-cylinder cars vibrated less than four-cylinder cars but understood that four-cylinder cars were the most popular, luring the biggest market. Chrysler thus broke with its exclusively upper-scale clientele by designing a "floating power" motor mount that reduced vibration in four-cylinder models; with it, the company entered the expanded market in 1931.[77]

Sales yielded neither rich incomes nor easy working conditions. A survey among dealers in 1921 by a company in Toledo said salesmen should be paid according to the size of the population they served. In towns of less than 10,000 people, annual salaries of $2,000 to $2,500 were considered sufficient. In towns with populations of 10,000 to 25,000, salaries of $2,500 to $5,000 were the norm. For towns of 25,000 to 100,000 people, it was $3,000 to $5,000. Historian Robert Genat took the rare opportunity to find out from a long-term salesman that they put in, on average, fifty hours a week, with some individuals reaching seventy-five hours per week. Schedules were split between two teams who worked from eight in the morning until two in the afternoon and two in the afternoon until closing. Two systems operated within each block of time: the "up" system and the "open floor system." In the first, each salesman was assigned a place in a rotation system and greeted the customer entering the showroom when his number was next on the rotation list. In the open floor system, the first salesman to reach an incoming customer worked with that customer. Indicative of competition in the latter system, it was also known, in a colloquialism derived from wild-game hunting, as the "open season system," wherein salesmen were allowed to pursue an objective without restraint.[78] Sales in this system bordered on unstructured aggression, notwithstanding the profession's growing trend toward rules and professionalism.

Gender Issues

Automobility seemed initially to be fully male dominated. Until the passage of the federal Equal Credit Opportunity Act in 1974, few women could obtain the credit to purchase an automobile.[79] Then, for the few women who could afford the purchase, gender entered most prominently into sales at the point of bargaining for the final price. As Steven Gelber has convincingly shown, the centuries-old male practice of haggling over the sale price of a horse continued on into the automobile trade, while the sale of all other products followed the retailing reforms of the late nineteenth century: a "female orientation" of offering set prices.[80] Automobiles were complex machines requiring, many believed, a male appetite for things mechanical. As the thinking went, men naturally "took the wheel," controlling the car's course just as they as they did with the circumstances of public life in general. In practice, however, women were equally, if not more important, when it came to buying cars. A good salesman with the acumen for intuitively unlocking individual prospects' personal needs and interests—what might be termed psychological pressure points—understood women's critical role in car sales. Our concern here is not with the broad topic of cars manufactured with or without gender bias but with the previously untreated ways in which sales are known to have worked.[81]

Virginia Scharff, who has contributed the most to understanding women in the early auto age, confirms that electric cars were thought to conform more to a female market because their mechanical traits were less like the gasoline-powered car that was best suited to men. In practice, women did seek mobility, and some perceived gasoline-powered cars as dirty and more concerned with power, speed, and long-distance service. Electric cars, on the other hand, were comparatively simple, clean, quiet, and comfortable, featuring enclosed passenger compartments earlier than did gasoline cars.[82]

An article in *Electric Vehicles* on the eve of America's entry into World War I confirmed the pervasive faith that "the electric is preponderantly a woman's car": its superlative coachwork, interior appointments ("air of daintiness, refinement, and elegance"), and "simplicity and ease of control" enabled the electric to become "a woman's car by adoption without any special effort of its own." To this generally agreed-upon link between gender and types of automotive power, however, the *Electric Vehicles* article explored the almost secret practice of women's quiet authority. The magazine held that men appreciated the refinements women enjoyed in car design and, as a result, induced manufacturers to make them standard. Prices rose as a result but without complaint. "Many a man could be satisfied with a car costing three hundred and sixty dollars were it not for his wife and family," the magazine stated at a time when some cars did sell for mere hundreds of dollars.[83] Indeed, the influx of consumers wanting family cars brought manufacturers' attention to the qualitative aspects of look, color, and exterior and interior design.[84] Ford's reluctant and belated cessation of the legendary Model T and replacement with the Model A is the best-known case.[85]

Dealers soon realized that women certainly influenced car purchases,[86] but a 1921 article in *Motor World* was prescriptive. An "astute automobile dealer" in Detroit, according to the magazine, simplified the complex interplay between culture and individuals in negotiations for a particular car: "sell the woman and you sell the car." This was especially true if the car was for a family. With uncommon sensitivity to women in the car market, the dealer outlined two groups of female buyers—namely, those with no experience in previous shopping and those with previous experience. "Women . . . if they are looking over a car for the first time, want two things, appearance and comfort. They don't care a hang about the mechanics of a car." This was not to suggest that women were incapable of grasping mechanical knowledge. The author of the article said that he talked about the car's appearance to an experienced female driver but switched at length to the features of "acceleration, flexibility and riding comfort. She knows what a quick getaway means in traffic and she appreciates ease in handling for she knows the difficulty of parking, and she has experienced driving fatigue." Men achieved parity in the shopping experience, the Detroit dealer judged, because men will have done the "preliminary scouting," or working through alternatives to place one or more under serious consideration; then, however, they would back away from the interplay in the sales experience until the final stage, when they reemerged to pay for the purchase (fig. 4.7).[87]

Females shopping alone were rare.[88] The few existing accounts of female customers, however, suggests that the experience was different for those women who did not conform to the usual pattern of teaming with a man to shop, their respective responsibilities uniformly assumed. Describing her experiences as a lone shopper, a woman named Alle Mac wrote in *Motor World* in 1923 that salesmen should find what appealed uniquely to women and sell them on those features. Mac's article suggests that she had shopped with at least several salesmen before purchasing her car and may have had previous experiences spending another person's money before she shopped for cars on her own. She was put off by the succession of car salesmen who came to her house during World War I, knowing that she possessed Liberty Bonds, which they offered to accept

Figure 4.7. A leading sales primer still pictured women in a secondary public role at mid-twentieth century. From *Planning Automobile Dealer Properties* (Detroit: General Motors Corporation, 1948), 20.

at their depreciated value so that she might purchase one of their cars. They "chloroformed my intention of buying. . . . But my last salesman was wise," Mac wrote. She perceived each encounter with this last salesman as an "interview." The first interview included nothing about the mechanical features of the car but was concerned instead with its durability, the manufacturer's fine reputation, and how similar customers (those with about the same amount of money to spend) had enjoyed it. She drew closer to the car itself as the sales proceeded, first looking from a distance at the car's exterior features, then inspecting its interior, then sitting at the wheel "and [feeling] the ease with which it turned." On a demonstration ride, the salesman, however, drove the car. By the time he showed the motor to her, she had already been "sold." No longer was it a frightening machine.[89]

Motor World's exceptional attention to the female market was also underscored in an article published three years earlier. That piece, titled "'Takes a Woman to Sell to a Woman,'" focused on the experiences of a female salesperson in Cincinnati and argued that women could be even more effective in sales than men. A saleswoman could encourage a sale because she would not only demonstrate that a particular car was easy to drive but would also chat about the advantages of a car in a woman's life while she and her customer sat side by side in the front seat. Unexpected friends phoning to say they would come by for lunch, for example, could be accommodated at the last minute because the hostess could drive to the market for groceries. In demonstrating the car's ease of handling, the saleswoman could take the customer's hand and place it on the steering wheel or brake. *Motor World* thus wanted to open the door for other dealers to employ some saleswomen based on this example in Cincinnati in 1920.[90]

Only the Maxwell Motor Company appears to have thought of employing a group of saleswomen; some suffragists also launched a program. But no evidence has survived of their results. Individual saleswomen who worked on their own, and not part of any widely based effort, did make news, however.[91] Eva Jewell of Antigo, Wisconsin, was one. Not only a saleswoman but a dealer, Jewell found that customers were initially reluctant to talk to her because she was a woman but that this barrier was overcome with time.[92] She learned in selling to women that she was more effective when she got women to disclose exactly what they were looking for in a car and then playing up its appearance: "Every woman wants her car to be noticed as she drives down the street, although she will not always admit it." Actually, status associated with the ownership of certain marques was a general trait understood early in the market.[93] Jewell reinforced the experience of others that women felt unfamiliar with things mechanical and that these features should not be emphasized in the sales experience. Jewell also insisted that flattery should be avoided because it could be taken as an insult to the customer's intelligence. Further, she urged salespeople to talk about price with the woman customer "because the bargain instinct is inherent in her": women were shrewder buyers than men. They also liked to outdo their neighbors. Even as these alleged gender-based traits made selling to women a specialized proposition, Jewell strongly encouraged dealers to take on the female market.[94]

Accessory and parts sales seem to have been less grounded in a female profile although not in inherent psychological differences, the scant bit of evidence from the time suggests. Again in *Motor World,* the same Alle Mac mentioned above for her advice about women shopping alone for cars described how she routinely shopped in department stores "just plain hunting for temptations." She believed that "[t]he first answer then in selling motor accessories to women is to create fads that will add to the attractiveness of her machine." Garages also erred by featuring accessory displays that resembled a man's workbench, she shuddered. Instead, Mac advised that accessories should be shown with "pictures of classy looking cars wearing them and prices easily read, quite in the department store ways."[95] But women were no different from men in the mind of a female tire dealer in Fort Worth, Texas, who held that both sexes were attracted to odd prices. A $50 hat marked down to $49.98 was no less attractive to a woman than a $22.50 tire marked down to $22.22 was to a man. In general principles she drew no distinction between the sexes: deal in the best accessories, keep the price as low as possible, keep your promise with the customer, be honest, and refund money cheerfully to the dissatisfied.[96] *Motor World Wholesale* cited the case of Elsie D. Marr, a former stenographer in an automobile part dealers' business who converted to such a business under her own ownership. It touted her for applying a woman's "natural born" housekeeping talents to the business: systematic and compact stock arrangement and cleanliness.[97] Yet, instances such as Marr's parts business and the female-owned tire dealership were in fact no different from male-managed shops that were also held up in the trade magazines as examples.

Sales Floors

Nothing in the automotive industry contrasted more with its vast workings than the place where dealers displayed their final products. Complicated mechanical contrivances, schemes for mass production, friction-filled labor-management relations, the calculations of how best to trigger latent public appetites for mobility and status, and the cunning craft of making deals with buyers—to name but the most obvious of the industry's complex processes—could barely have been imagined when buyers walked into a showroom in quest of their ideal car.

Convenient access was a primary consideration. Buick, for one, counseled that salesrooms be close to where buyers worked, thereby adding yet another meaning to service. Of an exemplary showroom in Seattle, the *Buick Bulletin* explained that its downtown location particularly suited it to "the busy motorist who wants to make an inspection of new Buick models during business hours but who cannot get away from the business district for any length of time." Big cities quickly witnessed the construction of "auto rows," well-trafficked streets with dealers in their own tall buildings positioned beside one another and across the street from one another, thus creating a unique corridor (fig. 4.8).[98]

Figure 4.8. Early motor row on South Michigan Avenue, Chicago. From authors' postcard collection.

The very concept of a showroom itself was a departure from the earliest practice in which cars were purchased directly from the manufacturer. Some dealers did renovate buildings of other prior use. In contrast to later automobile shows in large halls, the early showrooms were appreciated for their capacity to help customers concentrate. Dealers and buyers "were free from interruption at the same time, and the prospects had all the chance to examine closely," the *Marmon News* reported of its dealership in Boston in 1918. And aisles were not crowded as they often were at successful shows.[99]

Effective sales, it was understood from stores before the automobile, benefitted from proper display. "Its [sic] the psychological kick," the *Hoosier Motorist* said. Cars in their own right were felt to be pretty enough "to arouse the human desire for ownership," but a "really modern setting" augmented the "very primitive and wholesome desire to own one of them."[100] In 1928, the *Accessory and Garage Journal* succinctly reinforced Marmon's claim of nine years before: "A beautiful car is made even more beautiful when properly displayed with a background that enhances the beauty."[101] It was thought that even the *bete noir* of car sales, the used model, would benefit from its own showroom, as noted above. It was emphasized that buyers instinctively assumed that "a car left standing out of doors is not very highly regarded by the dealer and the prospect's valuation of the car is likely to suffer correspondingly."[102]

Showroom grand openings were major public events publicized in news columns of papers collaborative in civic growth and could include invitations mailed to select townspeople.[103] Events like Ford's first showing of its Model A could flood showrooms with curious observers and customers.[104]

Mass consumption was made feasible in part because of the alluring stages inside and regal architecture outside that architects, not building contractors, were commissioned to execute. Exterior treatments ran to numerous florid styles, all eye-catching in their intent. Corner windows with entrances were standard at first. Windows along the street side from the corner were wide and positioned to frame the car behind the plate glass like a picture. After all, it was the interior that was most elaborate and fetching. Recommended plans uniformly placed the showroom at the front of the building and service repair at the rear. This front-back pattern emphasized just how magical, how free of effort, the showroom was intended to be. Of palatial treatments, which historian and cultural heritage conservationist Chester Liebs has likened to banks and hotel and apartment-house lobbies, a fine example was the showroom for Marmon automobiles in Pasadena, California, modeled after those in Los Angeles and featured in a 1917 issue of the *Marmon News*. The two-story interior where cars were displayed had a towering affect, pronouncing admission into the epicenter of the building's activity. A balcony at the back of the room across from the entrance was said to "relieve the monotony of a room without any variation in the walls." Might it also have suggested an opportunity to position oneself above the whole and survey the majestic assemblage in one vista in the fashion of the serene God's eye view of an outdoor landscape? The *Marmon News* was more restrained in pointing out that it offered "a quiet and restful retreat for ladies. Pretty wicker furniture is used here, a writing desk being placed along a wall." On the floor beneath was a fireplace with a large table and chairs in front. "Harmonizing with these pieces are settees about the room," the publication noted. A restful ambiance pervaded the setting, with something of the implied relaxation usually associated with domesticity. Stairs joining the two levels rose in separate flights before converging after several steps for the final ascent on stairs broader than each of the two separate flights. A fountain was positioned at the juncture of the two stairways.[105]

Details of the Leymon Motor Car Company showroom in Louisville, Kentucky, expands understanding of the representative case. It extended 105 feet along the street front and was 50 feet deep. A ceiling 26 feet above the interior floor towered over a decorative scheme of mahogany, bronze, and light brown with steel blue hangings. As in Pasadena, a staircase rose to a balcony across the showroom from the entrance. The Leyman staircase was of marble (fig. 4.9).[106]

An eight-story distributorship in San Francisco centered on a main-floor showroom. Rebuilt used cars were sold on the second floor. (This model was mentioned above for its exemplary service and is mentioned below in chapter 6 for its overall organization.)[107]

Figure 4.9. The palatial showroom of the Leyman Motor Company, Louisville, Kentucky. From *Motor World* 74 (Mar. 28, 1923): 18.

Changes relentlessly swept over these majestic markets. An article in *Automotive Industries* in 1925 advised, "Pass the Word Down to the Dealer—It's Slick-Up Time"—"slick up" being the vernacular for the renovation of interior decor. Locations also migrated to changing downtowns, away from older center cities as populations moved to the suburbs in the early automobile age. With new locations came new buildings in the latest architectural fashion. In time, too, showrooms were built off the immediate right-of-way and housed in buildings that allowed an array of cars outside for public viewing as had earlier been reserved for used cars.[108]

Used Cars

In an economy of mass production wherein ever-greater profit from the newest version of a product was considered success, what was to be done with older products of minimal value? Used cars fell into that questionable category and were not often seen buoyantly for commercial opportunities. In a somewhat self-defeating sequence, because the depression of 1920–21 had persuaded manufacturers to create constant demand with an annual model change, they were also faced annually with the previous year's cars that had gone out of style.[109] Henceforth, "the used car problem" bedeviled the industry.[110]

In the 1920s, many dealers were pleased if they could "break even" on used cars. Across the used car market, trade talk was not optimistic. The National Automobile Dealers Association estimated a loss of $155 per dealer on each used car. The vehicles depreciated rapidly too. In 1926, it was calculated that the average one-year-old u sed car could be resold for only 49 percent of its original value, 35 percent after two years, and 7 percent after five years.[111]

Perhaps used cars should be shunted off the dealers' grounds altogether. In 1913, the Automobile Dealers' Association of New York believed that it could adopt a "no trading plan" if the dealers dealt fairly with prospective customers of a new car when they put the seller in touch with a purchaser. Too often dealers in the association figured they lost money in an overall deal if they factored in the resale price with the amount required to service the car for sales.[112] Dealers also spoke of the "trading evil" described in the literature.[113] One trade magazine uttered the obvious: "Sooner or later . . . the man who owns a second hand car and who trades it in, receiving a high price for it, will realize the price of the car which he has purchased has been inflated in order to meet just such a consideration."[114]

Simultaneously with New York's anticipated solution, a member of the Philadelphia Automobile Trade Association proposed a scheme thought worthy of adoption throughout the city. Much more elaborate than New York's, Philadelphia's would have required a plot of land and a building large enough to house all the association members' trade-ins. As a condition of the trade-in, each owner would be required to give several categories of information, principally a full history of the car, including its owner's name, the vehicle's approximate mileage to date, and the service it had received. This was supposed to alleviate the problem of customers who lacked funds for a new car but were suspicious about the true condition of a second-hand one. A trustworthy reputation for the new program would be the necessary underlying component achieved by this step. If the association undertook their members' proposal, agents could be assigned to sell cars throughout the Philadelphia region and a big used car market would open.[115] It would also free dealers' funds from lying idle in a used car inventory over an uncertain duration. But who, after all, would finance it: the association or a stock company? It was only a proposal.

No solution formed a consensus. *Motor World*'s editors felt compelled to sternly lecture that dealers should show cars indoors in a neat, clean, and well-lit setting. Obviously this was not often heeded.[116]

Trade magazine reports on various successful used car dealers definitely indicated the persistent nature of the challenge but outlined a combination of several features in each case. Building public confidence in a class of highly suspect vehicles was foremost. In the early 1920s, the Dodge dealer in small-town Spencer, Iowa, created publicity in an annual spring auction whose final prices were guaranteed by a one-hundred-dollar reward for anyone who could prove that the dealer had fixed the bidding in any way. Another small-town dealer in Iowa profitably specialized in used cars, selling the residents of Pella and vicinity carefully rebuilt models. This was done in a well-equipped and specially arranged shop. On the second floor was the most unusual feature, a used-parts department whose inventory derived from those cars that had been determined after purchase to be unfit for rebuilding. Service in the automobile dealerships of the time meant preparation of a new car for the owner, but Pella Motor Company also applied it to repair work enabled by the extensive used-parts inventory. A Chevrolet dealer in the small town of Wyoming, Pennsylvania, made used cars the basis of his trade, first by the best service he could offer according to two grades of trade-ins. High-priced models were completely overhauled and cheaper ones were renovated and touched up before being displayed in an unusual feature that attracted attention: the sidewalk in front of the dealership was filled with used models grouped close beside one another. This was an uncommon scheme at the time, and it forcefully made automobile dealerships a part of the dawning roadside commerce. Like Pella's dealer, the shop in Wyoming was well equipped and its work carefully done. The dealer saw to that because he was very knowledgeable in automotive mechanics, inspecting his staff's work at intermittent and unannounced times to keep them diligent. On the eve of World

War II, a dealer in Louisville, Kentucky, was known for similarly meticulous care, personally inspecting the trade-ins to decide what they required (fig. 4.10).[117]

Big-city dealers drew notice for their unusually profitable business in used cars. "Shelton Stores—All Over Dallas" was the slogan for a chain of five used car businesses under common ownership; these were entirely separate from the new Chevrolets the dealer sold at another location under its own manager. In a single reconditioning shop, the used car chain employed the huge number of twelve to fifteen mechanics and body and fender repairmen who had previously operated in its separate repair shops. Complete records were maintained for buyers to review if they wished. The pressure for sales was great; if a used car was not sold in thirty days, the price was reduced for quick clearance.[118]

In pursuit of advice for its readers on the used car question, *Automobile Topics* concluded about advertising that no one formula could be proposed. Considerations about the classes of buyers in an area, the general volume of used cars available in a given place, the stance a dealer took in general on used cars, and the reputation of the dealer made only general advice possible.[119] Physical features of display also varied from place to place. Just as the dealer in Wyoming, Pennsylvania, learned that curbside display drew customers' attention because

Figure 4.10. Used car lot of the Cooke Pontiac Company in Louisville, Kentucky. From *Automobile Topics* 137 (Oct. 7, 1940): 339.

of its novelty, the Capital City Auto Company of Baton Rouge and New Orleans emphatically endorsed outdoor sales. The "yard market" implicitly threw open an invitation to come and look at the stock, as though just browsing, and was found most attractive to those shopping for low- or moderately priced models.[120] Doors leading to a display inside a building embodied a psychological barrier, *Motor Age* reported. Those of "the more particular class of trade" preferred a used car display inside, and Capitol City Auto Company kept that variation as well as the outdoor display.[121] This anecdotal evidence supports other evidence gathered by the end of the 1920s that used car buyers made up a group of their own and were not purchasing used cars as part of two-car ownerships.[122] In 1923, *Motor Age* illustrated the floor plans for two ideal dealerships that located a used car salesroom on the second floor of a building that featured new car sales and service on the first floor—an arrangement that ran counter to the Baton Rouge–New Orleans dealer's experience only two years later.[123] The Chevrolet dealer in Detroit recommended that others adopt its use of an "elevated salesman's shanty," an eight-by-ten-foot frame building raised four feet above ground, not only because it gave the used car salesman a broad surveillance of the open-air lot but because it was believed to lend "an air of dignity and permanency to the lot." Might these features have enabled salesmen to see and approach the idle shopper as well as engender respect for products that were otherwise of little esteem? Beyond guesswork, the dealer's survey confirmed that used cars in certain rows sold faster than in other rows. This might well indicate how impulsive used car shopping was (fig. 4.11).[124]

In some locales, the siting of used car sales was not simply a business problem. Rumblings in California against "used-car dealers, that rent a vacant lot as near the business section as possible, stock it with second-hand cars of doubtful ability and sell them 'as is' to all comers" caused an outcry in Berkeley to ban such dealers. These disreputable dealers moved from city to city and never stayed long in any one place. Used car sales thus embodied the lower echelon in selling, as well as a kind of roving slum on the landscape.[125]

Used cars could also be resold or dismantled for parts to be sold, but this was not commonly done. However, in the early 1920s, the Wroten-Hundley Motor Company, a Dodge dealer in San Antonio, undertook the tedious option of adding an extensive used parts component to its new parts sales in the early 1920s. Careful management of this component eked out a small profit, but it won other ad-

Figure 4.11. Used car lot of the Mack-Gratiot Company, the Chevrolet dealer in Detroit. From *Accessory and Garage Journal* 19 (Aug. 1929): 39.

vantages as well. Small commercial garages and wrecking companies had cast a bad reputation over used cars in the city because of little or no rebuilding before resale. As a Dodge dealer, Wroten-Hundley especially wanted a good reputation for rebuilt vehicles bearing the marque. Learning that it was more economical to salvage some models for parts instead of rebuilding and reselling them, Wroten-Hundley based its used parts department on parts that could be resold to make a safe car. The overall impact was to improve used car sales throughout the entire city. Admittedly, it also diminished the used parts business of disreputable commercial garages and wrecking companies.[126]

Economic considerations motivated manufacturers to address the used car problem from the viewpoint of selling their annual models. In 1925, a reliable survey discovered that the used car surplus was so extensive that not just one but, in some cases, four cars were being offered by customers seeking a new car purchase. From Pittsburgh to Spokane, Washington, dealers were beset with the surplus. The problem could be traced to a glut of open cars at a time when new car production had shifted to closed models. Studebaker developed a plan to support its dealers in used car sales by making them agree to offer only reconditioned cars and give buyers a five-day period, after which they could return their purchase if dissatisfied. Ford developed a similar plan simultaneously. Programs to acquire second-hand cars and sell them for parts or destroy them at the expense of a cooperative company developed among some dealers nationwide and also encouraged dealers to advocate that manufacturers should do the same by adding a cost to each new car sold.[127]

Over the span of time, from the Great Depression through the end of the early automobile age, dealers continued to face ebb and flow in the used car market. When the supply of new cars ended during World War II, used cars stocked the seller's market. Prescient manufacturers in late 1941 encouraged dealers to trade wisely for used cars and work into the repair and service business. Anecdotal evidence abounds of drivers stopped on the street and offered a substantial amount above the original price. Before the full resumption of car production after the war, there were cases of people who entered the automobile trade by dealing in used cars exclusively. The recession in the late 1950s encouraged the used car market again because used cars were cheaper to buy.[128]

Architectural questions about used car displays also continued to be asked. After mid-century, covered displays were popular with dealers, their canopies offering shelter to the inventory and to shoppers, their long edge high above ground coincidentally but strategically positioned for signs. The ensemble signaled not an afterthought for an undervalued product but a place of its own for a respected one (fig. 4.12).[129]

* * *

In some ways, the high and low points of the automobile industry were achieved at the sales level in car dealerships, both in the automobile rows of the big cities and in the lone dealerships that marked numerous small towns. There were those who heralded car ownership as a sign of American greatness and accomplishment, as well as those who saw in it the worst aspects of the industrial economy and a consumer culture run rampant. The sale of automobiles certainly does not deserve the condemnation of Neil Lewis Morfitt, manager of the biggest and oldest dealership in Astoria, Oregon, who said, forty-two years after its founding, that selling cars was "the dirtiest, most unethical of all large-volume businesses."¹³⁰ It is most fair to say that it was a tough business, with prospects of big profit but also of dismal failure—an enterprise from which everyone sought maximum advantage and very few comprehended. The foregoing treatment, thus, amounts to something of an exposé, having penetrated the inner workings of car sales as a high-volume, high-finance business awash in the complex interpersonal dynamics of buyer and seller on which the entire industry's success ultimately hinged.

Duality defined this tough business that Americans had so quickly decided they could not do without. In contrast with lavish showrooms stood used car lots filled with less-preferred products and at times representing the antithesis of the dignified and sumptuous settings contrived to dazzle buyers. Financing was one of the most widely questioned aspects of sales, routinely leaving the buyer in doubt about how good a deal she or he had really negotiated for a product that precipitously lost value within the first year of ownership. Behind the showroom or used car lot stood the repair and maintenance garage, hardly a glamorous scene but a stalwart contributor to the automobile industry. Dealers continually wrestled with how to organize and staff these garages and sometimes whether to even have their own. We turn next to the essential role of this most ambivalently received type of garage.

Figure 4.12. A leading sales primer at mid-century also proposed a "foreground sign" without canopy to add prestige to the used cars for sale by linking them, via the sign, directly to the new car showroom. From *Planning Automobile Dealer Properties* (Detroit: General Motors Corp., 1948), 23.

5

THE DOMESTIC GARAGE

Nothing more dramatically reveals the garage's multifaceted uses than attention to its historical place as a residential adjunct grown from repair and storage to storage only. This chapter touches briefly on the first combination through the winnowing out of residential use alone and its refinements over a century. In the current United States, what else but a garage allows people to eat, sleep, and live alongside a huge machine (separated from them by a thin wall in most cases), whose full potential they are able to arouse at a moment's notice? Where else a century ago was such a machine also often at rest with a special servant, the chauffeur, before being called into action? How did the unlikely combination then and now come into play?

The Chauffeur in Residence

From the slight history of the chauffeur in the scholarly literature, it can still be reliably asserted that chauffeurs most often served the wealthy in the early years of the automobile—a time when it was generally characterized as a plaything of the rich. *Chauffeur*—another French word in American automobility—meant one who literally stoked engines when steam-powered automobiles were common. Some chauffeurs doubled as mechanics in garages provisioned with appropriate tools and, like retainers on mansion estates, lived in the estate's garage. In 1911, a former mayor of Cincinnati, Ohio, employed four chauffeurs who resided on the garage's second floor. At the elite extreme, one early car owner provided accommodations for the several chauffeurs of his three cars, including a second-floor apartment of four rooms and a bath for one chauffeur and his family. Insofar as chauffeurs attended to repairs, they were retained not only to drive but also to take the family car to a public garage for service, thus preventing problems common to early cars such as paint loss and mechanical problems due to mud.[1]

At the interface between chauffeurs and public garages, problems arose that tainted some early repairs. Chauffeurs did occasionally take advantage of their employers by expecting "kickbacks" from the garage in order to ensure their business. This was part of the "chauffeur problem" that resonates in early popular automotive literature. Conciliatory garage men counseled car owners that they, at least occasionally, deal with the garage owner in person. Many times they were simply known to the garage men from the names on the checks given to them to pay for work. Several states also addressed the chauffeur problem in court cases and legislation that carefully monitored chauffeurs to prevent their "joyriding"— that is, reckless or unauthorized personal use of the cars in their care.[2]

Two factors converged by the 1920s to reduce, if not end such abuses: providing a home for chauffeurs in the domestic garage and repairs shops in that same space. Commercial repair garages increased in numbers simultaneously with the onset of mass automobility in the 1910s, and in the following decades chauffeurs became drivers only. The abundant number of middle-class car owners, especially after World War I, turned to commercial repair garages.[3]

The Standard Domestic Garage

Utility sheds or converted stables first housed their vehicles in commercial storage garages, as noted in chapter 1, but many owners wanted their vehicles more readily available. Commercial garages were distant, requiring transportation to and from them, and how did one accomplish that feat when the car was inoperable? Most owners thus preferred not to depend on any transit system and were quite ready to exercise their skills as handymen or hire builders to adapt existing structures. Convenience surpassed cost in car owners' minds. In the western United States besides, car owners had sufficient land on their house lots for garages and did not want to pay the costs in public garages driven high by labor in the region. Through the 1920s, the garage had acknowledged uses but had not become a special building in its own right, one deserving of careful design rather than a leftover space in a family stable or out building, as two designers advocating the architectural trade agenda saw it.[4] Elaborate conversions that contractors completed are the best documented cases of the early era.

John B. Knox's stable in Hartford, Connecticut, which was remodeled for a garage-stable and described in *House and Garden* in 1908, demonstrates the expense and trouble automobile owners willingly paid and endured to base their automobile in state-of-the-art conditions. "A well appointed car requires more attention than a pleasure carriage," Knox's architect, A. Raymond Ellis, admitted. A stable with concrete foundation stood across a center aisle or "carriage room" from three vehicle stalls, but elaborate precautions were taken against gasoline fires in contrast to the more simply drained and vented stable. Hard-plastered metal laths encased the carriage room. Used petroleum products dictated a ventilated cabinet in the workshop. The gasoline pump had to be connected to a distant gasoline tank to comply with fire insurance requirements. The probable imbalance in favor of the automobile was clear. "If in the future, the owner should desire to have more than one automobile, it would be an easy matter to remove the partition between the stable partition and carriage room," Ellis reported, and it was recommended as cheaper to incorporate the piping, storage tank, and repair pit for a space later completely given to a garage than to install those elements later.[5] Ellis did not envision immediate economy for a subsequent reconversion to a stable only. Spare no expense for what was likely inevitable, Ellis seemed to say. Was a self-fulfilling prophecy at work?

Although no surveys were reported widely to assert a number, a significant percentage of early automobile owners persuaded themselves to adapt existing structures rather than build new garages. William A. Radford, principal of the Radford Architectural Company in Chicago and editor of several building-trades publications and his own series of building plans, offered one on garages in 1910. It was the first garage-design plan book published. Although only one of fifty-five different plans in the volume, the barn converted to a garage merited Radford's special mention for the space suitable for a workroom upon the horse stall's removal (figs. 5.1 and 5.2). Economy lured interest. A commentator held that one of the advantages of a garage at home was the incentive it offered to repair one's own car rather than pay a mechanic who was apt to call for continual repairs on cars stored under his care. Furthermore, it was better to invest one's money than to pay for a service. Whereas an annual storage fee of $550 was the sum that could be earned at 1908's interest rate on $11,000, a two-car garage cost $1,500 to build.[6]

Early garages were places where men asserted themselves. As the commentator on the advantages of a garage at one's home suggested, it was a place a man was invited to manage. Men made the early automobile theirs; they had the "ever-present pleasure of being skipper of one's own ship," as one commentator described the act of automobile driving.[7] The garage also was a place where a

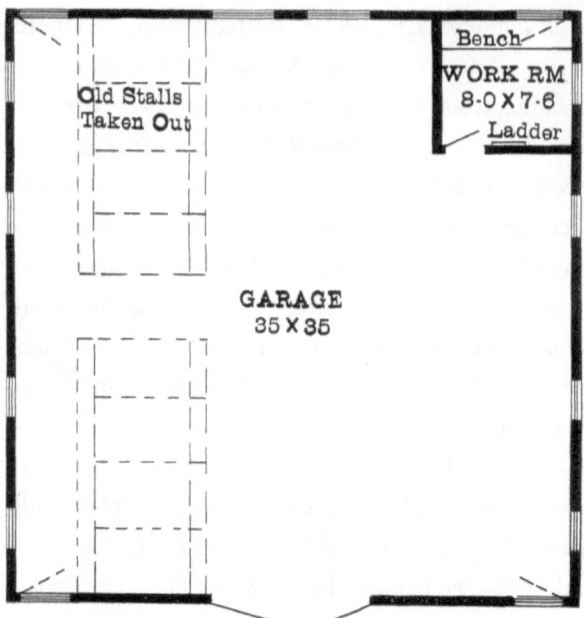

Figure 5.1. Radford diagrammed a 35-foot by 35-foot barn whose conversion to a garage was made to look easy. Note the reference in the upper left to the horse stalls removal. From William A. Radford, *Radford's Garages and How to Build Them* (Chicago: Radford Architectural Co., 1910), 62.

man could exercise his mechanical skills to restore the vehicle to its full physical potential. Hosts invited their male guests to inspect the garage's provisions.[8] For the wealthy automobile owner who retained a chauffeur, the driver-mechanic's living quarters, often above the garage, reinforced the gendered assumption about the garage.[9] Increased numbers of women drivers and women's advocates, however, lessened the domestic garage as an exclusively man's world. Advocates contended that women were capable of maintenance and some repair so long as these activities did not require muscle (fig. 5.3).[10]

Values played out importantly in the conception of the garage. Its location at the owner's residence has drawn the most study. "An automobile to be most enjoyed must be within easy reach," one motor journalist encouraged. "It must be where it can be taken out at a moment's notice when the spirit of the road is upon its owner."[11] Impulse and the romance of unfettered travel linked the garage to house sites. Easy access for business use was certainly an influence. Doctors, lawyers, teachers, and other professionals, for example, could afford the early twin luxury of automobile ownership and the added expense of a garage. Financial calculation remained important yet was seldom fully articulated.[12] Consumer guides for the comparative cost of commercial and home car storage were scarce

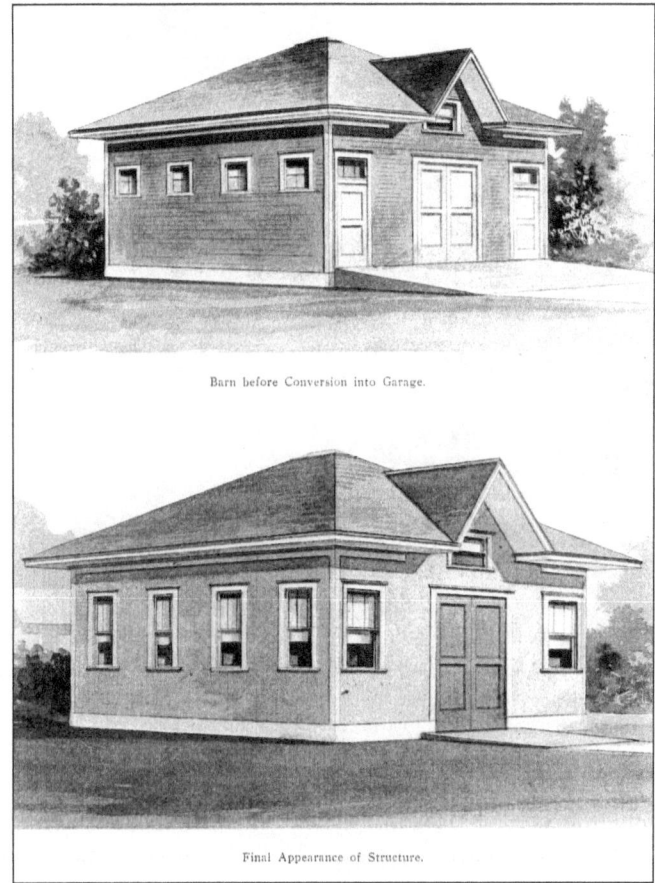

Barn before Conversion into Garage.

Final Appearance of Structure.

Figure 5.2. Radford's conversion of a barn to a garage looked unmistakably service-oriented. From William A. Radford, *Radford's Garages and How to Build Them* (Chicago: Radford Architectural Co., 1910), 63.

in the literature of the day. Given the early automobile's role as a novelty, one of the chief intangible benefits was for the owner to demonstrate his mastery of modern technology by fixing his own car when possible. Then, too, the automobile avoided the stench, disease, and volume of waste that pushed many to stable their horses away from home in commercial liveries.[13] Notwithstanding the automobile's peculiar liabilities—poisonous fumes, acrid smells, noise, and incendiary potential, most especially in the repair pit into which gasoline mixtures settled—a fair number of owners welcomed the machine beside their home.[14] Cars soon designed for repair without requiring a pit[15] and fireproof building materials eased many minds. Space thus given to a comparatively hygienic machine, as opposed to the carriage and riding horses, gave little reason for owners to hesitate about welcoming the car to their home.

Figure 5.3. One electric automobile charger advertised a woman using it in her garage. From advertisement, General Electric Company, *Motor*, Apr. 1910, 164.

Review of Radford's designs used to build garages reveal that from a third to a fifth of the floor space was assigned to tools and workbench, a bath and/or sink, and a "man's room." Caretakers for larger houses or chauffeurs were domiciled in the latter. At this upper end of the garage scale, owners picked between motor repair in a pit or a chain tackle to lift one end of the motor for mechanical work. Turntables with drains to rotate the vehicle under repair were common in Radford's multicar garages. Turntables were necessary to turn a car in very confined quarters or in locations lacking sufficient space outside. Turntables also facilitated movement in those conditions because the reverse gears on early automobiles were difficult to operate or were absent in some models. Lighting and spatial clearance for maneuvering the car were essential. Large and elaborate garages could cost up to three thousand dollars, but cost varied according to where in the nation the garage was built. Less-wealthy owners eager to repair their single car were advised not to purchase power machinery and many tools but to rely instead on commercial repair shops. Countryside residents, on the contrary, often calculated that it was cheaper to maintain more repair equipment than to travel the distance for work in towns. The emphasis in a small garage was on fireproof construction, concrete flooring, drainage, doors that were easy to open and shut, and fuel pumps with underground gasoline storage. Elements of construction, not pretentious size or styling—that is, functionalism—informed design.[16]

With the origins of the specially designed garage entered the commitment to space for more than automobile repair and storage. Owners occasionally adapted garage plans to preserve existing landscaping.[17] The courtesy of housing a guest's car, however, was one of the most convincing initial pressures to expand the space beyond the bare minimum. "This display of hospitality will be a benefit to your friends who will occasionally call," ironically wrote an advocate of the principle that the garage should be kept simple.[18] Pressure on adapting an earlier house sited on a lot before the need for a garage encouraged adjustments. Other outbuildings were avoided by consolidating their function with the automobile-inspired garage.[19] Here was a step tantamount to the later conversion of the garage into living space, which became common beginning in the 1950s. Houses were not retrofitted for garages, but garages could be converted for living. Garages have proven the most malleable of all residential structures, their malleability enhancing their utility.

Beauty was a highly arguable matter of affordability. Numerous brief columns in the building-trades and motoring magazines testify to the fact that wealthy owners of single-family houses consciously made choices for their garages. "The garage lends itself delightfully as an architectural element in planning the group of buildings of a country place or town house," posited a writer for elite home and car owners.[20] Styling became a central calculation, and when it did, the advice was usually taken to build in the same style as the house.[21] Radford charged new garage owners with a moral responsibility; their "purpose should be improvement and betterment" of their neighborhood.[22] Many wealthy owners likely found selfish as well as social reasons for holding high their property's values. By the 1920s, architectural harmony between house and garage was a given.[23] All manner of period-revival garages were built to accompany their period-revival homes in exclusive suburbs through the 1930s (fig. 5.4). Snobs looked down on the portable garage as "small and unsightly"—that is, for its incongruence with the house in both mass and style.[24] Most freely admitted that the portable garage satisfied demands for economy and convenience.[25]

Figure 5.4. A shingle supplier chose a Tudor revival house with attached garage to distinguish its product, a common advertising strategy in the 1920s. From advertisement, Preston Roofing, *Building Age* 47 (Nov. 1925): back cover. Courtesy of Simmons-Boardman Corporation.

Numerous manufacturers of portable buildings for various industrial uses added their varieties of garages with hope to increase profits. A few were these: the Wycoff Lumber and Manufacturing Company of Ithaca, New York; Mersohn and Morley Company of Saginaw, Michigan; E. F. Hodgson Company of Boston, Massachusetts; and the Metal Shelter Company of St. Paul, Minnesota. Mersohn and Morley boasted that a wrench and screwdriver, common tools, were sufficient to assemble and disassemble their model. Where people often relocated to a new house within the same city, the portable garage was especially appealing (fig. 5.5).[26] Thus, automobility was extended beyond personal conveyance to the structure protecting the conveyance, another installment of a highly mobile society.

Garage location in relation to the house also became a key calculation, regardless of the garage's size or the protection it afforded. One building expert ranked garage construction second only to the house itself by the early 1920s and gave consequent weight to the garage's proximity to the home. Municipal fire ordinances dictated that garages not fireproofed must stand at least fifteen feet from the house, and this single demand left considerable discretion as to the exact position. Some designers situated the garage far from the access road and perpendicular to it, while others preferred to situate the garage at the end

Figure 5.5. The Finlay-Wheeler company of Buffalo, New York, sold its portable garage "Quixet" on the basis of a product that was cheap, clean, fireproof, durable, close, and easily moved. From advertisement, Finlay-Wheeler, *Buffalo Motorist* 13 (Oct. 1920): 55.

of a curved driveway with a screen of foliage muting, but not obstructing, plain view from the access road. Aesthetics increasingly became important although considerably diverse opinion has prevailed about what is best.[27]

Only with the increased marketing of enclosed cars in the 1920s did thought begin to be given to leaving cars outside with no storage in a garage.[28] Soon after the garage's emergence, however, it came to be integral to the house itself. "Automobile house," "the garage in the house": various names indicated that many Americans questioned how fully to embrace the garage.[29] "Garage," unmodified, and not "automobile house," gained general currency by 1910.[30] But this did not reflect emotional distancing. One writer offering advice on the construction of garages verbalized what remained probably inchoate in many: "The motor car has become so deeply intrenched in our American life that it is appropriate that we should give it a place under the same roof that shelters us."[31]

Attached garages and freestanding garages were both popular as soon as the garage became a specialized building. The tendency of horse owners to stable their animals away from home did not long dissuade car owners from garages in close proximity to their house, contrary to some opinion. Architects, both radicals seeking to integrate the garage into the house and conservatives championing the primacy of the house, controlled the exchange in professional circles over the garage's proper role from about 1910 to 1935. It was resolved in favor of the originally radical views. Among the great mass of people, however, convenience, fire codes, personal taste, but, above all, economy determined the choice between freestanding and attached garages. Freestanding garages incurred greater costs than attaching a garage, and although the few early automobile owners were wealthy and less deterred by expense, the automobile's wider adoption introduced more cost-conscious garage owners in the 1920s. Rare in 1919 by one contemporary account, the attached garage grew popular in the following decade. Increased construction costs early in the century also made family expansion into an attached garage converted to living space a frugal expedient. On society's way to deciding firmly for the attached garage, three arrangements competed for dominance: access via a covered passageway, placement beneath the house, or connection as a wing. After World War II, the attached garage of whatever variety prevailed in new construction.[32]

A word is in order about the domestic garage used purely as a parking space: this consideration consistently remained a silent partner in all the automobile's elaborately proclaimed benefits of convenience, economy, and even romance of the road.

The great garage door debate, on the contrary, drew attention among contemporary garage designers and, later, scholars. Of the many window and panel arrangements, perhaps inspired by the desire to avoid the look of barn doors, which was best? Which of the improvements to prevent ice and snow blockage of double-hinged doors was best? Three-part doors, one of which opened independently for exclusively human use, became common. In the 1920s, automatic garage door openers came onto the market but did not gain common usage. By the 1930s, overhead doors emerged as the most popular.[33] "Many people are tired of struggling with sagging, sticking doors, and are interested in the new and improved garage doors, and hardware now available at reasonable prices," one building contractor's magazine asserted in 1932.[34] What were the common denominators of the shopper's cornucopia?

The ways and extent to which prospective garage owners came to rely on concrete in providing the enclosure and access instructs us about objectives.

Many early garages were of wooden frame construction, relics of retrofitted stables or new efforts at blending the automobile's utilitarian implication into a picturesque home site where wood seemed sympathetic. Concrete, however, satisfied the U.S. Commerce Department and the Underwriters Laboratories, which influenced insurance rates and fire codes throughout the nation. Of six rules for attached-garage construction, which Ira H. Woolson, consultant to the National Board of Fire Underwriters and chairman of the Commerce Department's Building Code Committee, published for the latter in 1923, three mentioned concrete specifically. The other three outlined construction details rather than materials. Concrete came in preformed blocks. Radford declared that the virtues of concrete block were economy and wide availability. Although he cautioned that poorly made concrete block deteriorated from moisture, he seemed sanguine that high-quality blocks could be obtained and outlined the option of a stucco finish, another fire-resistant material, if owners desired it. Stucco was likely a new consideration of owners who wished to mask the otherwise industrial ambiance of a concrete block garage, here setting aesthetics in third rank behind durability and cost.[35]

Garage access involved driveways as well as doors, although the latter gained far more attention in the building trades and scholarly literature about the garage. Concrete's applications in the United States dated from the late nineteenth century when its success in monumental edifices invited more modest uses.[36] Concrete's virtually unanimous choice for driveways by the early twentieth century contrasted markedly with the myriad relative advantages that fueled the great garage door debate (fig. 5.6). Poured concrete seemed perfect; it was plastic, durable, and inexpensive. Some driveways remained gravel, but they required more regular maintenance than concrete. Flagstone was recommended for parking spaces for multiple cars in a garden setting—or "courtyards," as they were called.[37] Elite arbiters of taste wrestled with how best to use concrete. Writing in *House and Garden* in 1913, a detractor of cement driveways did not deny their advantages—the avoidance of "weeding, sprinkling and macadam repairs"—but limited his reservations to the perception that one particular design showed too much cement and too little grass "to give a pleasing result."[38] An article in a 1928 issue of *House and Garden* noted what seemed the too-frequent tendency to make an afterthought of the garage's approach, a convenience as the first object seen.[39] It has been observed that the Prairie style, *avant* in the early twentieth

Figure 5.6. This model garage of hollow tile with applied stucco defaulted to two common concrete features: driveway and floor. From "When I Build a Garage," *American Builder* 24 (Mar. 1918): 41. Courtesy of Simmons-Boardman Corporation.

century, seemed especially suited to concrete garages.[40] Thus, concrete carried aesthetic associations but ones arguable among the elite who exchanged views about them.

Garage design was far less often the architect's or the building contractor's realm than the received wisdom of the examples and principles espoused in the home beautification, architectural, or building-trades literature would suggest through the 1920s. When business plunged in the 1930s, the building-trades literature, which openly called for aggressive salesmanship, disclosed that perhaps many people—certainly too many for the trades and professions seeking control of the garage construction market—did not keep cars in garages or garages that professionals had designed and built.[41] In 1931, a contractor's magazine complained that several million cars were not parked at home in garages. Owners were accused of parking their cars in but one "modern, firesafe, convenient, private garage" for every ten garages in 1933 (fig. 5.7).[42] Handymen hired for various jobs, as well as do-it-yourselfers, built many garages. Portable garages were popular with those shopping to avoid professional costs.[43] Garages—cheap, close, and unadorned because they were free of costs deemed unnecessary—informed their landscape.

Figure 5.7. *American Builder* magazine disparaged the vernacular garages shown above. From "Millions for New Cars—but Where Are They Kept?" *American Builder*, Sept. 1933, 19. Courtesy of Simmons-Boardman Corporation.

Garages for apartment dwellers generally followed the same aesthetic, with the garage-building industry, as judged from the trade literature, demonstrating little interest in reforming this trend. The "garage court" was an early and rare deviation (fig. 5.8). Advocated in one building-trades magazine in 1920, the garage court was suitable for older urban areas into which automobile traffic squeezed (fig. 5.9). These back lots were accessed from the street through corridors lined by existing buildings and were irregularly shaped because of their siting on remnant parcels that owners of these courts could adapt in strategies to maximize income from modest garages. The use of fireproof materials—whether brick, tile, or concrete—to assure safety and the interior's function was paramount, not the outside appearance. Each garage in the court was to be provisioned with "every practical convenience that car owners would require in a garage of their own."[44] Meeting needs that other interests in the neighborhood ignored, the garage court owner was motivated by profit from rentals, not the pride of ownership that a concern with aesthetics would imply.

The general absence of ordinances for parking at multiple-occupant buildings until the late 1930s invited entrepreneurship with little concern for garage appearance or function. Beside the blocks of apartment flats closely adjoined in

Figure 5.8. The garage court was plain but purposeful. From "The Garage Court," *National Builder* 62 (Aug. 1919): 37.

the Bronx were examples of the "garage flat," an auto fan magazine reported in 1913. Those garage flats were lamentably unsuitable by the standards that single-family house dwellers would require for their garages, but they provided the basics—namely, shelter, workspace, running water, electric light, and fuel storage. They rented for fifteen dollars per month.[45] In 1934, attempting to elevate expectations, residential designer Thomas Adams advocated parking in the ground floor of buildings on lots thirty feet wide.[46] Practice was far more mundane. The plan for future growth in Chicago's Woodlawn neighborhood based on a 1940 survey reported that few residents rented garages. Because many of the garages were unusable and because the neighborhood's dark alleys invited mayhem, forty-four hundred cars were parked at the curbs on an average weekly night between 11:30 PM and 1:30 AM. Shoppers at the outlying shopping district competed for parking space. "Thus, day and night, Woodlawn streets were lined with parked automobiles," the report noted.[47]

In 1940, garages and parking for apartment house dwellers mobilized various local governments' attention to produce a national survey. The Public Administration Clearing House of the American Society of Planning Officials reported on the ordinances of thirty-five cities. While many big cities had adopted them, so too had many small cities. A typical ordinance was that of Evanston,

Figure 5.9. Drivers reached their parking destination in a garage court through a narrow off-street passage to arrive in an equally constrained space. From "The Garage Court," *National Builder* 62 (Aug. 1919): 37.

Illinois: each new apartment building was required to provide a garage or surface lot within or adjacent to the building's lot with capacity for one vehicle for every two units. Los Angeles and Santa Monica, both key contributors to Southern California's legendary car culture, enacted a one-to-one ratio. Interestingly, the public administration magazines summarizing the report accepted its premise that apartment house parking was a commercial consideration akin to ordinances for parking-customer ratios at hotels and theaters. One of the magazines added remarks about parking at industrial sites. Official consideration clearly turned to making entrepreneurs responsible for helping end traffic-congested streets and did not see parking as a courtesy in the tacit manner in which it was extended to shoppers or assumed by single-family homeowners. Residential parking was a concept still evolving.[48]

During the last half of the twentieth century, garage design and construction remained key contributors to making a home livable wherever one resided in America. Some building contractors believed that the majority of low-priced homes built during the construction boom immediately after World War II did not include garages.[49] The building trades and architectural profession continued boosting the notion that the garage was an essential component of every properly built home, and most Americans concurred. The Federal Housing

Administration, which so profoundly influenced the availability of mortgage money and the social composition of neighborhoods, implied its agreement in the spatial standards set for garages as a condition of money loaned.[50] Decline of the alley (a commonplace with or without a garage), expansion of residential property widths often beyond fifty feet, the car's enhanced status as a social symbol, and virtual acceptance of the car as a family member helped clinch the garage's—and with it, parking's—centrality in homemaking.[51] *House and Garden*'s typification of one family's house in a 1954 article was evidence that the pastoral paradigm reappeared in new words: "Suburban living is about equally divided between indoors, outdoors, and behind the steering wheel of the family's Lincoln 'Capri.'"[52] Thus, it was after mid-century that the suburban garage significantly impacted the landscape and made the once-prominent garage screened from extensive public display in alleys an antique artifact.

With this assurance dawned the era of parking's most visually bold place at the home: the showcasing once more of the domestic garage's versatility.[53] Assignment of the garage as the house entrance abounded in literature that offered advice on ideal house construction.[54] Even advice not uttering the garage-as-entrance premise *displayed* it in drawings of proposed houses and photographs of built ones.[55] Whereas earlier designs recommended curvilinear driveways often concealed with landscaping, newer proposals commonly put the sight line of the driveway straight from the garage to the street, underscored by the uninterrupted contrast of concrete with the leafy surrounds. *House and Garden* came forward with several layouts for "planned homeparking," not only for the homeowner but for guests as well.[56] The attached garage, which predominated in the last half-century, lent itself to this rendition that designers made of parking. Furthermore, one garage at each single-family house was virtually unquestioned. As the authors of one study of landscape design observed, the space- and money-saving option of pooling garages or carports into multiuser "car harbors" that would take advantage of compact paved areas conflicted with homeowners' "desire for individuality and for having direct access from car to kitchen in any weather."[57] Critics of the immediate post–World War II suburban sprawl recoiling against the one-garage-one-house rule were few. People commonly parked in their garage and entered their house from the garage (fig. 5.10). The garage was also the structure that passersby most commonly viewed at home. Little effort was made to avoid the family auto on display on the concrete driveway in building-trades magazines. A parked vehicle indeed complemented the bucolic scene. Concealed beneath the concrete lay wire fabric to strengthen construction and heating coils to keep the driveway clear in winter (fig. 5.11). The magazines advocating these construction techniques felt confident in running illustrated advertisements that placed the driveway in the forefront.[58]

With the attached garage triumphant in most new construction, the discussion in the trade literature turned away from the style of the garage: it was a foregone conclusion that the garage style would be the same as the house; in that way the house retained a semblance of priority. The aesthetic debate turned instead to the garage interior, where the stored automobile became but one determinant. Pressure on parking space at home mounted no less than it had on downtown commercial sites through the entire half-century. Whereas land banking had been conscious in those downtown parking sites, the spatial explosion of living space into the garage in the last half-century followed the earlier tendency to build garages larger than necessary for the vehicle or vehicles owned at the time of construction. It has been pointed out that in the adaptation of carports in Brookside, Delaware, the displacement of cars from their shelter in favor of newly claimed living space challenges the common scholarly belief in the automobile's hegemony. Suburbanites did subordinate their automobile to the role of mechanical servant, but nevertheless it was a necessity whose need for parking made significant spatial demands, whether in or out of a shelter.[59]

Figure 5.10. A typical ranch house with attached garage. From *Modern Ranch Houses Designed for Town and Country Living* (Elmhurst, IL: National Place Service, Inc., 1951), 2.

Figure 5.11. In this ad for heating coils, the driveway waiting for a concrete covering seems also to yawn wide in anticipation of cars. From advertisement, Bell & Gossett Company, *American Builder* 74 (Oct. 1952): 285. Courtesy of Simmons-Boardman Corporation.

Many owners wanted their garages remodeled. Architectural, building-trades, and home-improvement magazines documented numerous cases and further encouraged remodeling through alternatives of their design. "Remodel Your Garage to Gain an EXTRA ROOM," charged the title of one of many such articles in *House and Garden* in the 1950s.[60] Remodeling required few structural changes. Folding doors could replace the partition between the garage and the house. Wallboard could cover walls and trussed ceilings. Numerous floor materials could be laid atop the concrete floors. In one apparent advantage, utilities were relatively easy to extend into an attached garage being adapted for living space; in some cases, those utilities were fully present before adaptation. In 1969, *House and Garden* featured a garage converted into an entertainment center in Houston. Needing a place to entertain guests without disturbing their children at sleep, the owners converted their garage entirely to an entertainment center and added two bays. "Everyone nowadays seems to have more friends than facilities for entertaining them," *House and Garden* editorialized.[61] This represented an upper-class expectation and architect-designed extreme.

It was far more common in the trade magazines to offer plans for accommodating automobile parking and living space within an existing garage. Encroachments on space heretofore reserved exclusively for the automobile began with better-organized space. "Unclutter the Garage," commanded the title of one 1978 magazine article, which advised homeowners to systematically rid the garage of stored tools and equipment that had remained unused for some time. Then, it continued, the owner should organize the remaining necessities in cabinets and on specially arranged wall hooks. The urge to compact space became urgent. One family utilized more efficiently stored tools and equipment to add a dining table, drafting and writing desks, and book bins downstairs and a bedroom and a bathroom upstairs. The garage then housed two cars, a boat, and bicycles. *Mechanix Illustrated* presented another option in 1980, the "over-garage apartment," exemplified by a case in Fairfield, Connecticut. It could serve as extra living space for the owners until it was later rented for added income. Outside the building-trades literature, a widowed artist in semiretirement offered two examples in an *American Artist* article, thereby verifying the wide extent of popular interest. She pushed her car's storage to one side of the garage and converted the remaining spaces into her studio.[62]

Carports, a partially open variation on the garage that became popular in mild climates and with the advent of more reliable automobiles after mid-century,[63] held special advantages for conversion. *American Home* magazine sold one-dollar plans for seasonal conversions. In the winter, the magazine advised its readers, shelter your car. Then, with screening in the summer, the carport could become a place "where the whole family can play, relax, have out-door meals and parties" (fig. 5.12).[64] In 1972, *Mechanix Illustrated* presented a carport with room for a large station wagon and two small rooms.[65] It harkened to the earliest garages that were provisioned for mechanical work. In the 1970s, however, favor turned against the carport, shifting back to the garage for its protective capacity and the storage space it added to the house.[66]

Garages remained significant male domains even though adaptations for family living ended exclusively male occupancy. Although some women were carpenters and cooperated in designing garages, the trade magazines spoke almost invariably to men of new building.[67] Although many women drove automobiles, the garage remained a place associated with male legerdemain, perhaps a carryover from earlier times when many men exercised mechanical talents in automotive repair. As if to ward off women and unmanly males, *Mechanix Illustrated* said that it was possible to convert the carport to multiple uses but that it took "muscle."[68] Perhaps *House and Garden* exercised the most flagrant stereotyping when, in 1958, it said this about the items constituting garage clutter:

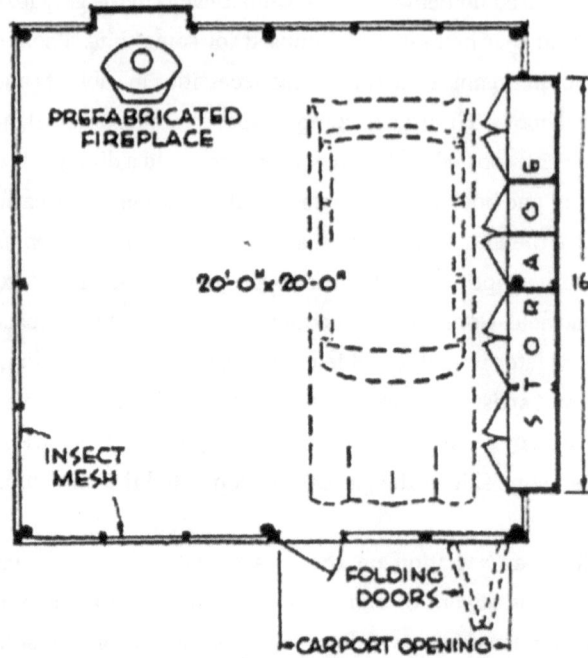

Figure 5.12. The floor plan of the carport-screenhouse envisioned in the segmented outline where the car can find room amid space for habitation. From Hubbard H. Cobb, "Versatile Carport Converts to Summer Fun House," *American Home* 61 (Apr. 1959): 42.

"They wind up in the garage because you are reluctant to make the hard decision to discard them and because this is one area of the house that escapes the proud and probing eye of its mistress."[69]

Parking for apartment dwellers became a matter of serious attention with systematic planning in the last half of the twentieth century. Parking demand in multiunit dwellings rose along with the increase in parking everywhere. Demand, however, was very acute in high-density urban areas where multiunit dwellings predominated. In 1959, *House and Garden,* offering remedy for single-family homeowners, observed that many suburbs enforced ordinances against curb parking overnight or should enact them. Where were apartment dwellers to park if they could no longer use the street as they had before? The conviction grew that local government had to stipulate the parking provisions, thus expanding a trend begun in the late 1930s.[70]

Garages returned to center stage in the debate. Realtors and developers of apartment houses were advised to view the provision of parking as a competitive edge no less than merchants of outlying shopping districts had realized twenty to thirty years before. New York's area of multiunit dwellings for up to 35,000 people, built in the first half of the century, seemed pitifully obsolete in part because they lacked parking provisions. By contrast, the 116-car underground garage serving 300 units at the skyscraper apartment built in 1951 at 860 Lake Shore Drive in Chicago seemed farsighted in the 1950s for its ratio of 1 stall for every 2.6 units in the apartment house. The ideal was 1:1. The largest provision at the time was for 3,150 cars at an apartment house complex for 3,500 people at the edge of San Francisco. That city introduced the "San Francisco–style" apartment house, its garage occupying the ground floor, near downtown (fig. 5.13). Designers struggled with how best to combine parking convenience for inhabitants with clean air and good looks. Medium-density sites appeared to present the grandest challenge because the volume of parked cars seemed to envelop the entire complex. Too many garages were as unappealing as too many surface lots. The tendency was to shift parking to the rear entries of residences where they had often been when alleys were common.[71]

Figure 5.13. This view made in 2000 at University Heights, California, illustrates the diffusion of the apartment above the garage. Authors' photograph.

Suburbia as built through the mid-twentieth century came under serious criticism for many reasons by the end of the century. Traffic and its consequent parking provisions were but one. In 1963, in Beverly Hills, California, where traffic congested streets nonetheless built for automobile traffic, the city council and planning commission denied homeowners the right to construct "asphalt lawns"—front yards paved between the sidewalk and house for parking. In other similarly prestigious areas, "asphalt lawns" seemed an unavoidable concession.[72]

The "snout house" summoned particular contempt in the 1990s. Projection of the garage directly toward the street, often challenging the house in its mass, enjoyed great popularity for new house construction in the 1950s through the 1960s but engendered a backlash among elitists. Their disgust often expressed itself positively in historic preservation as an effort to regulate conditions from an idealized past, the "first motor age."[73] The reformers were strongest in Portland, Oregon, where, in 1999, the city enacted an ordinance outlawing the "snout house" in new construction. No garage could be wider than 50 percent of the house front and the front door had to be within eight feet of the front wall. "It's more welcoming," one reformer asserted.[74] Builders and developers unimaginatively countered that larger vehicles and the two-car family norm dictated their design.[75]

Opposition to the "snout house" was but one article of faith among the rising consensus known as the New Urbanism. Its adherents sought to reclaim streets for multiple uses of recreation and neighboring, as well as vehicular traffic. They believed a wholesome balance could be struck. Garages were included but minimized in size and prominence, often recommended for location behind houses or apartments for a more pedestrian-oriented landscape. The garage had come to symbolize a rampant automania. Jane Jacobs was alone when, in 1961, she published her advocacy for renewed street life, *The Life and Death of Great American Cities*. Gathering force by the 1980s, the New Urbanists included planner Donald Appleyard, traffic engineer Walter Kulash, and architect Mark Childs.[76] About parking, Childs argued that the car and street life could once again be made to yield good living space. In a chapter on residential parking, he expressed faith that his "recipes [would] suggest ways to accommodate the automobile at home and the formation of a neighborhood."[77]

* * *

That the paramount concern of car owners for convenience has always rendered the garage at home seems a natural conclusion. Many activities occurred there, depending on each period's restless reorientations. Inside its enclosure or beneath its sheltering carport, motorists have taken on varying degrees of auto repair and maintenance. At the dawn of automobility, some chauffeurs resided in the garage, and considerably more work was performed there than in later times, when motorists more confidently turned their needs over to professional mechanics in shops removed from home. The car, thus, became the object of concern in multiple places, each with its exclusive purpose. Outside the domestic garage, community members increasingly imposed their demands on its looks. Domestic renters were swept along in the changes. Inside the garage, homeowners shuffled goods in storage, found space for privacy, and attended to their cars' needs to the degree they saw fit. By century's end, the New Urbanism's reformers wanted it pushed to the background. Still, throughout the nation, the domestic garage remained the most ubiquitous artifact of automobility except for the car itself.

6

COMMERCIAL GARAGE EVOLUTION THROUGH SPECIALIZATION AND DEPARTMENTALIZATION

At first, car dealers took responsibility mainly for repairing the cars they sold, honoring, for example, automaker warranty agreements. Dealers might sell gasoline and offer lubrication service but mainly for the convenience of customers who had purchased cars; car servicing in general tended to be left to others. After World War I, automobile manufacturers began to encourage dealers to emphasize maintenance as well as repair, and not just for car buyers but for the public at large. Garages not associated with car sales, on the other hand, had always emphasized car maintenance while also engaging in repair work, with most shops involved only in making light repairs but others also tackling heavy repair work such as engine rebuilding. Accordingly, what garage buildings housed—or, in other words, what services they rendered—varied substantially. Nonetheless, all car repair remained at first a generalized endeavor with the entire car a focus of attention. After World War I, garage specialization quickly became the norm, as many garage owners opted to emphasize only one thing. Within the remaining general repair garages, on the other hand, especially in dealer shops, departmentalization rapidly came to the fore. Departmentalization involved the bundling of specialized repair operations under a single roof.

Improving Technical Competence

In the first ten to fifteen years of motoring in America, a wide range of expertise was brought to car maintenance and repair. Historian James J. Flink has outlined a period when few mechanics, especially those trained by automobile manufacturers, were available. Car owners turned to bicycle repairmen, blacksmiths, and even plumbers, or simply the mechanically inclined, to service their motor vehicles.[1] This last group were, as historian Kevin Borg has dubbed them, "ad hoc mechanics."[2] Many motorists necessarily fell upon their own skills for want of better remedy, necessity prompting a quick learning curve. Ad hoc mechanics might work in their own shops, bicycle clubs, or storage garages. Of course, minor repairs were certainly within the skill range of many people, especially farmers experienced with farm equipment. The typical mechanic, in other words, tended toward the "jack of all trades."

Employment of carefully trained mechanics in well-equipped repair shops occurred first in the nation's major cities led by the automobile manufacturers, certain large dealers, and the larger automobile clubs. Initially, manufacturers created branch operations with sales floors and repair garages accompanied by storage facilities. As early as 1901, the Winton Motor Carriage Company was operating six such facilities in New York City.[3] The Banker Brothers, distributors for some nine automakers, maintained similar venues in New York, Philadelphia, and Pittsburgh.[4] Automobile clubs, such as New York City's American Automobile Club, provided repair services in its elegant storage garage in midtown Manhattan, but only for members.

Early on, only a few manufacturers provided instruction in car repair, whether for car owners or for those intending to become commercial mechanics. In retrospect, early motoring would have been made far easier if such instruction had been available. The first automobiles were notoriously unreliable, being subject to frequent breakdown. To fill the information void and, indeed, to develop repair expertise, various institutions stepped in. Mechanics' schools were organized from city to city much like the numerous business colleges that taught typing, shorthand, and other skills to would-be office workers. To help achieve its stated goal of "character building," the Young Men's Christian Association began a program to train mechanics, local chapters usually cooperating with a local automobile club or mechanics' school. Boston's YMCA was the first to do so, starting its program in 1903.[5]

The coming of mass automobile production based on standardized car parts fostered standardized repair procedures in garages specifically outfitted for the purpose. But much ad hoc activity remained, engaged in mainly by repairmen making the transition from working on horse-drawn vehicles or, indeed, from shoeing or otherwise working with horses. As late as the early 1920s, as we have said, many a blacksmith split his time between traditional horse-oriented business and some aspect of auto repair, some running garages as a side activity but most utilizing their original facilities.[6]

Trade journals were an important means of diffusing technical advice not only about car repair per se but also about how to market repair service. In the early days, motoring was very much a seasonal, warm-weather activity across much of the United States; cars taken out of winter storage always required servicing.[7] Trade journal and auto club magazine articles appeared with titles like "Getting the Car Ready for Spring" or "Overhauling Time Here."[8] Each year the *American Garage and Auto Dealer* published a "winter overhaul chart," which along with other technical articles kept repair shop operators, and motorists also, abreast of relevant servicing needs from one car make to another.[9] Such reporting only enhanced the demand for "professional" work done by mechanics whose work could be "guaranteed."

Many early car owners thought that the automakers, and certainly the dealers where cars were purchased, ought to provide recurring maintenance and even to do it free of charge. Manufacturers and dealers did offer warranties and thus stood to make good on equipment failures. But the financial onus for regular car maintenance fell quickly on the car owner, although discussion continued in the press well into the 1920s as one article—"Where Shall We Draw the Line on Free Service?"—demonstrated.[10] Owners soon learned their car's capacities in terms of anticipated repair costs as well as operating expenses. And they learned that a car's life expectancy, especially before World War I, was not very long.

Long-distance driving required special preparations. *The Official Automobile Blue Book* of 1923 (published in cooperation with the American Automobile Association) not only provided route descriptions, maps, and a listing of service garages but also a section on "Getting Ready for Your Tour." A car's engine needed to be tuned, its fuel system tested, its lighting system examined, its clutch and transmission adjusted, its axles checked, and new tires and tubes installed.[11] Additionally, long-distance motoring posed problems of trust and reliability regarding where one should have repairs made when engine, axle, tire, or other difficulties occurred. Away from home—away from where the car had been purchased—how was one to choose a repair garage? Articles appeared in popular magazines with titles such as "Ali Baba and His Forty Thieves." Too often, they warned, mechanics who found a customer with no real understanding of the problem at hand would assert the worse and go on to charge exorbitant fees, often for unnecessary work.[12]

The car servicing industry was very much aware of such criticism. Caring garage owners—those not merely running a business but concerned with avoiding customer dissatisfaction—began to innovate accordingly, separating out, for example, the diagnosis of problems from their fixing. Into the vocabulary entered the term "contact man": one who bridged the mechanic's and the car owner's worldviews. A mechanic, as competent as he or she might be, was not necessarily well suited to dealing directly with customers. "Discourtesy and uncouthness on the part of the trouble shooter will very often incur a customer's dislike for the whole organization," the editors of *Motor Age* observed in 1922.[13] A ballooning number of customers in what was by then a mass market were coming to garages with considerably less knowledge of the car's inner workings than that possessed by earlier motorists. They were decidedly vulnerable and needed protecting. Guaranteed repair work was something dealers were promoted as best prepared to render.

Dealer Repair and Maintenance Guarantees

Repairing customers' cars had always been the dealer garage purview, car maintenance falling more to independent general-service garages. But by emphasizing both, and by maintaining high standards of workmanship, carmakers saw a mechanism for enhancing buyer confidence in company products. Such encouragement brought dealers added headaches, particularly added expense. The Buick Division of General Motors advertised "Authorized Buick Service," requiring that dealer garages be equipped with tools specially designed to handle Buick cars and that dealer mechanics be "factory trained." This included not just initial mechanic schooling at a company facility (in Buick's case in Flint, Michigan) but also mechanic participation in periodic clinics, usually held regionally. Dealer participation was advertised on special signs displayed at garage entrances. Each garage stood as if part of a chain, which in fact it was. "Traveling men" exercised Buick's authority, enforcing company standards through regular inspection.[14]

Thus, the larger car companies sought to convince the car-buying public that dealer garages were superior to independent garages that did not employ, or could not be forced to adopt, standardized repair and service procedures. Convinced of the soundness of strict garage oversight, manufacturers began to liberalize warranty agreements regarding guaranteed repairs. So also did they begin to package long-term service agreements. The Star-Durant Company was one of the earliest firms to sell "maintenance service plans" built around regular lubrication and engine tune-ups. Stickers reminded car owners of the odometer readings at which prepaid servicing was scheduled.[15] The Franklin Motor Company promoted monthly car inspections, the reasoning being that it insured both the owner's confidence in a dealer and a steady demand for the dealer's services.[16]

By the end of the 1920s, most dealership garages were divided between front and back spaces, not just separated from sales but divided between those who dealt with customers and those who actually did car repair and servicing. It was a division much encouraged by the carmakers. Mechanics dominated the back space, undertaking repair work and, with increasingly specialized equipment, following standardized procedures. Dominating the front space were the contact men (increasingly called "service salesmen")—people with mechanical knowledge, but also sensitive to customer thinking.[17] There, cars were received and also returned to customers. It was there that costs were calculated and customer bills prepared and presented. Early in the twentieth century, most garages calculated charges according to the parts and other supplies used and then by the amount of time consumed in servicing the car. After 1920, "flat rate" charges were popularized, with bills calculated according to standardized job requirements, parts and time calculations being preset.[18]

Individual auto dealerships were themselves responsible for much innovation. A Detroit Packard dealer regimented work by assigning each customer to one of three repair teams. Cars were marked accordingly on one headlamp bracket so that it could be referred to one group or another immediately upon entering the garage. A team inspector gave a list of required repairs to a garage service manager, who then approved a work order. Team members came to know each car, the system fostering more of a personal relationship between mechanics and customers.[19] A Hudson dealer in Chicago offered "servicing and selling, instead of selling and servicing." Ninety percent of the dealer's three-story building, he advertised in 1923, was devoted to car repair and maintenance rather than to car display and sales. Each floor, constituting an acre of space, made the building one of the largest structures of its kind in the city. It was promoted as a "service station" in the new vocabulary of the day. The first floor was dedicated to quick service, the second floor to preparing new cars for sale, and the third floor to major repair work and car painting. Also located there were lockers, showers, and a restroom for the male work force, as well as a restroom for women employees. An "auto-call" telephone system connected the entire building through a central switchboard. Boys on roller skates brought parts swiftly to mechanics from storage rooms on each floor. *Motor Age* reported that, notwithstanding the building's enormity, everything had been done "to smooth the path of the customer."[20] In new garages, focus was also placed on employee comfort and productivity. Mechanics at the regional Oakland branches of General Motors worked in daylight, work floors being generously provided with wall and ceiling windows. Fans cleared away smoke and cooled work spaces in summer.[21]

Innovation also involved business management as, for example, through the novel embrace of flat-rate accounting. At O.K. Motors in Louisville, Kentucky, a Studebaker dealer, two-thirds of each customer charge went to the firm to pay overhead and other costs, while one-third went to pay salaries, making its mechanics better paid than at any other dealer in the city.[22] Improvements in managing personnel slowly accrued. The Ohio Buick Company of Cleveland, Ohio, launched regularly scheduled service department meetings, subsidized annual picnics, and, most important, offered a mechanics school on the premises.[23] Other dealers experimented with customer relations. At one dealer in Texas, the employee who accepted a car for servicing returned it once servicing was complete, thus to build a personal bond with the customer. "By doing this, it is easier to strike up a friendship with the customer and get him to come in more often, or suggest the sale of accessories," it was reported. In addition, the garage adopted a policy of "wiping down" every car after a service call, thus to return vehicles "sparkling clean."[24]

Innovations came from small-town as well as big-city dealers. Change to meet competition was constantly required in places both large and small. In Clarinda, Iowa, a town of some five thousand people in 1910, mechanics Paul and John Opitz rented space at the back of a storage garage, broke with their lackadaisical accountant and a landlord resistant to making building improvements, obtained a loan from a local bank, and then built and moved into a new building of their own, one equipped with the latest technology. In 1919, they obtained a Ford franchise but on condition that they build and move into an even larger structure. As reported in the *American Garage and Auto Dealer,* a methodical system of repairing cars, flat-rate charging, and scientific "time studies" honed the firm's reputation.[25]

The Mechanic

Without mechanics garages could not function. That was obvious. Yet the mechanic was not a driving force for garage evolution. New technologies and management decisions to embrace them always dominated trade-journal reporting. For the most part, technology in every industry was adopted largely to cut labor costs, reducing in the process skilled laborers to little more than machine tenders in many enterprises. This was especially true of assembly-line work in factories, something substantially innovated in the automobile industry. But at the level of the repair garage, how did new technology play out? Historians, and other scholars for that matter, have been reticent to comment. Indeed, only relatively recently has the mechanic become a focus of attention in this regard, specifically Stephen L. McIntyre's 1995 PhD dissertation ("'The Repair Man Will Gyp You': Mechanics, Managers, and Customers in the Automobile Repair Industry, 1896–1940"), as well as his recent article in *Technology and Culture* and Kevin L. Borg's 2007 book, *Auto Mechanics: Technology and Expertise in Twentieth-Century America.*[26]

McIntyre explored the mechanic through the lens of social-class friction and the potential for conflict engendered through class division, at least in the early years of motoring. Even in independent repair garages, "labor" was generalized as a cost of production—something that management sought to reduce through technological innovation. Put differently, management needed to constantly enhance worker productivity, putting mechanics increasingly to work as machine tenders rather than as skilled artisans using traditional tools. Certainly for the elite automobilists early on, the mechanic was a subject of suspicion—if not resentment. Like the chauffeur (or the chauffeur-mechanic) at home, the garage mechanic could easily take advantage of those without technical knowledge. In many ways, garage-floor labor, garage management, and customers stood in potential conflict. In a sense, the mechanic straddled the intellectual domains of production and consumption, falling, perhaps, into the abyss separating the two.

Automobile mechanics shared a historical trajectory similar to that of repair people in other fields, as sociologist Douglas Harper has outlined. Repair was initially much more intuitive than it later became. Kinesthetic, or bodily, knowledge prevailed initially.[27] Borg, himself a mechanic when he was young, explained that the identification of engine problems in automobiles, for example, required mostly the sight or feel of broken, loose, or leaking parts, along with listening to the sounds they made and smelling spark plugs for combustion.[28] But, as Harper emphasized, tools such as screwdrivers and wrenches extended the body's capacity to feel and to know. Internalized and largely nonverbal in nature, such skills propelled mechanical thinking and success at auto repair well into the 1920s.[29]

Increasingly thereafter, mechanics learned their trades in schools where the emphasis switched from feelings and intuition to analytical thought aided by a rapidly increasing array of diagnostic devices that measured things objectively. Learning in trade schools expanded from learning by watching and attempted replication to learning by problem solving based on objective measurement. Such schools certified graduates so that they might go directly into the job market with their journeyman apprenticeship vastly shortened. Rationalization, as Harper called the new learning process, also entailed replacing broken parts or components rather than repairing them, with repair and maintenance increasingly turning to "off-the-shelf" solutions. Indeed, problems were increasingly anticipated and solved in corporate research laboratories through experimentation. Having surrendered their intuition to externalized schemes of reason—a shift from an inductive to a deductive approach—mechanics indeed became substantially "deskilled." Also, standardized procedures dictated by automakers, as well as standardized parts readily available from wholesale jobbers, further decreased garage managers' dependence on their mechanics' knowledge and skill.[30]

Automobile maintenance and repair was thought of mainly as a masculine enterprise, as was motoring itself. Such a stereotype was largely rooted in fact. The 1930 U.S. Census counted 66,536 male, but only 257 female, "garage workers."[31] However, one woman's particularly lucid 1936 account of her career as an auto mechanic and commercial garage owner (along with her husband) is insightful, especially with regard to the very small garages that continued to thrive both in large cities and small towns through the 1930s and '40s and into the '50s. Matilda Black, a mother of grown daughters who had both graduated from college, worked beside her husband for some twenty-five years, and for eight hours each day during the five years before she wrote her account. She repaired almost everything from dented auto bodies to overhauling nineteen-cylinder engines, while still keeping house and tending to other domestic duties. She defined her daily work as "systematized," first putting account books in order, making sure that tools and equipment were in their assigned locations, and then preparing work sheets and ordering parts. She inspected cars both before and after completed work, and cleaned tools and equipment at the end of each work day. "I realize that a woman, in her insistence on details, can be a nuisance in the shop," she wrote. Hence she refrained from detailing to male employees their work. Although she was a good diagnostician, she refrained from appearing beside her husband when he was "selling a job." As she asserted, "Customers don't like the idea of a woman butting in."[32]

Specialization and Departmentalization

The journeyman mechanic—the "jack of all trades"—continued to flourish in the small, independent repair garages, especially in rural areas. There, mechanics tended to engage in any and all repair work that came their way. It was what kept many independent garages going, unfettered as they were from automaker oversight. But as brand loyalties grew and as the automakers extended through their dealer networks enhanced warranties and service agreements, independent garages became increasingly disadvantaged. True, they did not have the extra expense of special tools and specialized training required of dealers' mechanics, but then they did not have the power of national advertising working for them either. And increasingly, independents were forced to invest more and more in tools as cars became increasingly sophisticated. One way to cut operating costs was to focus on some specific aspect of auto repair and service.

Through the 1920s, independent garages turned increasingly to specialization in one or another kind of maintenance or repair work, activity that was usually linked to sales of related parts and accessories. Some of it was customer driven. "Customers like to place their business with different companies," the *National Petroleum News* reported in 1932. "In place of buying all services and merchandise for their automobiles at one place they like to buy gasoline and oil from Bill Smith, tires from Johnny Jones, and batteries from Bud Thompson."[33]

Specialization, of course, was encouraged by the greater technical sophistication of the motorcar itself. There was more for the garage mechanic to learn and know, and not just increasingly sophisticated tools to use. Covering repair and service without the benefit of manufacturer advertising became ever more difficult for most independent garage owners. Focus brought relief. Specialization potentially brought economies of scale to a narrower range of activity and enhanced profits not only in terms of services rendered but also in terms of related replacement parts, accessories, or other commodities sold. Lower prices could even attract customers who had previously been quite content to do their own car servicing and/or undertake their own replacement chores. "No longer does Father put the car in the drive Sunday morning, wash and grease it and look after the battery in addition to making minor repairs," noted one trade journal in 1927. "Greasing, battery watering and the repair jobs are done by professional workmen now. And so the car owner is getting a few dollars together to have his auto washed rather than do the job himself."[34]

Garages that did just one thing climbed in number through the 1930s, with proprietors focusing their business on tire repair, battery recharging, or some other market niche. Leading the way were the tire and battery manufacturers that created factory-owned chains of stores and/or franchised chains of independent dealers. However, the specialized garage was but one response to changing times. Garage departmentalization was the other. This involved creating focused shops that operated separately but nonetheless in close association with others, often on a single work floor. Auto dealers very much sustained the general-purpose garage. But they did so through bundling—in other words, through creating and sustaining separate shops for tire, battery, and other services in close proximity. The 1939 Census of Business reported some fifty-two thousand independent general repair shops in the United States and some thirty-four thousand dealer shops, but only five thousand so-called specialized shops. Additionally, however, some seven thousand body repair and radiator repair garages were also counted.[35] Thus, once again was statistical reporting unreliable. More confusion than ever reigned as to how auto repair garages ought to be categorized.

At the New York World's Fair in 1939, the Ford Motor Company displayed a "model garage" that was "decentralized" with specific spaces reserved for various operations. The exhibit was designed to show dealers as well as the public how efficient planning and utilization of floor space made for better service. Departments were clearly labeled "Engine Repair," "Body Repair," "Chassis Repair," "Engine Tune-Up," "Brake Service," and "Wheel Alignment."[36] Most repair and maintenance functions, indeed, lent themselves to bundling through garage departmentalization. Thus, the activities emphasized by Ford at the World's Fair very much remained part of the company's dealership scene.

Highly specialized stores, and highly specialized store chains, evolved to cover various narrow market niches. By the end of the 1950s, dealer garages with their "jack-of-all trades" implications were facing keen competition from specialized garages that were also backed by large corporations, companies that were perfecting very impressive economies of scale through franchising. Brand names like Firestone, B. F. Goodrich, and Goodyear, for example, had become as well known as Chrysler, Ford, and General Motors. Names like Aamco and Midas also became household words. But, too, corporate names like Gulf Oil, Standard Oil, and Texaco became firmly associated with car repair and thus with garage work. As the Texaco slogan put it, "You Can Trust Your Car to the Man Who Wears the Star."

Departmentalization tended to play out in new buildings. Specialization, on the other hand, came to characterize both the new and the old. Indeed, specialization sustained many an older garage building. No longer large enough or in some other way no long suitable for a general repair and service business, old garage buildings found renewed life by housing, for example, a tire store, a body shop, or an auto parts store. How then did specialization and departmentalization play out over time in the garage scene? We now turn to the various auto repair and service specializations that evolved through the 1950s, some important to the garage as an institution and some not.

Gasoline

Sale of gasoline was always problematic in the traditional garage. At first it was the associated fire hazard, but later it was the difficulty of customer access and convenience. In the earliest years, gasoline was stored inside garages in barrels delivered by jobber tank wagons. Not only was hand transfer of gasoline from barrel to automobile gas tank time consuming, but it also involved much evaporation, especially when it was filtered, as was common, through a hand-held chamois. Dangerous were the leaks and spills that spread layers of greasy dirt on garage floors. "Thirty-nine cars were completely destroyed by a fire which completely demolished the frame garage and salesroom of L. E. Huddle at Lancaster, O.," the *Horseless Age* reported in 1915. "The fire was caused by some gasoline on the floor of the building becoming ignited by a spark from a backfire in one of the cars."[37]

After 1910, underground storage tanks were required by law in most localities. Constructed of galvanized metal sheathed in concrete, they were to be located outside of garage buildings and buried several feet below ground. Gasoline was then pumped inside the garage for distribution by hand or, as quickly became standard, distributed by pump and hose into automobile gas tanks. Various manufacturers, including the Vac Liquid Equipment Company of Cedar Rapids, Iowa, whose system is pictured, competed to perfect the technology (fig. 6.1). At most garages, gasoline storage came to be located under front sidewalks in conjunction with curbside pumps. Cars with internal combustion engines were considered the most dangerous in terms of fire potential. Steam cars, whose boilers operated on kerosene, were considered less so. Least dangerous were electric vehicles. But necessary in every garage, irrespective of the kind of car serviced, were chemical fire extinguishers, ideally backed up by buckets of sand, often hung from ceiling rafters. And, of course, garage construction changed. After 1910, new garages were increasingly built with masonry walls and metal roof trusses—what garage owners invariably advertised as "fire proof" structures.

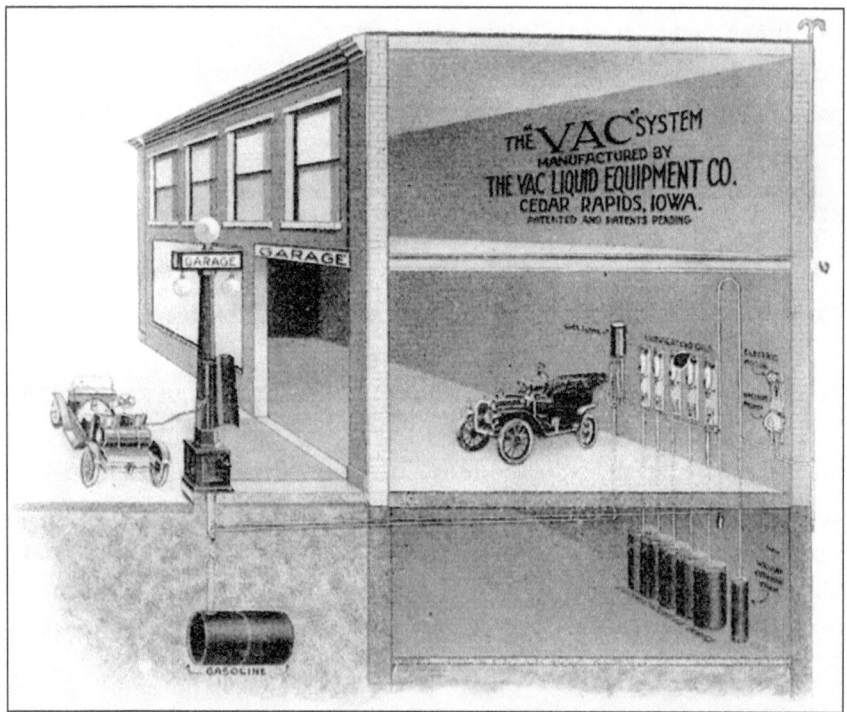

Figure 6.1. "Vac" system of gasoline storage and distribution. From "Gasoline Storage Systems," *Horseless Age* 29 (May 1, 1912): 805.

Figure 6.2. Advertising illustration for the Guarantee Liquid Measure Company of Rochester, New York. From *Motor World* 65 (Dec. 29, 1929): 144.

The "visible" gasoline pump revolutionized gasoline retailing (fig. 6.2). Not only was it safe, but it also offered an important guarantee against garage dishonesty. Gasoline was pumped up into a glass reservoir that was clearly calibrated as to the amount being dispensed, thus enabling the motorist to verify his or her purchase. Electrically driven, the pumps were also fast. But when such pumps were moved to off-street driveways at filling stations, buying gas became even more convenient. No longer did the customer have to stop along a congested street, honk for service, and wait for an attendant (possibly a mechanic diverted from other work) to come outside. At gasoline stations, attendants dressed in smart uniforms provided instant service, including cleaning windshields, checking oil, and even checking air pressure in tires.

Although most garages eliminated gasoline sales, some in the 1920s and '30s, as we have seen, sought to copy gas station formats. More or less separate gas stations were appended to existing buildings. New buildings were constructed, often with a clipped corner to accommodate a driveway with a pump island (see figs. 3.5 and 3.6). Some garage owners operated gasoline stations as fully separate businesses, thus to hedge against losing gasoline sales completely. R. S. Sperry of Emmitsburg, Maryland, as reported in the *Accessory and Garage Journal*, embraced both the old and the new: "He not only sells oils and gas from the vantage point of the garage site, but he also bought out a gas station on the opposite side of the street, where he now has a special gas station for the exclusive sale of *Good Gulf* and *NoNox Gas* and *Gulf Supreme Auto Oils*." "A great many motorists prefer the drive-in station," Sperry was quoted as saying, "because it takes them out of the line of traffic of a busy thoroughfare where machines are passing all the time, and it also affords a much stronger feeling of safety."[38] To sell gasoline, garage owners found that they had to conform to corporate retailing standards, including the sale of only one gasoline brand—the company's brand. But bringing the garage up to standards also required appropriate signage, assigning attendants to pump islands, and, of course, the same high standards of cleanliness and orderliness demanded of filling station franchisees. Retailing gasoline needed to fit within corporate marketing strategies in both look and function. It needed to conform to the dictates of place-product-packaging.[39]

Lubrication

Initially, automobile engines were engineered to low standards and thus consumed as much, if not more, lubricating oil as gasoline. To prolong engine life, early motorists were encouraged to change oil at least every five hundred miles, but then every one thousand or two thousand miles as engine specifications tightened (fig. 6.3). Once oil filters were introduced, they, of course, needed periodic changing. And so also transmission and differential oils required replacement with each seasonal change, hot and cold weather requiring different grades of oil. Springs and other moveable parts needed periodic greasing. Thus did lubrication, with its constant repeat business, represent an important garage mainstay, something very much sustained even after gasoline retailing moved on.

At first, the dispensing of lubricants was, as with gasoline, quite primitive. Little more was required than a drum of oil, a calibrated tin container, a funnel, and a wrench. Small oil tanks with hand pumps atop them were popularized in

Figure 6.3. Advertisement for the Standard Oil Company of Indiana's Polarine Motor Oil. From *Wisconsin Motorist* 8 (Dec. 1916): 9.

Figure 6.4. Lubricating rack. From advertisement for the Bowen Products Company, *Automotive Industries* 52 (June 25, 1925): 179.

the early 1920s. Then came oil in cans. At first, cars were jacked up and engine oil simply drained out into flat pans, with the mechanic crawling underneath. Then came the drain rack made of wood or metal, onto which cars were driven (fig. 6.4). Often racks were placed over concrete-lined pits, enabling the crouching mechanic to fully grease the car as well. Thus was the so-called grease monkey born (fig. 6.5). The final improvement, first widely adopted in the 1930s, was the vertical hydraulic lift that enabled the attendant to stand beneath the car (fig. 6.6).

Lubrication was an activity that enjoyed a fixed location in every shop, and became, thereby, the first specialized department in many garages. By 1920, special-purpose structures, called "lubritoriums," were also being built, the first in Omaha, Nebraska, in 1917.[40] Some of these buildings were quite large and quite elegant—for example, the Western Oil Refining Company's *White Flash* "lubrication Station" in downtown Indianapolis, Indiana (fig. 6.7). Built in 1923, the building was actually part of a one-stop super service station, with the gas pumps and a gas station house located immediately adjacent to it. Nonetheless, lubrication was clearly the complex's main purpose. Twenty cars could be serviced simultaneously. "It is an entirely fire-proof construction," the *Hoosier Motorist* reported, "the sides and roof being of glass, supported by structural iron work."

Figure 6.5. Cartoon illustrating the garage greasing pit. From *Motor Age* 65 (Feb. 1946): 76.

Rather than the conventional oil racks and pits, the basement was one large room that permitted station attendants to freely move underneath from car to car. Oil was drained into "swinging basins" connected by hoses and pipes to a central discharge tank. At night the building literally glowed in the dark, a large electric sign up top.[41]

Several large petroleum companies experimented with lubritoriums. In Chicago, the Sinclair Refining Company opened several "greasing palaces" in connection with several of its gasoline stations. The Standard Oil Company of Indiana quickly followed suit. At one station, "practically everything was done by air pressure," the *National Petroleum News* reported. "In one corner is a big compressor which furnishes air for spring sprays, pressure for grease guns and air for tires which is available through an overhead reel."[42] Several automobile manufacturers also embraced the idea, encouraging dealers to install modern lubricating plants within or adjacent to dealer garages. The Ford Motor Company, a decade before its display at the 1939 New York World's Fair, outfitted a demonstration lubricating floor at its plant in Highland Park, Michigan, thus to instruct dealers.[43] By 1940, all General Motors dealers featured lubrication floors

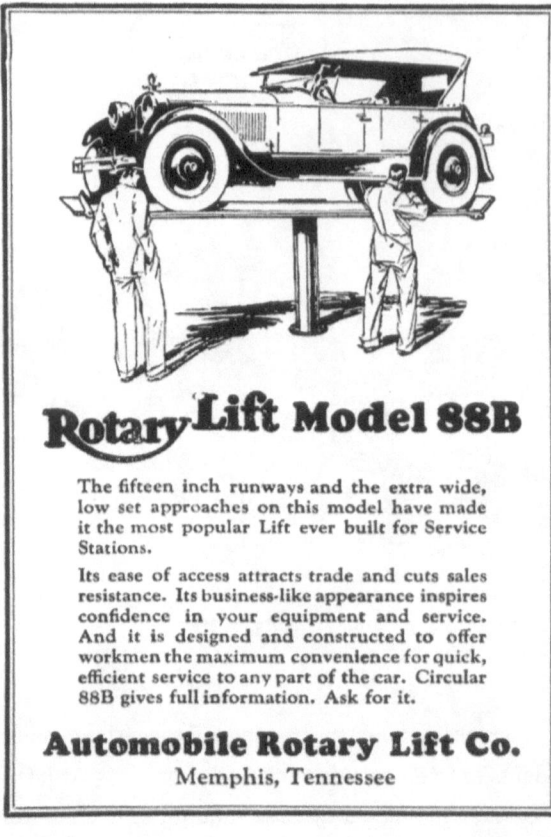

Figure 6.6. Advertisement for the Automobile Rotary Lift Company. From *Accessory and Garage Journal* 18 (Dec. 1928): 64.

(fig. 6.8). In the 1950s, necessary lubrication equipment included a vertical lift, separate pressured chassis, transmission and differential lubricating units, and a "quick changer" oil draining apparatus as well as wheel-bearing and tire-servicing tools.[44]

BATTERY SERVICE

Cars with internal combustion engines were not the only automobiles on the road before World War I, but they were fully the most popular. Steam cars burning kerosene were greatly disadvantaged by the amount of water that could be conveniently carried, generally only enough for thirty or thirty-five miles of driving. But their engines were of the utmost simplicity, many with only fifteen or so moving parts. Few had more than three dozen moving parts overall. They required much less maintenance, therefore, and very little lubrication. They ran

Figure 6.7. Lubritorium, Indianapolis, Indiana. From "New Lubrication Station Presents Unique Appearance," *Hoosier Motorist* 11 (Feb. 1923): 25.

smoothly and quietly due to very low engine speed. Low gear ratios meant that drivers could accelerate evenly to high speeds without need of shifting. Steam cars did not carry complicated transmission and clutch mechanisms.[45]

Electric vehicles proved popular longer, especially the use of electric delivery trucks. In 1915, there were an estimated twenty-five thousand electric passenger cars and twelve thousand trucks on the road in the United States, making battery recharging an important branch of the garage business. But use of electric vehicles was restricted largely to cities and their immediate hinterlands, there being a general lack of recharging facilities in rural America. Out along well-traveled highways, for example between New York City and Philadelphia, recharging stations were available at intervals (fig. 6.9). But off main roads there was little or nothing. In Chicago, Commonwealth Edison maintained a network of emergency recharging stations (fig. 6.10). However, most electric vehicle recharging took place elsewhere—truck recharging at fleet garages and private cars (approximately thirty-two hundred in 1915) at one of seventy commercial garages.[46] The service floor at Jacob's Detroit Electric Service Station in Savannah, Georgia, pictured in 1916, was typical (fig. 6.11). Recharging panels and switchboards lined the wall of the second-floor service floor reserved for electric vehicles. A Detroit Electric is shown undergoing recharging at the right.

Figure 6.8. Lubrication floor at Lansing, Michigan, Pontiac dealer. From "Lubrication Department Brings Increase in Sales," *Automobile Topics* 127 (Aug. 16, 1937): 102.

Of course, electric cars and trucks also had limited driving ranges; for most vehicles the range was less than eighty miles between charges, making them primarily city cars. The greatest drawback, however, was the time required to recharge—rarely less than four hours for quick charges. To fully charge, a car needed to be plugged in overnight. Electric cars were suitable for shopping or for an owner's commuting to work, but not for long-distance touring. They were, for the most part, considered ideal for women, being quiet, clean, and very easy to drive, albeit always at rather low speeds. Battery recharging stations were mainly in what one journalist called "electric neighborhoods": "the better apartment districts, exclusive communities fronting on boulevards, and suburbs within a reasonable distance of central localities directly connected by paved roads."[47]

Batteries also found universal use in gasoline-powered vehicles, first to power headlights and then to power electric starters once they displaced hand-cranked magnetos. Through the 1920s, most automobile manufacturers were primarily car assemblers, buying engines, bodies, and, indeed, most car parts from specialty manufacturers. Batteries were very much included. The Electric

Figure 6.9. Electric vehicle recharging stations in the New York City area. From "Electric Vehicle Recharging Stations," *Electric Vehicles* 6 (Feb. 1915): 45.

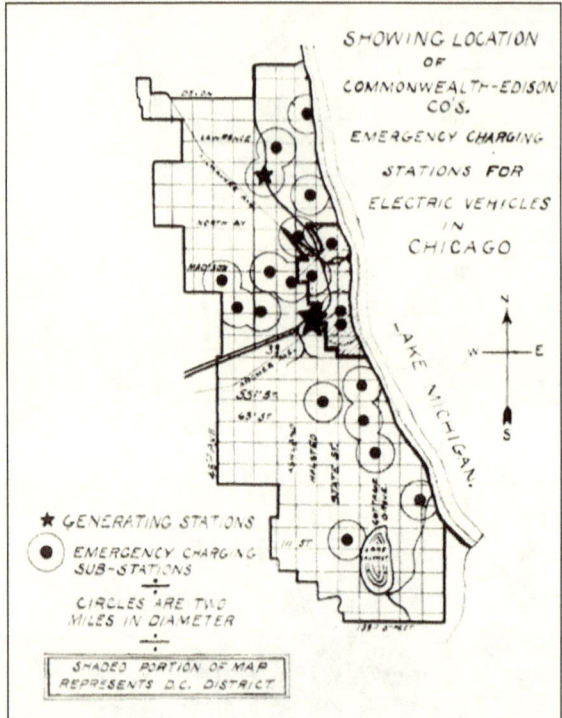

Figure 6.10. Commonwealth Edison's emergency charging stations in Chicago. From *Electric Vehicles* 6 (Apr. 1915): 128.

Storage Battery Company of Philadelphia became the largest supplier of lead acid batteries for automobiles, all marketed under the Exide brand. The word stood for "Excellent Oxide." The company not only supplied original equipment to carmakers but also sold its products through a network of retail stores and service garages, together numbering some thirty thousand locations by 1940.[48] Dealers proudly displayed the Exide logo (fig. 6.12).

Detroit's Ford Motor Company and General Motors Corporation led the way to vertical integration in the manufacture of cars. Companies were bought out and made into subsidiaries not only to eliminate dependence on suppliers but also to reduce the cost of automobile components. The Willys Corporation of Toledo, Ohio, bought the Electric Auto-Lite Company, which, as its name indicated, began as a maker of automobile headlights. In 1915, the company also produced batteries and electric starters—of course to equip Willys-Overland automobiles but also to sell them through a network of franchised dealers. Dealers were

Figure 6.11. Charging Floor at Jacob's Detroit Service Station, Savannah, Georgia. From "New Station Insures Future," *Electric Vehicles* 7 (Dec. 1910): 229.

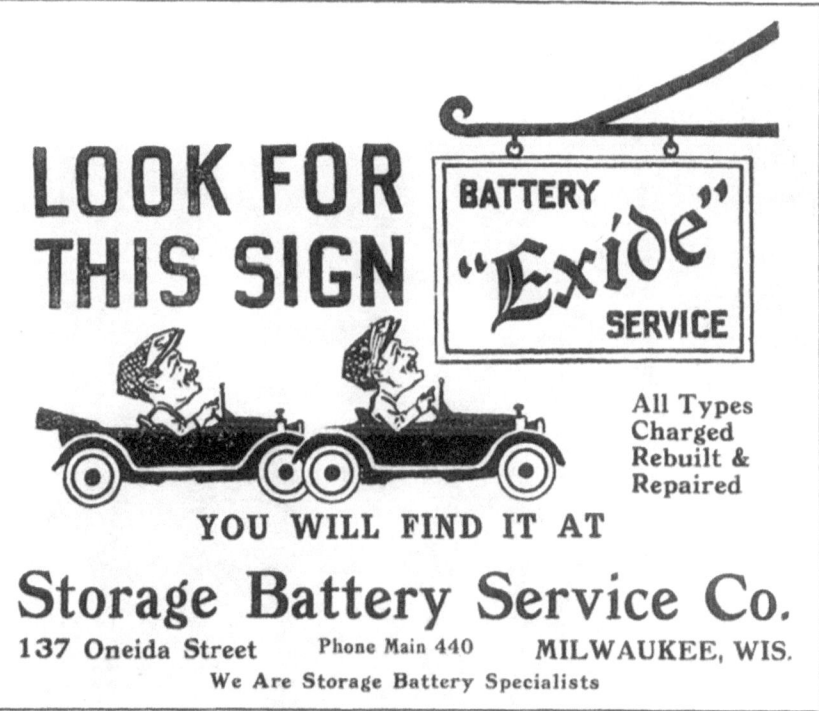

Figure 6.12. Advertisement for the Storage Battery Service Company of Milwaukee. From *Wisconsin Motorist* 7 (Jan. 1916): 103.

supplied through factory branches in New York City, Kansas City, and San Francisco.[49] Pictured is an Auto-Lite Dealer in Omaha, Nebraska (fig. 6.13).

The typical recharging outfit was not expensive, making battery work something of a universal, just like lubrication. "Of course," advised *Motor World*, "a lead burning outfit is essential and a battery steamer is desirable, but other repair equipment is more or less optional. A common sink may be used for the drainage rack." Also necessary, of course, was a charging bench upon which batteries removed from cars might be placed, benches provided with electrical panels logically. And then there were the adjacent shelves for storing distilled water and battery acid.[50] Small storage batteries initially required slow charges lasting upwards to twenty-four hours. By 1923, however, charging time had been reduced to some eight hours.[51] However, an early car battery that serviced only lights and a starter could last for thousands of miles of driving over months and even years.

Figure 6.13. Farnam Ford Repair Garage, Omaha, Nebraska, circa 1938. From authors' photo collection.

Tune-Ups

Lubrication and battery recharging took motorists to service garages on a recurring basis. So also did minor engine tune-ups. It is interesting that motor tuning, one of the original fortes of the general-purpose shop, became a kind of specialization (fig. 6.14). Today we think of the minor tune-up as an oil change, a new air filter, cleaned or replaced spark plugs, cleaned and adjusted points, checked belts and hoses, and a topping-off of various fluids. But for cars early in the twentieth century, it also included such things as chassis lubrication, brake inspection, wheel-bearing repacking, and the tightening of bolts and screws both in a car's engine compartment and across its body and undercarriage. Engine work included flushing out the cooling system, checking valve clearances, inspecting cylinder heads, and, most important, adjusting the carburetor.

Figure 6.14. Lacy L. Redd & Company, Philadelphia, Pennsylvania, tune-up specialists. From "On Watch for Failing Batteries," *Motor Age* 60 (Aug. 1941): 39.

Indeed, it was the increasingly sophisticated carburetor that tended to make the minor tune-up a kind of specialty. Garages linked their carburetor servicing to the products of one or another manufacturer through franchise contracts. The Bendix Stromberg Carburetor Company, a subsidiary of Bendix Aviation of South Bend, Indiana, was one such franchiser (fig. 6.15). As noted in the *Accessory and Garage Journal* in 1928: "The carburetor is a scientific mechanism which requires special study—and it must be right. Far too many years have seen it tampered with without understanding and with hit-and-miss theories. Likewise, the carburetor manufacturer more than welcomes the carburetor specialist and he is being given every help and encouragement."[52]

Major tune-ups remained primarily a function of the large, general-purpose garages, and especially those of auto dealers. In the 1950s, the following was recommended for most cars at the thirty-thousand-mile mark: thorough cylinder work (including the grinding of values), an overhaul of the distributor, a rebuilding of the carburetor, a cleaning or replacement of the fuel pump, a checking of the starter, and brush replacement in the generator. At fifty thousand miles, addi-

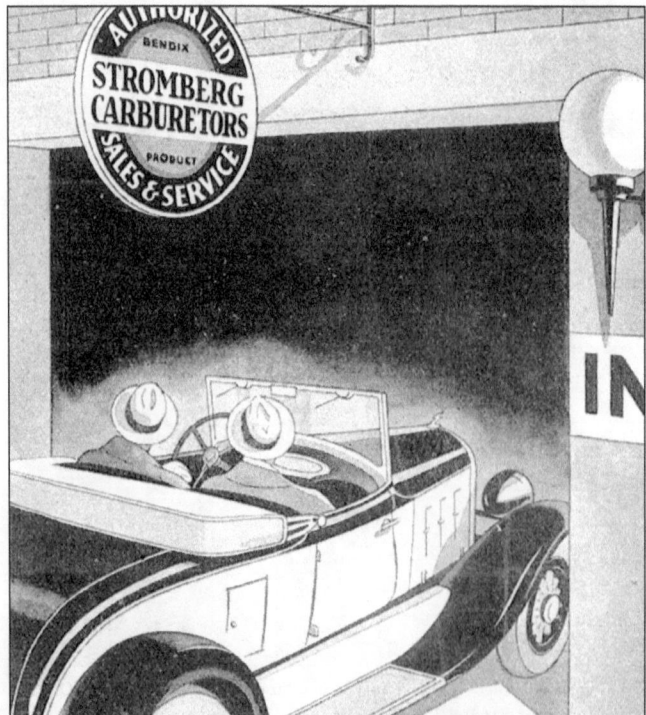

Figure 6.15. Advertisement for the Bendix Stromberg Carburetor Company. From *Automobile Topics* 105 (Mar. 5, 1932): 315.

tional work included "re-ringing" the engine (again grinding the values but also installing new wrist pins, resizing the pistons, and installing new connecting rod bearing and oil seals), adjusting the voltage regulator, overhauling and/or installing a new starter motor, and adjusting the transmission bands.[53] Earlier in the century, it was expected that engines would be removed from cars, disassembled, and every part cleaned. "The cylinder bloc should be examined for cracks, tested for warpage of base and measured for wear of cylinder bore and valve guides," advised the *American Garage and Auto Dealer* in 1925. Main bearings and connecting rods or crank pins needed to be measured for amount of wear, and the crankcase checked for cracks. "Camshaft, camshaft bearings in crankcase, timing gears, idle gear studs, idle gear bushings, magneto and water pump shaft bearing should be checked . . . [and] connecting rods should be examined for fractures and all bolts and nuts should be given special attention."[54]

Tire Repair and Sales

Perhaps the tire store epitomized the specialized garage if only for its numbers. Before 1910, many cars were equipped with solid rubber tires mounted on wooden or metal rims. But by the 1920s, pneumatic tires with inflatable inner tubes and heavy outer covers (the latter being what most Americans thought of as tires) were standard. Variously did tires "clinch" with raised beads in the rubber firmly fitting into grooves cut in the wheel rims. It was not until the 1950s that tubeless tires became the norm. Pneumatic tires, being inflated, absorbed much road vibration. They were plagued initially, however, by frequent punctures, blowouts, rim cuts, and valve leakages. Early pneumatic tires also failed to grip road surfaces firmly, especially in wet weather. Over the years, tire manufacturers changed the chemistry of the rubber used, added layers of alternating cloth and rubber, and improved heat-curing methods (vulcanization), thus to strengthen tires and prolong life. They also experimented with novel tread designs calculated to increase driving stability.

There were ninety-four tire makers in the United States in 1911, along with fifty-three rim manufacturers and thirty-five makers of inner tubes.[55] Most manufacturers wholesaled tires through regional jobbers, who then supplied retailers, most of whom carried the brands of several companies. However, the largest tire makers—such as Goodyear, Firestone, Fisk, and the United States Rubber Company—distributed their products through their own factory branches, and additionally created company-owned and/or franchised retail chains. Like the petroleum companies in their use of place-product-packaging, tire companies promoted look-alike stores that shared not just logos but also color schemes and even architectural styling, although building design, as with gas stations, steadily evolved from year to year.

Before 1920, most tire dealers operated from traditional storefronts—building facades usually cluttered with signs. Witness the Progressive Tire and Rubber outlet in Philadelphia pictured about 1925 (fig. 6.16). With its gas pumps featuring Atlantic and Tydol gasoline, the store was, nonetheless, primarily in the tire business, carrying the McClaren brand. As with many early storefront tire stores, new tires were installed on customer cars outside at the curbside. But dealers were encouraged to modernize and that meant adding garage floors, thus to service cars under cover. Outside they were encouraged to add updated equipment—for example, compressed-air pumps for inflating tires in conjunction with gas pumps.

Figure 6.16. Progressive Tire Company, Philadelphia, Pennsylvania, circa 1925. From authors' photo collection.

Figure 6.17. Illustration from a Romort Manufacturing Company advertisement. Ad copy reads: "Romort Air and Water Station installed in front of your place of business will bring you hundreds of new customers that would otherwise drive by." From *Automobile Dealer and Repairer* 31 (Aug. 1921): 56.

If gasoline sales attracted tire customers, so also would "free air" (fig. 6.17). United States Tire Company dealers were given an array of fascia, projecting, and roof signs (fig. 6.18). But fully modern buildings with new materials and up-to-date architectural styling (with signs carefully integrated into facade treatments) were what the Fisk Rubber Company idealized (fig. 6.19).

After 1920, new tire stores invariably contained not only front-of-building sales floors but also back-of-building service garages. Sales floors contained sales counters (which usually fronted storage rooms), but also display cases and racks where tires and at least a small array of automobile accessories were displayed. The company-owned stores of the Goodyear Tire and Rubber Company even sold home appliances in what the firm called "Car and Home Stores." Also at car dealerships were display cases and racks variously distributed in both front and back regions (fig. 6.20). At dealer garages, at least one of the service bays constituting a separate repair department was usually set aside to handle tires and related services.

Tire-Related Servicing

Closely associated with tire work, which included tire balancing, was wheel alignment, frame straightening, spring and shock absorber replacement, and brake service. Often these activities were bundled together with tire work in a specialized garage. Usually, however, each was given a separate space. The same held true, of course, in dealer garages. Again, parts manufacturers led the way, developing and patenting not only distinctive products but also distinctive

Figure 6.18. Advertisement for the United States Tire Company. From *Automobile Topics* 47 (Aug. 18, 1917): 105.

Figure 6.19. Advertisement for the Fisk Rubber Company. From *Automobile Topics* 44 (Dec. 9, 1916): 437.

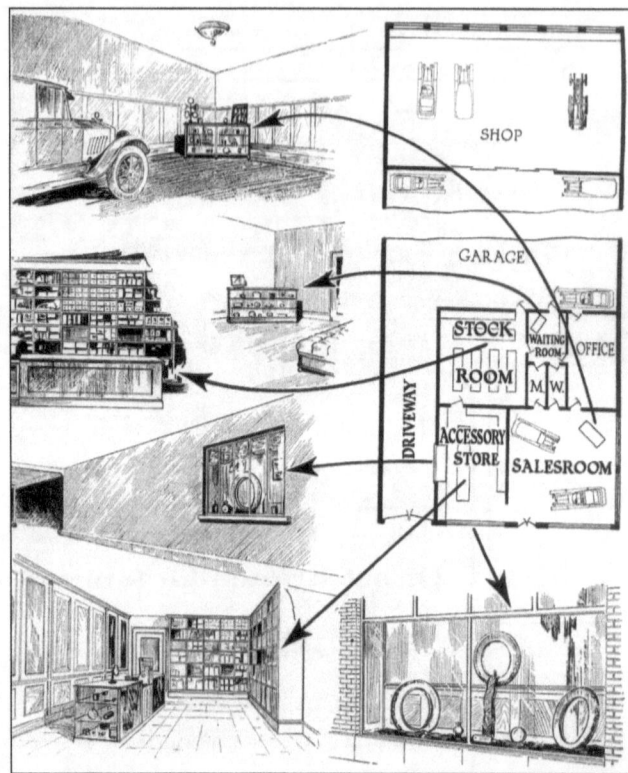

Figure 6.20. Six places for car dealer to display tires. From "Put Displays to Work Selling Equipment and Tires," *Motor World* 71 (Apr. 26, 1922): 52.

installation equipment. For example, the Bear Manufacturing Company of Rock Island, Illinois, promoted "Specialized Bear Service," even changing (and trademarking) the word "alignment" to "alinement." Offered to garage owners was a complete prefabricated setup (fig. 6.21). In 1924, it was calculated that each year one spring broke for every four passenger cars in service. With 15 million automobiles in use, that translated into a demand for some 5 million replacement springs annually.[56] The Harvey Spring Company of Racine, Wisconsin, sold springs through franchise contracts, forbidding its franchisees from selling any other brand. Dealers were required to prominently display the company logo, employ its methods of installation, and, importantly, use only its specially crafted tools (fig. 6.22).

It was calculated that fifteen out of every one hundred cars on the road in 1940 needed brake reline work, and thirty-three needed at least a brake adjustment, or so reported the editors of *Motor Age*. Reportedly, fifteen cents out of every service dollar were spent on brakes. Fully justified, in other words, were

Figure 6.21. Illustration from a Bear Manufacturing Company advertisement. As depicted: (a) frame service, (b) front-end service, (c) headlight tester, (d) wheel alignment tester, (e) wheel "truer" (to eliminate wheel wobble), (f) "On-A-Car wheel "truer," (g) "On-A-Car" wheel balancer (or "jiggler"). From *Chilton Motor Age* 76 (Dec. 1956): 28.

garages that specialized in brake repair. And all garages, for that matter, were justified in setting up brake departments. "There is profit to be made from truing brake drums, brake fluid, grease retainers, front wheel bearing lubrication, hydraulic brake parts such as cups and cylinders, brake cables, hand brake ratchets and pawls, wheel bearings, brake drums, etc.," *Motor Age* argued.[57]

Axle, Radiator, and Tailpipe and Muffler Repair

Garages might have welding equipment. Certainly, in the early days of motoring, broken axles and leaking radiators were prime motorist complaints. So also were broken tailpipes and damaged mufflers. Axles were generally replaced rather than repaired, something that general-service garages everywhere handled. But only in the larger cities, and only after World War I, could one find specialized radiator shops (fig. 6.23), and only after World War II did specialized muffler shops come to the fore. Required welding (as with metal work generally) involved expensive equipment and highly trained and thus well-paid welders, something that most garage owners resisted as unaffordable. Welding by and large was something they jobbed out to welding shops, operations that did auto-part repair

Figure 6.22. Illustration from a Harvey Spring Company advertisement. From *Automobile Dealer and Repairer* 22 (Feb. 1917): 10.

but did many other things as well. Early on, particularly in small towns, welding might be done in a blacksmith shop. In cities, it might be in a machine shop. In 1921, the Briskin Manufacturing Company of Indianapolis advertised in the *Hoosier Motorist*: "Radiators Properly Repaired. All Kinds of Welding and Brazing. Quick Machinery Repairs. Hurry-Up Service. No Job Too Large, None Too Small."[58]

Body, Paint, and Fabric Shops

Car bodies, and especially fenders, frequently came to grief. As often as not, replacing an extensively damaged fender, hood, or other body component was cheaper than repair. Sending pieces out to tinsmiths or other metal fabricators

Figure 6.23. Advertising blotter for the ABC Auto Radiator Works, Chicago, Illinois. From authors' collection.

was also common. But when only small "dings" were involved, in-shop handwork sufficed. Such bodywork required special but not particularly expensive tools. "Reasonably soft hammers are needed, and some means must be provided to support the dented surface while hammering," advised the *American Garage and Auto Dealer* in 1925. Forms, called anvils, supported large surfaces, while beading and spoon tools were used in supporting small, difficult-to-reach surfaces.[59] Soldering closed small gaps, although, after 1930, caulking with plastic resins was also used. Nonetheless, most service garages discouraged bodywork because it was so specialized. Indeed, it was not until the 1950s that auto dealers in any numbers added so-called collision work to their services. Today the business is again being shunned by auto dealers, stung by expensive equipment and expensive training for personnel as before, but now also by environmental issues.[60]

Closely related to metal bending (or "banging") was painting. Early on, it was the lack of technical expertise and the undue length of time required to paint cars that discouraged most garages from doing bodywork. When varnish finishes predominated, hand painting with brushes was the rule, with coat after coat being very carefully applied over days and even weeks. When fast drying lacquer finishes came into vogue so too did air brushes, which, by spraying paint, vastly sped up the process. Large baking ovens were also introduced, making for almost instant drying. Manufacturers outfitted entire paint plants. By the 1950s, the fully equipped paint shops sold by the DeVilbiss Company of Toledo, Ohio, could process upwards to fifteen paint jobs a day. To be profitable, however, a paint shop had to attract a volume business, which, in itself, promoted specialization.

Auto glass replacement was another enterprise that favored the specialized shop over the departmentalized garage. Mainly it had to do with inventory, since glass had its own peculiar storage and handling requirements. But glasswork also required a volume business to be profitable. Before enclosed auto bodies were fully popularized in the 1920s, most cars were either entirely open or sported only convertible tops. Working with fabrics to repair or replace soft car tops was another highly specialized activity, one given over mainly to specialized garages. Pictured is an advertisement for an Omaha, Nebraska, firm engaged in selling and installing auto tops with glass inserts (fig. 6.24). The firm also did bodywork. Frequently, bodywork, painting, and car-top repair were bundled. Note that the business originated as a carriage works. With the coming of enclosed cars, many car-top repair shops turned to repairing car upholstery.

Figure 6.24. Advertisement for the Wm. Pfeiffer Auto and Carriage Works, Omaha, Nebraska. From *Motorist* 20 (Dec. 1918): 38.

Car Washing

Cars could be washed anywhere. And they were—in traditional commercial garages, at dealer garages, at gasoline stations, and, of course, at home. At the new "super service" gasoline stations, lubrication bays were usually paired with wash bays. In the former, minor tune-up work might also be done, but wash floors were almost always just for washing, lacking as they did hydraulic lifts and the other accouterments of light engine repair and maintenance work. Departmentalization, therefore, was of the essence. At most garages, as at gas stations, washing was done by hand, albeit with pressure hoses. Usually a section of a garage was partitioned off as a wash floor complete with drains (fig. 6.25). Of course, wash floors could also be used for engine and chassis cleaning. Nearby was a drying floor that provided space for car polishing and light touch-up work with quick-drying lacquer paints if needed. So also might car tops be dressed there. Car washing not only lent itself to garage departmentalization but also to business specialization, specifically to the rise of the car wash.

Figure 6.25. Idealized wash rack. From "Washing and Polishing the Automobile," *Motor World* 72 (July 26, 1922): 29.

Certainly, the car wash was not a kind of garage, but clearly it was a garage derivative. In the 1920s, garage-like buildings appeared containing only wash bays or racks. One entrepreneur, W. A. Moyer, opened an eight-stall "Auto Wash" in Cleveland, Ohio, in 1928. Moyer was a builder specializing in residential garages. Thus, the structure that he erected was very much of the "domestic garage type," containing eight side-by-side wash floors, each with its own door. Hand washing with a mixture of water and kerosene employed eight workers.[61] Moyer's facility was one of approximately one hundred commercial wash racks then operating in Cleveland. "Many service garages, gasoline filling stations, tire dealers, and car agencies are washing all the way from 6 to 20 cars per day," the *Automobile Trade Journal* noted.[62] The Glendale Auto Laundry of Glendale, California, represented an important next step in car-wash evolution—car washing in assembly-line fashion. "Cars enter from the rear of the building on a guiding track," again reported the *Automobile Trade Journal*. "They are powered through the laundry station at the rate of 8 ft. a minute by a revolving link belt chain, operated by an electric motor." Overhead jets of water began the washing process, followed by four workers hand scrubbing with hoses, and then two workers hand drying. Each car took about twenty-five minutes.[63] At the Cunningham Company in Chicago, however, cars passed through in only twelve minutes (fig. 6.26).[64]

Parts and Accessory Sales

Auto supply stores proliferated across the United States after 1910, not only to sell replacement parts for cars but, perhaps more important, to sell automobile accessories. Few had garage service floors, but they enter our discussion here as suppliers and thus sustainers of actual garages of all kinds. Auto parts stores deserve to be considered as part of the garage supply chain. Of course, no dealer garage was without its parts department, a necessary adjunct of parts and accessory sales nationwide. And full-service independent garages maintained them also.

Accessories were not viewed as original equipment so much as add-ons that made cars look better, if not function better. Most early auto supply stores were established in traditional storefronts in central business districts (fig. 6.27). John King operated one such store in Poughkeepsie, New York. It sported a large electric sign projected out over the sidewalk that proclaimed: "John King the Gasoline King." A single gasoline pump stood at the curb. Although new, and unique in the city's downtown, the store was not considered out of place, or so argued

Figure 6.26. Cunningham Company car wash employees run conveyor line. From "Cars Are Washed in 12 Minutes," *Motor Age* 47 (June 11, 1925): 13.

Donald Blanchard in *Motor World*: "King's store belongs on Main Street, in company with the other leading merchants of the town, because he is one of them, just as much as the furniture dealer who occupies the store on one side of him or the produce man who has the store on the other side. He has earned a place among them because of the soundness of his methods and the success that has attended his efforts."[65] That a question of appropriateness was even raised seems to suggest that, even as late as 1923, auto-oriented retailing was still very much the new kid on the block.

By 1930, merchants were cooperating in voluntary auto supply chains that were variously branded, most of them organized by auto part wholesalers. One such was the Allied Independent Dealers (AID) chain headquartered in Newark, New Jersey.[66] But by far most stores remained fully independent, although most

Figure 6.27. Interior of idealized auto supply store. From "Winter Business—Cold Weather Made Profitable," *Wisconsin Motorist* 9 (Dec. 1917): 11.

were associated with nationally advertised brand names, most being the franchised dealers of parts and accessory manufacturers. Manufacturers sold their products to carmakers as original equipment but usually at little profit. Money was made primarily on replacement sales at auto supply stores. Thus did companies brand their products for sale through franchised dealer chains, supporting dealers with aggressive advertising spread across trade journals, popular magazines, and newspapers. The Champion Ignition Company of Boston, Massachusetts, was the first to manufacture spark plugs in the United States. General Motors bought the firm in 1909 but not the rights to the Champion name. GM marketed with the AC brand (to honor the firm's founder, Albert Champion) through both its car dealers and independent auto supply stores. The new Champion Spark Plug Company also went the franchise route, establishing dealers across the country as exclusive Champion dealers. Supplied to retailers were signs for outside and inside posting, as well as other advertising paraphernalia such as counter display cabinets (fig. 6.28).

Figure 6.28. Counter spark plug display. From advertisement for the Champion Spark Plug Company. From *Motor World* 68 (Sept. 28, 1921), front cover.

With garages coming to dominate replacement part sales, auto supply stores turned increasingly to selling accessories. Henry Ford sought to create with the Model T a quality-built, but nonetheless "no-frills," automobile affordable by America's middling classes. Ford thus inadvertently lay the ground work for the accessory industry. "It is to be assumed," editorialized the *Automobile Dealer and Repairer* in 1921, "that every Ford owner is in the market for some sort of an accessory. The car is a complete unit for transportation, as it comes from the factory, but there are few Ford owners who will be content with the ordinary equipment." The Ford owner's favorite hobby, they surmised, was buying accessories.[67] Pictured is an array of products aimed at Ford owners by the Superior Lamp Company of New York City (fig. 6.29).

New car sales fell off during the Great Depression. Americans simply drove their cars longer or, alternatively, bought used cars. Either way, the market for replacement parts and accessories increased. An estimated $500 million market was based on Americans owning some 24 million automobiles. According to

Figure 6.29. Advertisement for the Superior Lamp Company. From *Horseless Age* 40 (Jan. 15, 1917): 86.

Business Week, auto dealers got half the business and independents half.[68] Ten years before, in 1923, 45 percent of all car dealers were said to sell automotive supplies, and that included Ford dealers. Indeed, 58 percent did so.[69] But after Ford's Model A was introduced in 1927, auto supply sales soared at Ford dealerships. By the 1950s, national advertising campaigns were vigorously promoting Ford's "Genuine Parts" (fig. 6.30). General Motors proceeded differently. In 1916, it created the United Motors Company to market the products of a host of its subsidiaries, including the Perlman Rim Corporation, Dayton Engineering Laboratories (Delco), Remy Electric Company, Hyatt Roller Bearing Company, New Departure Manufacturing Company, Harrison Radiator Corporation, and Klaxon Company, the last a manufacturer of automobile horns. Created was a nationwide chain of franchised garages under the United Motor Service logo (fig. 6.31). In each of twenty-three service territories, United Motor Service maintained a factory-owned store from which independent dealers were supplied. Auto parts and accessory sales were made integral to garage work; the question was how best to do the selling. Display cases could be placed on car dealer show-

Figure 6.30. Illustration from Ford Motor Company advertisement. From *Chilton's Motor Age* 71 (June 1952): 111.

rooms. Parts departments might be organized with storage spaces hidden from view but with sales counters fronting, for example, on customer waiting rooms. So also might display windows front on sidewalks or be placed just inside garage entrances to attract the attention of customers bringing their cars in for maintenance or repair.[70]

The St. Louis Automobile & Supply Company may have been first to start an auto supply business, having published its first catalogue in 1901. As the *Horseless Age* reported, "They aim to handle nearly everything that enters into the construction of an automobile, and make a specialty of their complete running gear, improved gasoline engine and transmission, which they sell to experimenters or those who wish to build vehicles for themselves."[71] In large measure, the auto supply business, at least at the wholesale level, grew out of the hardware business. Many hardware wholesalers, like the Philip Gross Hardware Company of Milwaukee, Wisconsin, had by 1915 substantially reoriented to servicing auto

Figure 6.31. United Motors–authorized service centers in the United States, 1928. From advertisement for New Departure Ball Bearings, *Motor Age* 54 (Nov. 15, 1928): 7.

supply stores (fig. 6.32). Regional wholesalers dominated the supplying of local garages. The reason was clear—the speed at which regionally based supply houses could receive, fill, and deliver orders, especially for repair parts needed literally overnight.[72] A 1927 study of where garages in seven Ohio counties obtained replacement parts substantiated that the bulk of those parts came from suppliers within a fifty-mile radius; Cleveland, Columbus, and Dayton figured prominently.[73] Order catalogs were distributed by mail to auto supply stores and service garages. Orders were placed by mail with emergency requests made by telephone or telegram.

Independent wholesalers sought to represent manufacturers as regional distributors. One San Diego supply house was described in the *Horseless Age* as follows:

> Gavin-Williams Co. has always been a progressive firm and has secured a number of exclusive sales rights for territory that place them in the forefront of the accessory business. Among the well-known and nationally advertised products which they represent are the fol-

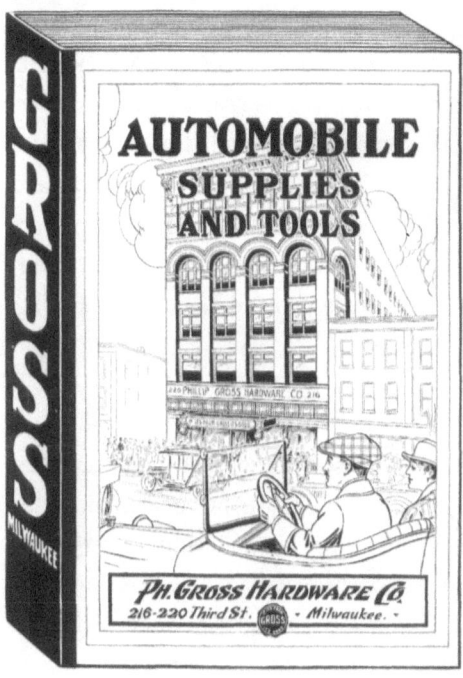

Figure 6.32. Advertisement for the Phillip Gross Hardware Company. From *Wisconsin Motorist* 6 (Apr. 1915): 16.

lowing: Firestone tires, Bosch magnetos, Rayfield carburetors, Veedol oils and greases, Red Seal batteries, Prest-O-Lite storage batteries and many others.[74]

Many a retailer's franchise agreement with a manufacturer was actually negotiated through a regional wholesaler.

There were, of course, wholesalers that distributed parts and accessories not just regionally but nationwide. The Western Auto Supply Company, based in Kansas City, Missouri, started as a mail order house, opening its first retail store in 1921. At its peak after World War II, the firm operated some twelve hundred company-owned stores, additionally servicing some four thousand "associate stores." Another Midwestern firm, the Boozer-Test Management Service of Indianapolis, Indiana, began just after World War I. By World War II, it was the nation's largest independent distributor of automotive parts, with branches in eighteen cities. The firm in 1925 was a founding member of the National Automotive Parts Association (NAPA) headquartered in Detroit.[75] By the 1950s, NAPA stores were everywhere across the country, an umbrella brand for independent jobber companies both large and small. Some jobbers, such as the Times Square Automobile Company, specialized in reconditioned used parts (fig. 6.33). Detroit's Puritan Autoparts Company, on the other hand, supplied replacement parts for so-called orphan cars, the automobiles of manufacturers that had gone out of business. By 1929, the company had accumulated, largely through purchase at liquidation sales, the parts inventories of 757 defunct auto and auto parts makers. Also bought were drawings, jigs, and patterns so that Puritan could manufacture anew such replacement parts as the market might demand.[76]

* * *

The commercial garage in the United States was an ever-changing business venue. By 1910, the general-purpose service garage, whether dealer run or independent, was to be found virtually everywhere, with the mechanic very much an emerging fixture in American life. Variously rooted in blacksmithing, carriage and wagon repair, and machine-shop work of an earlier era, repairing and maintaining automobiles became a widespread occupation if not a profession distinctive to its times. Especially important was the dealer garage where cars sold were repaired and maintained. Affluent car buyers, who dominated the auto market very early on, quickly found that maintaining service facilities at home, one overseen by a chauffeur, was not only overly expensive but not always adequate. When mass automobility came to fore, there was little choice in the matter. It was best to have cars repaired and maintained by competent professionals at commercial garages fully equipped and technically up to date, garages that could variously guarantee their work.

As automobiles became increasingly sophisticated, brand specialization became the norm, with specialized garages coming to emphasize different kinds of repair and maintenance work. In general-purpose shops, service departments evolved with separate work floors, special tools, and mechanics specially trained to take on specific kinds of work. After 1920, car manufacturers encouraged dealers to establish service garages not only for warranty work but for routine car maintenance also—and not just for customers but for the general public as well. In non-dealer garages, it was the auto parts manufacturer who led the way by branding such products as batteries, spark plugs, and tires and establishing dealer networks to sell them. A garage proprietor might not be a Ford, Chevrolet, or Willys dealer, but he or she might be an Auto-Lite, Exide, or Goodyear dealer.

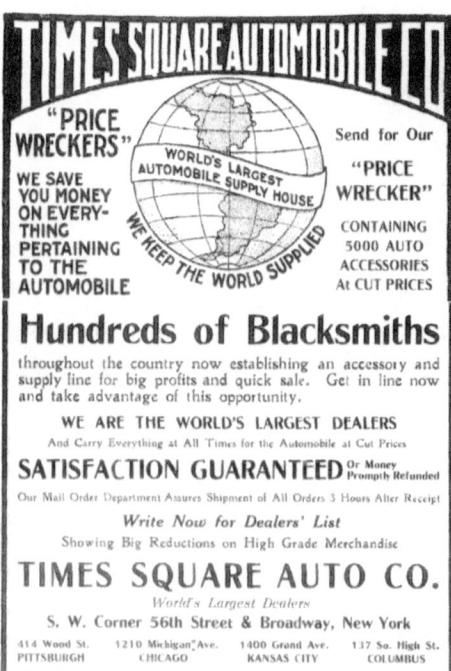

Figure 6.33. Advertisement for the Times Square Automobile Company. From *Blacksmith and Wheelwright* 73 (June 1916): 204.

Although there was much diversity from one garage to another, there was also much commonality, mainly through the bundling of related products and services. Tire stores sold and repaired tires but also offered tire balancing, wheel alignment, and spring and shock absorber replacement.

The traditional garage with open work floor lent itself to almost every kind of car repair and maintenance function. Spaces for separate service departments might be set aside but usually with only minimal structural implications—a greasing pit or hydraulic lift here but not there, for example. But body and paint work, and for that matter mere car washing, did require closed-off spaces and with highly specialized equipment. Thus were auto dealers as a class very slow to add "collision" work, sending it off to specialized body and paint shops instead. Washing bays, of course, could be installed almost anywhere, including the new "super service" stations of the 1930s that augmented the small "filling" stations which, in the decades before, had syphoned off the garage proprietor's gasoline sales and much of the lubrications work. But what came of car washing, of course, was the car wash. Variously, therefore, did different kinds of car servicing and repair sort themselves out in an increasingly car-dependent America. The commercial garage was an ever changeable thing.

7

A LANDSCAPE LEGACY?

Previous authors concerned with the automobile's impact on America's built environment have rather amazingly overlooked the garage. Certainly, early-twentieth-century commercial garages have been largely ignored and even by aficionados of early automobile travel—except perhaps by a few vintage car enthusiasts who found the buildings ideal for storing and even repairing old cars. Nonetheless, historic preservationists have been lax in recognizing the garage as a distinctive building form fully deserving attention—and this despite preservationists' belated recognition of the gas station as an icon of American landscape history. We believe that the vintage repair garage of the 1900–30 period, and its successors of the 1940s and '50s, definitely deserve the same recognition. And so also, for most matters, does the early domestic garage. This thinking motivated our writing this book. Would not the early sales and service of motorcars—and their distinctive architectural accommodations—merit stronger social memory?

The garage's neglect can be explained in part by what it was—or, perhaps better said—by what it was not. Essential to the garage have been its interior uses far more than its exterior look. Roadside fans drawn in their road trips to alluring or eccentric buildings along their way perceived garages neither as good looking nor associated with pleasant experiences. Garages, after all, either stood behind the other, more attractive roadside businesses, or were ordinary contrivances. They were rarely envisioned as attention-getting buildings in the foreground but, rather, as fully background structures in most locales. Much garage work was deemed unsightly for its purely utilitarian nature, something best screened from public view behind a polite facade or, as with automobile agencies, placed well behind elaborate sales floors—out of sight, certainly, although not necessarily out of mind. What attention garages bid for was either mundane or unpleasant. They were places to ready one's vehicle for travel or to repair it for a return to the road. Even early domestic garages tended to shrink into the background, placed at the rear of residential properties, behind the house. It was the "in-your-face" gas station, of course, that changed motor vehicle refueling from an activity inside a garage to an activity set up front. Later, however, auto maintenance and repair also changed to a fully visible roadside activity. So also by the 1950s had domestic garages come forward figuratively, attached alongside and even thrust out ahead of the new ranch houses. They helped symbolize the automobile as a new cultural imperative. The commercial garage, however, never earned such esteem. Commercial garages—what we have emphasized here—have always been screened, their management acting in various ways to improve their looks, cushion the customer's approach to them, and enhance the customer's comfort in them. This last objective was usually accomplished by keeping the customer out of the garage, making them a "back place."

Like all commercial enterprises early in the last century, success in the garage business required attention not only to customers' needs but to employees' needs as well. How was work to be assigned, approved, and compensated? What was labor's role? What constituted a safe working environment? How was space to be organized? What were the requisite tools? Who should own them—the mechanic or the garage owner? Who should decide? By and large, garage work, like factory work, came to be organized along the lines of least effort, with decisions based substantially on time and motion study—although in the garage, unlike in the automobile factory, moving assembly lines were never justified. Nonetheless, as in factories, highly skilled laborers tended to replace the marginally skilled or even the unskilled, something machines made possible. Both diagnostic and repair equipment constantly improved over the decades, thus making tasks simpler and quicker. At automobile dealerships, tools and repair strategies tended to be dictated by the manufacturer, and dealers were required to invest in expensive equipment engineered to the needs of specific car models. Not to participate ended in a voided contract. Even independent garages found it increasingly necessary to adhere "to the book," carefully following, in other words, car maintenance and repair guidelines. What started out as ad hoc repair shops closely related to, if not directly descended from, blacksmithing, carriage and wagon repair, and the like quickly became dependent on highly sophisticated technology, and its use required specialized training not only for mechanics but for garage owners as well.

Management and Labor Practices

Endemic of the repair garage from its inception, the issue of screening it from public view, except for the "contact man" or garage manager, has always presented a problem for management. At the outset of the mass market, *Motor Age* warned that the front part of an auto dealership put the back part at a disadvantage unless management enforced its sales department's proper regard of service: "future sales to the same customer depend upon the sales ability of their department, but [also] upon the service department, because the owner will decide soon enough after he has the car in his own hands whether or not all the salesman told him was true."[1]

Implicit in this awareness throughout was the primacy of vigilant managers, who had to attend to many details. These included enforcement of the best way to service a particular problem, availability of adequate equipment, efficient layout of the service department, keeping good records of labor and parts for every job, and operation by the flat-rate system of charges. Foremen should guide mechanics "just as good musicians in an orchestra must be led by a conductor so that the result will be harmony and not discord," to use the analogy of *Motor World* as it helped construct the mass market just after World War I. Above effective department managers, measured in terms of good profits, towered the entire business's manager. The exemplary manager of the C. U. Williams & Son Company in Bloomington, Illinois, insisted that his success rested with retaining a competent department manager. In practice, it was apparent that whatever the garage's hierarchy, all employees had to assume personal responsibility for executing their jobs as well as they could.[2]

Beyond generalizations about successful management, the automobile trade magazines that hoped to lead the way to efficient systems offered seemingly infinite prescriptive advice (fig. 7.1). For example, "straight-line" depreciation was recommended because it was fairly simple to compute; this meant that the estimated scrap value should be subtracted from the purchase price of equipment and then divided by the probable life of the asset. Garage owners and managers were told to push aside prices based on competition with neighboring businesses or to avoid the fear-based impulse to follow the general trend. One garage management manual warned in 1928 that mechanics' job applicants who did not own a tool kit and claimed that it was because they had not worked as mechanics for some time or that they had sold their kits were usually not dependable and likely to be poorly skilled.[3]

At the end of the 1920s, what were accepted as successful management practices were those of specific dealers and garages that the trade magazines had detailed earlier in the decade. Idealizing the tenet that growth was the clearest measure of success, exemplary small shops (fig. 7.2) were those for which the owners found it necessary to hire additional mechanics, meet customers, oversee incoming work and outgoing repairs, and prepare work orders. In practice, small-town garages lagged behind the lessons of the trade journal analysts and did not systematize their operations.[4] The standardized management principles that industry analysts advocated became characteristic of large operations.

Astride the resurgent postwar prosperity of the late 1940s and 1950s, aggressive and innovative dealers invoked various management techniques to spur profits. George H. Jones, the Ford dealer in Corpus Christi, Texas, developed an

Why Merchants Fail—36 Reasons

1. Indecision.
2. No records.
3. Poor location.
4. Poor equipment.
5. Too conservative.
6. Clerks not trained.
7. Self consciousness.
8. Open cash drawer.
9. No plans for future.
10. Too many mistakes.
11. Advertise in no way.
12. Wasteful with goods.
13. Carelessness of clerks.
14. Clerks run the business.
15. Slow service to customers.
16. Not enough help.
17. Creeds, not deeds.
18. Dimly lighted store.
19. Purchase too heavy.
20. Windows not washed.
21. Dishonesty of employes.
22. Unsystematic deliveries.
23. Will consider nobody's advice.
24. Too much attention to details.
25. Stock not moved often enough.
26. Too much credit on the books.
27. Not acquainted with customers.
28. Unsalable stock on back shelves.
29. Try to follow everybody's advice.
30. Forget to charge goods sold on credit.
31. Show window not used to advantage.
32. Customers' interest not borne in mind.
33. Fail to profit by their own experience.
34. Fail to carry what their customers want.
35. Antiquated system unfit for increased business.
36. Believe in the worn-out proverb, "Leave well enough alone."

Reo News

Figure 7.1. An early trade magazine gave thirty-six problems that dealers should avoid. From "Using the Appraisal Plan to Solve the Used Car Problem," *Horseless Age* 39 (Apr. 1, 1917): 28.

incentive plan for his staff. His general manager and each departmental manager received a salary plus a percentage of the dealership's profits. It was learned, for example, that mechanics could produce an extra one hundred dollars per month for the dealership if paid a third to a half of that. In sum, said Jones in a *Chilton Motor Age* article, people generally "don't give their best—without incentive."[5]

In 1949, a sales and service dealer in Iowa City, Iowa, launched a profit-sharing system publicized in the era's anti-Soviet ethos as "Democratic Profit Sharing Works." Each employee's vote determined each rule of the system. Owner Dean Jones did not attend many of those formularizing meetings, and employees contributed to its administration. Within two years, the adventuresome Jones swore that "the business operates better while I'm away since profit sharing began." In West Allis, Wisconsin, the Oldsmobile dealer sold a remarkable 302 new and 415 used cars in 1951. Management included a well-equipped shop that added to workers' satisfaction with their tasks. Benefits included a one-week vacation with pay for the worker employed for one year, ten days for two years' employment, and three weeks for three years' employment. Although these were exceptional practices at the end of the early automobile age, three-fourths of the mechanics in the nation at the time were paid a percentage of the flat rate that

Figure 7.2. Brothers Albert and Mart Thoele, typically versatile small-town mechanics, serviced farm tractors and milk hauler trucks in addition to servicing automobiles and selling gasoline, Teutopolis, Illinois, circa 1935. From authors' photo collection.

had advanced from an ideal early in the century to an ordinary practice by the early 1950s.[6]

Usually out of sight, friction between management and mechanics persisted. Notwithstanding their prevalence, flat-rate charges never gained general acceptance among mechanics, who found it a means to disempower them. As a result, mechanics either left the employer who implemented the system or pursued other types of work. It had been the trade journals that ballyhooed the flat-rate system. Inside the larger garages, enforced adherence to manufacturers' repair manuals met the resistance of mechanics who thought they knew their work better. Through the 1930s, independent repair shops, whose paid employees ranged from zero to four aside from the owners, held a significant market share. Less concerned with business volume than decent working conditions and a consistently tenable income, one master mechanic who owned his own small shop articulated in print—as few mechanics did—the faith that working on automobiles demanded close attention to detail and his final inspection of a completed job to ensure it was done properly. Mechanics rejected systems. In those cases where the public learned of mechanics' resistance to systematization, the reaction was less often to congratulate him for pride of craftsmanship than to brand him with the pejorative class stereotype of an insufficiently motivated proletarian male.[7]

Trade Associations

Concomitant with the automobile's mass production and consumption came the rise of business people's organizations to advance their trade en masse within large areas—namely, big cities, states, and the nation. Garage owners and managers were among the first. In New York City, a Garage Owners' Association was founded in 1910 but quickly failed for lack of interest. In just two years, however, the city witnessed the emergence of a very active successor. The New York Garage Association quickly addressed how to establish profitable storage rates and lower the cost of gasoline its members sold. Standard Oil Company's rates were particularly troublesome, and other suppliers were sought. The association also challenged legislation that required garages to be equipped with devices separating oil and gasoline from the water run into New York City's sewers. The association protested the expensive equipment because one association member found it ineffective and because owners could be ordered to replace the equipment at the seeming whim of the authorities. Insurance rates were also challenged because they took no account of the differences between cars stored in wooden structures such as reconstructed stables and those stored in fireproof parking garages built to standards specifically for parking. Interest in forming other associations was stimulated among garage owners in other cities.[8]

Illustrative of various problems for storage garages in different cities, Chicago and Philadelphia had actually organized storage garage associations four years before New York City's second (and more lasting) association was founded. The Illinois Garage Association was actually formed to deal with customers who parked in Chicago garages until they ran up a bill they would not pay and then moved on to another garage nearby. Devising their own remedy without seeking legal recourse, members of the Illinois Garage Association categorized customers in areas as "delinquents" and made the list available to the association's members. The Philadelphia Garage Owners Association formed initially to address a particularly acute problem in that city—that is, "joyriding," the practice of chauffeurs who abused the relationship with their employers by driving the cars under their charge whenever they wished. Any attempt to stop "joyriding" at one garage would simply result in the chauffeur taking the car to a different garage. Philadelphia's new garage association kept a chauffeur registry to weed out the bad from the good.[9]

Automobile dealers initially were unconcerned with an association to represent repair work. The National Automobile Dealer's Association, formed in 1917, confined its interests to fifteen thousand dealerships and not to any independent's repair work, claiming that the latter would confuse the mission. Garages independent of dealerships were thought to have a different set of issues. Dealers' chief concerns were achieving more cooperation with the car manufacturers, initially to help prevent a conversion of all manufacturing plants to wartime work in World War I. The new dealers' association then quickly established a full-time lobby in Washington, D.C. The association would later defend its own dealers' garages. After the initial formation, annual meetings included discussions about sales, business efficiency, record keeping, and even the tangential topic of good roads. The latter added weight to the Associated Highways of America, a union of thirty-eight highway associations formed within a few months of the end of the First World War to expand the agenda of the early automobile age.[10]

Finally, in 1954, independent garages formed their first national organization, the Independent Garage Owners of America. Local garage associations that sprang up in the early automobile age, such as those noted in Chicago and Philadelphia, often became defunct or restrained their work after they addressed their original complaints. However, the national organization in 1954 sought to consider the ongoing problems of auto repair standards and to address legislative solutions and their interests in the auto industry, as well as to improve relations with motorists. Members ranged across the numerous specialty shops that were treated in chapter 6.[11]

The Impacts of War and Economic Depression

Two world wars and a worldwide depression constrained what otherwise would likely have been an expansive sales and service industry. Short-term adaptations emerged to surmount the resulting problems (fig. 7.3). Even before America's entry into World War I, shock waves rippled through dealerships because of the shortage of railroad cars to transport the produced cars to dealers. Manufacturers improvised the solution of driving cars to the various dealers, while trains carried personnel from distributors to the manufacturers; these personnel in turn drove cars back to the dealers. Some companies had cars driven to cities with more shipping facilities. War commanded an urgent need for trucks rather than passenger cars and opened a manufacturing alternative. On the eve of the Armistice, manufacturers held 15,545 finished cars but planned production of 327,930 trucks. Production was wrenched back rapidly to passenger cars when the war ended.[12]

The Great Depression induced alterations in the automobile industry but did not shift its essential place in American life. The car was too important—the depression itself a consequence partly of car consumption—to push it out of place. Alterations in sales and service were witness not only to the car's importance but also to the ingenuity of dealers and repairmen determined to survive. Among manufacturers during the hard times, some forty became extinct. Others left the automobile business for other production lines. The Big Three emerged intact. Various apparatuses were developed in the search for cost-saving operation costs. Dealers declined in numbers as covered in chapter 4. Owners kept their cars longer, with the value of repair boosting the dependence on repair shops. Used cars naturally found a market.[13]

After America's entry into World War I, factories were initially converted to war products.[14] Dealers also turned more toward repair work, parts sales, and,

Figure 7.3. Frustrating limitations during World War II stimulated these jokes to help hurdle the difficuties. From "Laughs of the Month," *Motor Age* 63 (Dec. 1943): 39.

of course, used car sales to satisfy the public appetite whetted before the war. These conversions were repeated during World War II. *Motor Age* highlighted the Auto Parts Service Station that opened in Peoria, Illinois, in 1917, expanded its services between the wars, and was thriving as "a tremendous business" by the middle of the second war.[15] In 1942, Chevrolet announced the success of its policy to persuade dealers to expand beyond gas, oil, and tire sales, an expansion that included war contracts for its machine-provisioned garages plus the sales of home appliances and farm machinery.[16] With guarded optimism, it was reported in 1943 that four out of every five auto and truck dealers retained their franchises and that rural service shops were even better at surviving World War II than were dealerships in the cities.[17] Replacement parts quotas set by the federal government were but one indication of automobility's centrality to the national economy. Repairmen reaped a business benefit even when parts were too few because such shortages called upon the repairman's special skill to reuse a worn part rather than to simply install a new one.[18] In 1942, the Office of Price Administration granted small repair shops (those employing no more than eight people) permission to charge rates high enough to dissuade repairmen from reemployment at war plants where salaries were higher than they had been at such shops in the 1930s.[19] Dealers were worried. Beginning a year before America's entry into the war, some began to expand their service departments, but difficulties worsened when new car production ceased on February 1, 1942, and remained shut down until the end of the war.[20]

    The repair industry invoked other means to supply the necessary work force. A 40-percent drop in mechanics by the end of 1942 induced women to become mechanics and for dealers to put off any reservations they may have had about women's mechanical aptitudes.[21] Steve Ference, service director of the Chrysler factory in Pittsburgh, had the "courage to try this experiment on a large scale." He personally trained women with results that were wonderfully productive, with an estimated 80 percent of the women mechanics performing highly specialized mechanical work.[22] Women also filled in for the loss of the traditionally male workers who sold automotive products and staffed dealers' offices. Service managers regarded women trained for work in dealerships as "more alert" to car owners' needs, more cooperative about the time required for work, and less prone to complain about prices.[23]

    Madella Jenkins, owner and manager of a De Soto–Plymouth dealership in Kokomo, Indiana, exemplified women's capacity at it best for adaptive and successful entrepreneurship. Following her husband's death just before America's entry into World War II, she applied the lessons she had learned as the business's bookkeeper, and made her business exemplary by retailing and wholesaling replacement parts, a small number of used car sales, and service. She also succeeded by employing less than half the mechanics before the war.[24]

Successful automobile service and sales by the mid-twentieth century grew out of the financial slump in the 1930s and anticipation of the boom after World War II. Resilience was not merely possible but, of course, necessary for survival. Automobility's obvious centrality in the American economy promised a bright future even when sales had slumped and kept entrepreneurs busy at clever adaptations. For one, J. Grant Hyde, a former college professor, adapted existing practices and devised new sales and service techniques to get his Hudson-Essex dealership in Akron, Ohio, through the Great Depression. All the people he employed had to really work at their jobs, and that included Hyde himself. He did not help devise a new mode of operation and pass the rest on to his service and sales manager for implementation: he wrote repair orders and provisioned his office adjacent to the service department with a window from which he saw everyone who came into the garage. When not in his office, he was often on the shop floor talking with a newly arrived customer. Some thirty-five thousand dealers agreed to explore the advantages of standardized used car prices instead of high trade-in allowances to bait car buyers. Critics within the trade soon learned that while so-called wild trading may have earned some dealers good profits, the experiment of standardized trade-in allowances induced market stability. Hyde reemphasized a cardinal entrepreneurial principle. No system proven successful could be adopted without the prospect of astute adaptations. This required risks, truly, but not gambling. Successful entrepreneurship reminds the scholar to look at individual cases and not only at statistical overviews of the industry. Human agency's critical role will be addressed below in tracing some case studies.[25]

Resilient entrepreneurship during the Great Depression and wartime did not mean that gloomy advocates were few. David E. Castles, the president of the National Automobile Dealers' Association, was persuaded in early 1944 that postwar readjustment, whenever the war ended, would make the dealers' work the most complex of all retail businesses. Although declaring his optimism about recovery, Castles outlined in *Motor Age* several concerns: the uncertainty of the inventory on which dealers could rely, strong competition from surplus automotive equipment, and gasoline availability.[26] Sixteen months after Castles's hesitant prognosis, *Business Week,* which was freer of the automotive trade magazines' anxiety, reported that car dealers were ready for a "lush period" after the war, although, it noted, "the dealers have begun to worry once more in their time honored tradition."[27] The number of dealerships declined by 15 percent during the war, but only 10 percent of prewar profits were lost.[28] *Business Week* reinforced awareness of the fact that service had been roused to sustain dealers, making service even more profitable, in fact, than it ever had been.[29] It was widely anticipated that postwar service and sales would hit new highs.[30] Among mechanics, including both the lesser number who had been drawn into military service and the greater number who worked in war production industries, employment opportunities in their trade looked good.[31] By 1950, within five and a half years after the war's end, *Fortune* ran an article titled "Great Day for the Dealer."[32] It noted that dealers experienced their greatest year at mid-century in 1950. Nonetheless, it continued, the dealer "is not without his doubts and apprehensions," understanding that the period of abnormally high profits was a "transitory phase."[33] Success seemed sustainable but was always in doubt, whatever the market and surrounding circumstances.

Dealer Histories

What defined a successful garage? Success can be a measure of the owner's goals, such as earning a satisfactory income over a period of years that ends when the owner or his or her successors are pleased to leave the trade. Or, success can be measured by continual growth in profit and size of the physical plant—that is, the trade publicists' customary search for "bigger and better." The difficulty in defining success comes partly in finding narratives of repair garages that failed by anyone's definition. These are not chronicled in trade journals, and they are harder for pursuers of oral history to find because they require an intimate knowledge of local conditions not often shared with outsiders to satisfy a mission of objective knowledge. Hence, there is no real baseline.

Here we trace a few examples of the first category, including owners satisfied with their performance as well as a few of the dynamic-expansion type recorded in comparatively large numbers in the trade literature. Scholars should persistently seek out more because the record is rather meager.

L. A. Morgan Company, well known within a hundred-mile radius of its shop in Brookline, Massachusetts, submitted to the *American Garage & Auto Dealer*'s detailed questioning five years after its 1915 entry into the virgin market. L. A. Morgan learned his trade as a foreman in a Dodge dealership that grew rapidly from a small to a big shop but quit after a year and a half because he differed with ownership's opinions. Without funds to start his own shop and uncertain about the prospects of his own ownership, he accepted a customer's offer to fund the startup. Morgan kept accurate records, did bookkeeping and billing at night, and worked by day in the garage itself. The shared work with his employees earned him a friendly staff as well as his assurance that work was done properly. After six months, his steadily good profits enabled him to buy his partner's share. By 1920, Morgan operated in a one-story brick building (sixty by one hundred feet), well lighted and well ventilated, with an office, stockroom, battery-charging and repair shop, and a general repair shop. Tire repair was provided only as a convenience to customers but without aim for a major profit line. Advertising was done by mail and with only a few roadside billboards. When asked pointedly about what he attributed his success to, Morgan answered that it was honesty and hard work. He explained that he customarily gave dissatisfied customers work free of charge rather than have a job result in rancor. Let customers make their point and do not judge yourself perfect, Morgan counseled. He was earning the substantial annual sum of sixty thousand dollars at the time of the interview.[34]

Hulsebus Motor Company in Harlan, Iowa, was indicative of the garage successful in terms of expanding profits and shop building at the very outset of the virgin market. Additional income came from any available source, such as killing squirrels and pulling morning glories in 1895, to a shop producing miscellany such as baseball bats and a thresher. An outfitted machine shop in Defiance, Iowa, came next: it repaired threshers and automobiles between 1902 and 1909. The following year, the Hulsebus brothers operated a shop in a basement in Harlan and, in 1911, built a new shop and storage department. The years 1914 and 1915 witnessed a two-story addition with a half-basement. Provisioned with machines, many of which they fashioned themselves, the Hulsebuses eventually operated a garage and repair shop that included an office, as well as parts, accessory tire and repair, and power departments. They also operated a sales room.[35]

It was "[e]nthusiasm, energy, [and] experience" to which the reporting trade magazine attributed Hulsebus Motor Company's success—typical of the "country dealer." It was not profits the business embodied so much as the "evolution of a life project" attributable to hard work, ambition, the right kind of employees, and friends.[36] Here was a subjective definition of success, a blossoming of personality.

Crown Garage in Peoria, Illinois, bore traits of the big success story. In 1911, two Moutier brothers, employed as machinists and repairmen, joined with another brother who returned from Arizona mining country and contributed money to start the Crown Garage. Within six weeks, they had achieved a volume of business that necessitated two additional workers. Potential customers came to them instead of to the busier garages in Peoria's downtown. In buying one of the largest garages in Peoria, they acquired its customers. Another brother of the seven in the family who was eventually employed in the garage went to Cleveland to learn about batteries for an electrical department in the family business, while another brother, who was in the advertising business in Chicago, returned home to handle publicity for the Crown Garage. In three years, more space was required for the brothers' prospering business, and they added a second building. In 1915, during the winter when garage work regularly declined and storage carried the garage trade, the brothers purchased an existing garage in nearby Le Roy, Illinois, and, in the next year, added a building adjacent to their original one in Peoria. Business growth gave the Moutier brothers the opportunity for expansion; and on the eve of America's entry into World War I, their garage in Peoria was "one of the largest, most completely equipped, and most elaborate garages in the state," in the eyes of one of the watchful trade magazines. B. F. Goodrich Rubber Company helped fuel the automotive journals' ethos of ever-rising success in the garage industry. The Moutier brothers' story came to light because the Goodrich trade magazine had sponsored a "success" contest that awarded three hundred dollars to the best articles on the theme of "What It Was That Helped My Business." The same contest also made public the story of Bill's Auto Supply Company in Alva, Oklahoma, whose success came only after a series of serious mistakes in the garage business—one of the rare instances in which failures of any sort were detailed in public.[37]

The town of Romney in west-central Indiana was the scene of another version of success. Here Bill Balkema, son of an English emigrant and dairy farmer, was attracted to the mechanic's trade, and his is a nuanced tale that came to light through an interview with one of the Balkema family members by coauthor Keith Sculle. Balkema and his father both enjoyed working on motors, and the two of them went to an automobile dealer in Brookston, Indiana, asking about a job for which Bill might be suitable after he finished mechanics' school. Balkema was offered a position on the spot, at fifteen dollars per week, but declined it because he wanted first to graduate, which he eventually did after attending the McSweeney school in Cleveland, Ohio. He was hired by the same garage to which he had earlier applied—but for a dollar less than the amount he had originally been offered. Balkema worked for Allen Auto Sales for ten years, beginning in 1936, the middle of the Great Depression. Likely due to the decline in mechanical work during World War II, Bill operated a bus service for workers traveling to Kingsbury, Indiana, even as he continued as a mechanic at Allen Auto Sales. Then, Bill and his brother-in-law purchased a garage in Romney, which they operated for less than five years. Auto repair was profitable, but the shop's original sideline of lawn and garden equipment repair proved even more so. This, plus Bill's preference for sales, gave him the opportunity for an allied line of work. Hence, success proved greater in one field than in another, as judged by income in an area where hard agricultural work was the standard. Balkema's story, with its ups and downs, suggests something of a contrast to the trade journals' narratives of continuously rising success in small-town and rural shops.[38]

An interesting variation on the success story in the rural market is that of Duane Ulmer in Fulton County, Illinois. Ulmer was a largely self-taught automotive mechanic born in 1926 to a struggling farm family. Happy to tinker with cars, he enhanced his aptitude in auto repair classes in high school and took a job as a mechanic in a motor pool at a nearby army camp. After World War II, he bought an obsolete building from the camp and converted it into an automotive repair shop (fig. 7.4). He improved his mechanical skills by taking courses offered by Ford Motor Company, becoming a "sub-dealer" connected to a full Ford dealership. He subsequently bought his own Ford dealership from a dealer leaving the trade and achieved prosperity through the 1970s. The 1980s witnessed a decline in the local economy and dealers invading the local market via television advertisements. With more dealers selling to fewer customers, Ulmer sold his dealership in 1988 after nearly a half-century in business.[39]

In Detroit's contrasting big-city setting, Henry T. Ewald opened the Mack-Gratiot Company in early 1928. Ewald's dealership (see fig. 4.11) almost failed at first, and it took "a long time to correct the mistakes we made," by Ewald's own admission. A prominent location in a working-class neighborhood on Detroit's east side was important, and Ewald named the dealership for the busy street on

Figure 7.4. Duane Ulmer at work in his first garage, at Table Grove, Illinois. From authors' photo collection.

which it fronted (Gratiot) and another street at one end of the dealership (Mack). He was thankful for the sales tips he received from Chevrolet. He built a prosperous dealership after it had nearly failed and depended on the service department for much of the success. Work came from customers both near and far away. A salesman operated on the service room floor because almost as many cars were sold there as in the showroom. Chevrolet's corporate headquarters in Detroit praised Ewald's management for its cooperation with the company and avoidance of "stunty" promotions. Ewald had learned at the start that "wild trading," in the industry's jargon, was not profitable. His was a success story that began at the outset of the Great Depression.[40] Obviously, not all success stories were of people of modest means but included those with a strong mechanical aptitude drawn into businesses that they guided to ever more prosperous proportions.

Whether garage owners succeeded or failed, their buildings from decade to decade rarely stayed unchanged for long. Business failure left buildings vacant and thus open to different uses often totally unrelated to automobile repair. Business success was almost always tied to innovation, which as often as not changed building use—and sometimes dramatically. But so also was success tied to increasingly larger scales of operation. Both kinds of success, of course, contributed to the functional obsolescence of traditional buildings. And then there were the effects of time, as buildings after decades of hard use became physically obsolete. New structures at new locations, sometimes but not always, replaced buildings at old sites. As garage buildings were merely vacated rather than enlarged or replaced on site, a stock of residual garages grew on the American landscape. Perhaps it was only where the economy was flat, or even declining, that old garages survived with their car repair and servicing functions intact. And that was mainly in America's small towns and the older parts of its smaller cities. That is largely where early garage buildings remain today fully reminiscent of early motoring.

Dealership Survival

The periodic fragility of the automobile market is nothing new to the industry. But each episode has its distinctive traits. The biggest drop in dealerships, 22 percent, occurred in the 1950s and was due principally to the end of a group of smaller manufacturers, but continued in percentages of the high and low teens through the 1980s. By the 1990s, however, the number of companies owning dealerships dropped even more, and the trend was toward larger dealerships because of the decrease in profits per car sold. Auto dealers followed the examples of such discount retailers as Walmart and Best Buy, the so-called mass merchants who drove a large number of locally owned small stores out of business. Whereas each dealership in the past usually implied one owner and, at most, two locations, the Penske Automotive Group, founded in 1990 in Bloomfield Hills, Michigan, by racing celebrity Roger Penske, operated with 310 dealer franchises in nineteen states. Also in the early 1990s, CarMax staked out its claim as the nation's foremost "used car superstore." Based in Richmond, Virginia, CarMax drove Auto Nation out of the used car business in three years, after which the AutoNation giant retained its rank as the largest new car dealer.[41]

After the inflated economy of the early twenty-first century, the recession beginning in 2008 squeezed the market again. At the end of 2008, twenty-one thousand new car dealerships had not shown a profit in two years.⁴² General Motors and Chrysler gained an emergency bailout from the federal government.

What will the car sales industry look like in the future (fig. 7.5)? Predictions vary. The Internet may seize the shopping and purchasing of cars. Or, a slimly stocked dealer's lot might permit a basic car model for actual test drives, while computer graphics and big-screen televisions simulate the performance of the particular features in which a customer is interested. Or, cars could be made to order.⁴³ None of this is certain, but it can reasonably be inferred that each of these adaptations, as with adaptations in the past history of dealerships, rests securely in America's cultural constant of automobility. The recent trend toward fewer and bigger dealerships, in contrast to the smaller and more numerous dealerships of the past, will continue.

Historic Preservation and Adaptive Reuse

What will be the future of garages past (fig. 7.6)? They are, in fact, the most widely respected of all roadside buildings if they enclose large volumes of space comparable to other businesses requiring space or if they have pleasing aesthetic features. The *New York Times* generalized in mid-2010, following the bankrupt-

Figure 7.5. Pompano Beach, Florida, 2010. What will the future hold for this building that its relocated dealership left behind? Authors' photograph.

cies and closing burst in the automobile market, that dealerships with garages attracted several kinds of new occupants. "New uses for closed dealerships are as numerous as the properties," pronounced the newspaper.[44] A machine bottling company in Powhattan, Virginia, profitably adapted a dealership on 19.3 acres for its office, showroom, light manufacturing, and assembly site. Chain stores and schools—and not only technical schools—as well as automobile service and repair shops were among the first beneficiaries of garages' adaptive reuse. Diverse new uses did not imply absorption of the entire supply of available dealership buildings. The *New York Times* summarized: "It is unclear how many of the closed auto dealerships will find new uses, real estate experts said." Insufficient surrounding land, local zoning against certain uses, required cleanup of chemical compounds, and contaminants are negatives. But one of the best incentives for adaptive reuse has been their siting in locations with heavy traffic. In its report on twenty-three hundred closed auto dealerships occupying 70 million square feet in the buildings, the newspaper elaborately detailed one conversion to a grocery store in Whitehall, Michigan.[45]

Figure 7.6. A rare urban vestige of an automobile garage, this one converted to motorcycle sales and service near the city center of Minneapolis, Minnesota, 2010. Authors' photograph.

Even if buildings like dealerships remain idle, there are considerations other than adaptive reuse—namely, aesthetic and historical value—that must be included in the debate over their preservation. Various types of roadside architecture such as motels, gas stations, and drive-ins embody nostalgic attractions to fans of popular culture, despite their having eviscerated city centers as they catered to the out-of-town roadside trade. More recently, parking garages, definitely city-center structures and often exemplary of architectural styles, have begun to win learned advocates, as have dealerships of notable exterior design that earned places in local and state history.[46] Perhaps domestic garages that contribute to the appeal of older homes have won more acclaim (albeit of a quiet, sentimental sort) than any other garage type. In contrast, repair and service garages by themselves have seldom garnered comparable approval (fig. 7.7).

In *Remembering Roadside America,* a previous undertaking of ours, we argued for historic preservation to fully embrace the remainders of those businesses that enabled street and highway travel by car.[47] The reasons are clear if one accepts the transformative nature of any activity, whether for good or ill. Historic preservationists have long been advocates for beautiful buildings, as well as for great battlefields and the homes of important historical figures—sites

Figure 7.7. A merged livery and garage on display at Horn's Cars of Yesterday, Sarasota, Florida. Authors' photograph.

that mark America's progress as a nation of liberty and justice. The automobile lays no such claims to grandeur and greatness over the last century, but its impact has hardly been slight. Consider the very popular turn among progressive political adherents over the last half-century regarding the degradations to the environment caused by gasoline-burning vehicles and what they mean for the future: such frightening developments alone assert the automobile's importance. Moreover, we have argued in several publications for the automobile's geographical transformation of the nation.[48] And again, such transformation has not always been for the better, since it is clear that automobility has gutted the centers of many cities in favor of suburban and roadside sprawl, not to mention causing the death or dishevelment of numerous small towns. On a rather less dire note, cars have also redefined entertainment and Americans' image of themselves in highly personal terms: think of the road trip and the family vacation; think, too, of the automobile's vanity-satisfying role as a status symbol.[49] All of these, obviously, are significant impacts that the automobile could not have had without the enabling businesses arrayed along the roadside. And, in bringing these developments about, Americans exercised their freedoms and penchant for decentralized authority.

Garages remain newborns among historic preservationists. A casual survey along Route 66 is instructive about how garages considered "historic" are treated. Route 66 represents a good landscape to check because of its huge popular following and because it is the focus of the federal Route 66 Corridor Program, which has stimulated a comprehensive survey of resources and caused local people to ready these resources for historic-site visits or adapt them for other purposes. To date, of the eleven sites identified with garages, not one was a garage only. Is the garage by itself still too mundane to attract much attention? Does it remain a back place although potentially open to public view within a major historic landscape? Hope springs forth. At the time of this writing, the Route 66 Corridor Program is composing a comprehensive list of properties assigned to types. One of these is "Garages/Dealerships." Eligible, too, will be the outdoor service area where a ramp above a work pit or hydraulic life was built adjacent to a gasoline station or other roadside service.[50]

* * *

How can the new geography and culture of automobility be remembered without understanding—not necessarily celebrating—the garage? Is the roadside to be drained of its work implications and celebrated for its popular meaning as preservationists have done with places of aesthetic merit and sites associated with the greatness of the nation's founding fathers. Is the roadside only a playground? Is the roadside to be installed in public memory as just another theme park, with all that term's implications of uncritical and historically simplistic urges?

Garage preservation will be challenging. Often small buildings, garages will not be suitable for other uses except as shops. Adaptively reused auto dealerships that once included garages, conversely, will demand big investments. Those built in the virgin automobile market, before the construction of roadsides on the edges of cities, will be found—if they survive at all—in central-city locations with their depressed vitality. These minimally desirable locations are not where people want to go. Lastly, these early garages were not necessarily sturdy buildings. They were not meant to last. Their builders and owners often had intentions of just getting by, for the automobile had accelerated the role of landscape change. They were akin to early motor courts and motels whose rarity now is a sad reality facing preservationists. And, like those structures, they are disappearing rapidly. So, too, would it be perversely ironic not to avoid more labor and save for new purposes these buildings that housed past labor.

Car dealerships and independent garages survived or new ones emerged as they responded to economic changes. Auto palaces for display rooms, for example, were not built during and after the onset of the Great Depression, but this did not preclude show places in vast and otherwise empty lots with simple signs advertising an associated reliable garage. Regardless of their format, the repair garage is an index of an ever-changeful economy. Amid the numerous histories of roadside businesses, the dedicated historian willing to undertake not only archival research but the time-consuming assembly work of a base of oral histories will find the garage often run as a family enterprise whose members are proud of the productive results of their hard work, intelligence, and profitable success—in short, what they are glad to have known as their American dream. What made for a garage's success did not necessarily make them permanent fixtures. Their success is not so much an embodiment but an idea of improvised survival. For this reason, it falls to the responsibility of historic preservationists to point out their significance, add them to the list of landmark building types, and work for them as they can. Symbols of successful entrepreneurship, they should resonate no less today and into the future than they did in the past. Let garages not become lost patrimony.

The garage: what element of Roadside America is less understood? For customers having their cars serviced today, lingering on the floor of a commercial garage is a rather rare event. Most businesses that served customers arriving by car invited them inside, enabling them to look around and comprehend, at least for brief moments, how things worked. But entering a repair garage was, and is certainly today, a rare event.

Not true the gas station. Gas stations were and remain designed to attract attention. They fully invite customers in. It is there that the ring of the station bell and the smell of gasoline resonate in American memory. It was part of corporate America's place-product-packaging—the creation of networks of look-alike stores that, taken together, served to define marketing territories in landscape terms. (Place-product-packaging in the development of motel and restaurant chains did the same.) Initially, garages did dominate gasoline and lubricating sales and not just car repair, with many garages selling several brands simultaneously. But they tended to be disordered places. Petroleum companies found that they had little point-of-purchase influence. Only through carefully contrived gas stations could brand identity be controlled and thus brand loyalty sustained. Early commercial garages were "back spaces," often poorly lit and ventilated, where mechanics labored in bare circumstance. They excited little romance. No wonder today they have largely fallen beneath the radar of even those interested in roadside history. On the other hand, the garage that is well known is the domestic garage, the one that nearly every home dweller uses daily. Nonetheless, relic commercial garage buildings, perhaps by the tens of thousands, survive across the United States today. What are we to do about them? What are we to do with them?

EPILOGUE

Entering into older city neighborhoods or into small towns little changed over recent decades, thus to carefully scrutinize a passing scene for evidence of past automobility, the curious traveler, as well as the curious scholar, rarely goes unrewarded. For this book, one about early twentieth-century garages, certain questions loom for such observers. What do older garages look like? How did they function? Why have they survived? In a more philosophical vein, how should they be judged in terms of historical significance? Why are relic garage buildings today so little valued? Why do they go unnoticed and uncelebrated given that they are still so ubiquitous?

Look here at some examples. The following cases are not the definitive ones culled from an exhaustive national field survey. Rather, they came to the authors' attention quite accidentally as we motored about the country on excursions frequently taken to pay close attention to landscapes and places. Additionally, they have been documented as to origin, ownership, and changing use by our questioning locally knowledgeable people encountered along the way. It is our intent to encourage our readers in such exercise—to get them to look more carefully at the landscapes they encounter in travel and, more important, to the places where they live. Readers are invited to sleuth for themselves the traditional garage as an important fixture of the nation's automobile history. Neither the preservation of memory nor the preservation of buildings can be achieved without widespread involvement. Learning from exploring landscapes and places should be a widely shared enterprise involving all kinds of people. It can lead to important ends.

These examples reaffirm the kinds of knowing that newcomers seek in entering a new place. They are buildings that clearly stand out for what they are, or for what they once were. In the past, travelers, especially those experiencing motoring difficulties, evaluated garages primarily on the basis of utility. And much of that assessment was superficially visual. Did a garage look like a place where a problem might be readily solved? That is, did it appear to provide reliable service? Was it up-to-date? Was the business prospering? Was it advertised in believable ways? Today's tourists have less problems motoring than did earlier travelers, but today there is the added incentive of assessing historicity, at least should the tourist choose to do so. Does a garage or former garage stand out as being rooted in the past? Does it have heritage implications? Or is it merely old? Is it merely antiquated? Of course, to be an effective time traveler, what one needs to know is whether something seen is truly of historically significance. Does it stand out as fully symbolic of past ways and means? Is it a poor or a good example?

Common utility—rarely implication of historical value—is what locals tend to see in built environments close to home. This is especially true of common structures like garages. Appearances count for less. Knowing is based more on personal experience of the practical sort. Visual stereotyping enters little. Except for local history buffs, landmark status rarely attaches to ordinary things close at hand, including retail establishments in general and not just garages. It is, perhaps, today's antique car collector who is the most attuned to vintage garage buildings. They clearly feel an affinity for them. And many an old garage survives mainly to warehouse vintage car collections.

One remarkable case is that of the garage in Camden, Indiana, pictured and briefly introduced in the prologue (see fig. PR.1). It was born nearly a century ago and reborn some ten years ago. A collector, having restored it, now uses it to store old cars. We had the rare fortune, an almost serendipitous experience, of locating Pete Wagoner, whose maternal grandfather, Olpha Wyatt, established the enterprise with his oldest son, Harold, in 1916. Pete recalled for us in detailed and elegant prose the history of the business. Nearly forty years before the garage was founded, his great-grandfather, David Wyatt, came to Camden, now a town of some fifteen hundred people northeast of La Fayette, Indiana, to start several businesses essential to the town's growth as a frontier community: first a sawmill, then a cement-tile manufacturing plant, and later a retail merchandise store. Olpha Wyatt, an entrepreneur like his father, helped found the Camden Telephone Company and the Camden State Bank in addition to acquiring a couple of farms in the area. Only three years after starting the Camden Auto Company, Olpha died—ironically from complications of injuries sustained in an automobile accident. "There was no insurance," Pete recalled, "and most of Olpha's business holdings were liquidated."[1]

EPILOGUE

The Wyatt family had originally bought the building that housed the Camden Auto Company from a blacksmith, who first occupied it in 1913.² "When Olpha started Camden Auto Company in 1916, he intended it to be more than a garage," Pete Wagoner remembered. "It was also an automobile dealership where he sold Chalmers vehicles." Harold, however, lacked experience to run a dealership—he had just graduated from high school—and operated the business as a repair and service garage instead. Harold's younger brother, Floyd, helped with the garage work. The Wyatt homestead stood across the street from "The Garage" (as the family called it). Later, Harold built a new house just west of the building. Thus, following World War I, family life and family livelihood were tightly linked geographically.³

The garage provided a full range of services and light repairs, and for almost any type of automobile, truck, or farm tractor. It stocked selected parts and accessories and also sold tires and batteries, along with fishing tackle, tobacco, soft drinks, and candy and ice cream. The business continued to thrive when Mildred, one of Harold's sisters, married George Clem after World War II. Mildred began as office manager and bookkeeper even before her marriage, another case of a woman in the garage trade. She taught school as well, took care of her widowed mother, and fulfilled her dying father's directive to "look after the family." Pete Wagoner put it reverentially: "The garage was central to their way of life, and Mildred always remained involved."⁴

The Wyatt brothers—"both excellent mechanics"—could do virtually any type of repair, yet they tended to specialize in certain areas. Harold was the only welder. Floyd was skilled at rebuilding carburetors and also good at doing electrical diagnostic work. After Mildred's marriage to George Clem, the business began selling lawn mowers, and George became the specialist in small engine repair. "Harold," Wagoner recalled, "had the outgoing personality and was the person most customers wanted to see/talk to. . . . he lined up most of the repair/service jobs, sold lots of tires, pumped lots of gasoline, and continually gave away ice cream cones and candy bars to kids who came by with their parents." (Town children would eventually, after all, one day become loyal customers.) Wagoner continued:

> Floyd was warm and friendly, but more inclined to stay out in the shop doing the repair work that Harold lined up. Of course, there would be disagreements when Harold would commit to doing jobs

Floyd or George felt were too difficult, or they didn't think could be done when promised. George was good at his work, but had a short temper and would frequently "let off steam," which would cause Harold and Floyd to shake their heads, because this was very foreign to their Wyatt values/nature.[5]

The garage was more than a rallying point for the family. It was a place for community socializing also—a kind of community center. Harold, Floyd, and George were friendly with "'the regulars' who spent time 'loafing' around the garage."

They all liked to fish the streams and creeks around Camden, at the family's cabin on Indian Lake in the UP [Upper Peninsula] of Michigan, or on other fishing expeditions they might arrange with others to lakes in Wisconsin and Minnesota. The garage was a busy place Monday through Saturday. Harold would be there to open up before 7:00 am, be there all day, go home for a quick supper before Floyd and George called it a day at 5:30 pm, and then be back to trade stories with the evening "loafers," pump more gasoline, sell some hand-dipped ice cream, and line up more jobs until about 8 pm.[6]

Gary Robey bought and restored the building several years ago. A local, he always thought it was a great place. One day he happened upon the empty garage while hauling grain. The realtor's "FOR SALE" sign caught his attention. He and his wife looked at the building and were dismayed at how run-down it had become. Nonetheless, their instinct was "to bring it back to life just like it used to be." Besides the garage, they were able to purchase its original workbenches and many of the tools that had once been used in the garage. The Robeys have been restoring cars, trucks, and motorcycles in the building ever since, and, importantly, each year they put the building and its contents on display during an annual town festival. As Gary Robey acknowledged: "We love having the garage as it would have been in past times—it's like stepping back in time and Camden is the perfect setting for it. . . . The cars look like they belong in it."[7]

Family memory and concern for automobile restoration in a historical setting are by no means the only rationales underlying garage restoration today.

A survey of historic preservation agencies nationwide brings to light numerous local initiatives where preservationists, rather than property owners, have initiated garage restoration. But property ownership appears to be the key. Restoration of the 638 Building in Springfield, Tennessee, also discussed in the prologue, is a case in point (see fig. PR.3). The Draughton family has owned the building since 1920 and has recently overseen its refurbishing, carefully retaining much of the structure's original physical integrity as a garage. Jack and Louis Draughton first operated a hardware and seed store, adding, as previously mentioned, a filling station and a tire-vulcanizing operation in building additions. As at Camden, Indiana, the garage functioned as something of a community center as well as a business. The town's main bus stop was located there, as was the town's tourist information center. The building is listed as both a state and local historic site.[8]

Two other buildings are worth noting, both listed on the National Register of Historic Places; one is in Centerville, Iowa, and the other in Collierville, Tennessee. The Fisher Garage is one of several surviving close to Centerville's courthouse square, the town being the seat of Iowa's Appanoose County (fig. EP.1). Early in the twentieth century, Centerville was thriving as a farm trade center with an excellent railroad connection (and, as well, streetcars providing public transportation). Nonetheless, the sale and servicing of the private automobile became a mainstay of local commerce. The author of the form nominating Centerville's downtown to the National Register of Historic Places (as a historic district) wrote this of the 1920s: "The streets leading off the Square were crowded with new auto garages, both for sales and service, and gas stations were being built on corners in all directions from the square."[9]

The Fisher Garage itself, located one block west of the square on Van Buren Street, exemplified the local garage as a building type: it was described in the nomination form as a single-story masonry structure of minimalist architectural intent, built flush with the sidewalk and accessed from the front.[10] Set in terra cotta across the facade was the name Fisher, insuring that the building would be forever known by that name. The building was, indeed, erected in 1919 by one S. Fisher who intended to open a Paige automobile dealership. But a newspaper article that year noted that Fisher had lost his sales contract and thus had sold the building to one L. Morrison, who intended to operate a storage garage. Morrison had started out as a mechanic and garage owner in nearby Unionville.[11] Opening the garage for business was cause for a gala event. A dance band and refreshments

Figure EP.1. Fisher Garage, Centerville, Iowa, 2005. Authors' photograph.

attracted hundreds, perhaps the town's largest opening event in history, according to the newspaper.[12] A succession of owners sold a variety of automobile brands through World War II, particularly General Motors products. So also were various brands of gasoline brands sold from curbside pumps, prime among them Phillips 66.

In Collierville, Tennessee, the McGinnis Oil Company's service station and garage at 98 North Main Street has been, since 1927, a mainstay on the town's central square (figs. EP.2 and EP.3). W. W. McGinnis operated a lumber company (what today would be called a building supply firm) since 1898. It grew into a general contracting company that built many of Collierville's homes, retail storefronts, and public buildings between the two world wars. One of the buildings constructed was 98 North Main. It is described in Collierville's historic district nomination form for the National Register of Historic Places as follows: "a one-story, load-bearing[,] brick[,] corner 'drive-through' service station with flat roof extending over the entire structure, including the pump island. Its pressed tin ceiling covers the drive-in area and asphalt roofing covers the entire building."[13]

John Linn Hopkins, the form's author, considered the garage to be an important foreground structure and not merely a building supportive of the dis-

EPILOGUE

Figure EP.2. McGinnis Oil Company Service Station and Garage, Collierville, Tennessee, 2012. Authors' photograph.

trict's historical character. It fully symbolized the arrival of the automobile and its impact on town life, he wrote, being "the first automobile service facility in the town developed solely for automotive use, rather than converted from an earlier livery."[14] Bill and Jim Cox, who today own and operate the business, are descendants of the founder. They carefully delineate their building's pedigree on their business website.[15] Today, in addition to gasoline sales, they sell and mount tires and do lubrication work.[16] Collierville, once a farm service town, is today a rapidly growing suburban community of some forty-three thousand people, having been fully absorbed into metro Memphis. The town center has been redeveloped as a retail district with specialty shops, including art galleries and stylish boutiques. And yet the garage continues as an anchor in time.

The Knous Garage, located just off the courthouse square at Petersburg, Illinois, was opened in 1932 and, like the McGinnis Garage, remains in business, having continued under the uninterrupted ownership of a single family (fig. EP. 4). A town of some twenty-five hundred people northwest of Springfield, Illinois, Petersburg was originally surveyed by Abraham Lincoln. The town of Petersburg essentially replaced the village of New Salem, where Lincoln entered adulthood. Clyde A. Knous started as a Studebaker dealer with showroom and garage, the

Figure EP.3. View of central square at Collierville, Tennessee, from beneath the canopy of the McGinnis Oil Company Service Station, 2012. Authors' photograph.

family's apartment located above. Jack, Clyde's son, began helping his father at a young age; among his various chores was the towing of cars to Petersburg from the Studebaker factory at South Bend, Indiana. When Studebaker quit car production in 1964, father and son contracted to sell Dodge cars and trucks. When Clyde died in 1971, the business became Knous Motor Company, with Jack's son joining the business after his graduation from high school. Both new and used cars were stored in a newly built structure across the street.[17]

Thomas L. Knous, grandson of Clyde, remains in business (fig. EP.5). Up until 2009, he was a Jeep dealer for Chrysler but voluntarily gave up new dealer status to sell only used cars; his service and repair shop, of course, stayed open. The building has remained largely unchanged since it was built. Alterations include new shelving units inside the garage proper, the replacement of a single large showroom window by several smaller window casements, and the replacement of the front "accordion" door with a large overhead door. Thomas shares belief in the principle that the commonplace can be historic, even his garage. However, keeping his building largely unchanged over time has reflected not so much a penchant for pastness as an appreciation for a serviceable building that had provided excellent livelihood over three generations.[18] We, on the other hand, force-

EPILOGUE

Figure EP.4. Knous Motor Company Garage, Petersburg, Illinois, 2009. Authors' photograph.

fully see the past in his building. It reinforces our thinking that not all history is archival—that is, the notion that history is something revealed mainly through written documents. History also persists as material culture and even in buildings as ordinary and mundane as garages. The past is clearly visible in most landscapes and places. Buildings such as garages may not be thought of as essentially historic (or even historical), but that, nonetheless, does not make them any less symbolic of the past.

* * *

As America comes to grips in the twenty-first century with the consequences of the twentieth century's enthusiasm for automobiles, old garages persist, many if not most of them possessing resource value as structures capable of being recycled into new uses. Preserving old garages represents a form of conservation worthy of careful thought. Not only are they highly symbolic of one of the most important changes to occur in American history—the reorientation of the nation to car-dependent lifestyles—but they remain today fully automobile oriented (if not automobile convenient), something that commercial buildings in the future will continue to demand. As many an old garage has already proven, recycling into contemporary use or continuing in sustained use along traditional business lines can be profitable. Let us not allow the garage as a feature of landscape to remain obscure in the shadows, a vestige of place neither championed nor even thought of as valuable.

Let us not lose sight of the garage's symbolic value as historical icon. Without car service and without car repair, the dream of a nation in perpetual motion (the highly mobile individual placed squarely at its center) would have long ago evaporated. Perhaps not charming—but vital, yes—the commercial garage was an important promoter of automobility. The garage defined an important sense of place in the new auto age, a kind of place so common as to be largely ignored, then even forgotten, today. But time has come to give the lowly garage a rightful place in the iconography of American history, at least as it applies to the nation's emerging and now-dominant automobility.

Garages were highly personalized places, spanning the spectrum from the public to the private. They were busy places of work requiring command of newly emergent technologies. At base, their market niche was the troubled motorist. They were profit centers whereby entrepreneurial gambles played out in different ways for better or worse. Careers were made and lost. They were places where ordinary Americans defined new sorts of careers, particularly as mechanics and also as sales persons and business managers. Garages figured variously and prominently in American life. For all their commonplaceness, they should not be forgotten.

Figure EP.5. Thomas L. Knous, Knous Motor Company, Petersburg, Illinois, 2009. Authors' photograph.

NOTES

Preface

1. *The American Heritage Dictionary of the English Language*, 3rd ed. (Boston: Houghton Mifflin, 1992), 747.

2. See especially Kevin L. Borg, *Auto Mechanics: Technology and Expertise in Twentieth-Century America* (Baltimore: Johns Hopkins Univ. Press, 2007); Stephen L. McIntyre, "The Failure of Fordism: Reform of the Automobile Repair Industry, 1913–1940," *Technology and Culture* 41 (Apr. 2000): 269–99; and Stephen L. McIntyre, "'The Repair Man Will Gyp You': Mechanics, Managers, and Customers in the Automobile Repair Industry, 1896–1940" (PhD diss., Univ. of Missouri, Columbia, 1995).

3. Popular writing has focused mainly on auto dealers. For example, see Henry L. Dominguez, *The Ford Agency: A Pictorial History* (Osceola, WI: MBI Publishing, 1981); and Robert Genat, *The American Car Dealership* (Osceola, WI: MBI Publishing, 1999).

4. John A. Jakle and Keith A. Sculle, *The Gas Station in America* (Baltimore: Johns Hopkins Univ. Press, 1994).

5. John A. Jakle and Keith A. Sculle, *Lots of Parking: Land Use in a Car Culture* (Charlottesville: Univ. of Virginia Press, 2004).

6. John A. Jakle and Keith A. Sculle, *Motoring: The Highway Experience in America* (Athens: Univ. of Georgia Press, 2008).

1. Why the Garage?

1. "Sunday Afternoon in Gasville," *Motor Age* 43 (Apr. 26, 1923): 25.

2. "Automobile Storage and Repair Facilities," *Scientific American* 86 (Mar. 29, 1902): 226.

3. "The St. Louis Tour of the American Automobile Association," *Horseless Age* 14 (Aug. 10, 1904): 134.

4. Henry C. Schramm, "My Auto 'Tis of Thee," *The Spokesman* 31 (May 1915): 238.

5. Advertisements headed "Wanted to Exchange" and "For Sale" in *Horseless Age* 5 (Jan. 10, 1900), 22.

6. "U.S. Motor Vehicle Registrations, 1900–1958," *Chilton's Motor Age* 78 (Sept. 1959): 58.

7. "The Horse and the Automobile," *American Blacksmith & Motor Shop* 23 (Mar. 1924): 14.

8. C. W. Nash, "Motor Car an Essential," *Blacksmith and Wheelwright* 17 (Apr. 1918): 110.

9. Ibid.

10. "The Need for More Garages," *National Builder* 64 (Jan. 1921): 56.

11. "Big Building Bureau: Representative Buildings Erected by 'National Builder' Subscribers," *National Builder* 59 (Jan. 1917): 41.

12. "The Expansion of the Garage Business," *Horseless Age* 22 (Nov. 11, 1908): 643.

13. Nash, "Motor Car an Essential," 110.

14. Norman G. Shidle, "The Small Town—That's Where Biggest Automobile Market Lies," *Automotive Industries* 54 (Mar. 4, 1916): 397.

15. *Automobile Topics* 101 (Jan. 10, 1931): 824.

16. W. E. Williams, "The Kansas Farmer's Motor Cars," *Motor* 32 (June 1911): 37.

17. Donald McLeod Lay, "2,070,903 Cars in United States," *Automobile* 33 (Aug. 12, 1915): 272.

18. "Business and Sales, Statistics," *Automotive Abstracts* 5 (Feb. 20, 1927): 59.

19. "This Third Largest Industry," *Automobile Topics* (Jan. 5, 1918): 948.

20. "Facts Worth Knowing," *Accessory and Garage Journal* 18 (Oct. 1928): 60.

21. *Facts and Figures of the Automobile Industry* (New York: National Automobile Chamber of Commerce, 1931), 85.

22. U.S. Bureau of the Census, "Table 1-A, The United States—Retail Distribution, By Kinds of Business," *Fifteenth Census of the United States: 1930, Distribution*, vol. 1, *Retail Distribution* (Washington, DC: United States Printing Office, 1933): 47.

23. "Chain Stores are Important in the Automotive Field," *Automobile Topics* 104 (Nov. 28, 1931): 241.

24. "Automotive Wholesale and Retail Outlets, by States," *Automotive Industries* 104, Statistical Issue (Mar. 15, 1951): 98.

25. *Automobile Facts and Figures,* 3rd ed. ([Detroit]: Automobile Manufactures Association, 1951): 34.

26. "Automotive Business Guide," *Motor Age* 66 (Jan. 1947): 59.

27. For an introduction to the parking garage, see John A. Jakle and Keith A. Sculle, *Lots of Parking: Land Use in a Car Culture* (Charlottesville: Univ. of Virginia Press, 2004): 114–55.

28. "Minor Mention," *Horseless Age* 6 (Sept. 12, 1900): 24.

29. Advertisement for the Grand Circus Garage, Detroit, *Detroiter* 18 (Mar. 28, 1927): 46.

30. "Hoosier Motor Club's Road Markers," *Hoosier Motorist* 5 (Jan. 1917): 25.

31. Louis J. Jocelyn, "Common Sense for the Garage Man," *Motor* 19 (Mar. 1913): 95.

32. John A. Jakle and Keith A. Sculle, *Motoring: The Highway Experience in America* (Athens: Univ. of Georgia Press, 2008): 10, 18.

33. "Motor Liveries," *Horseless Age* 5 (Dec. 27, 1899): 9.

34. B. M. Ikert, "Some Faults of Southern Service," *Motor Age* 35 (Apr. 17, 1919): 18–19.

35. For an introduction to blacksmithing and its early twentieth-century reorientation to auto repair, see Kevin L. Borg, *Auto Mechanics: Technology and Expertise in Twentieth-Century America* (Baltimore: Johns Hopkins Univ. Press, 2007), 35–51.

36. "Prize Topic: Automobile Repair Work in the Black Smith Shop," *Blacksmith and Wheelwright* 73 (Jan. 1910): 19.

37. Elmer E. Roberts, letter to editor, *American Blacksmith* 15 (Jan. 1916): 101.

38. G. B., "Ready for the Smith, Automobile Repair Business and Conditions Leading to Success," *Blacksmith and Wheelwright* 74 (Sept. 1916): 315.

39. "The Modern Blacksmith," *Automobile Topics* 57 (Aug. 1957): 31 (reprinted from the *Chicago Post,* c. 1910).

40. Thomas A. Kinney, *The Carriage Trade: Making Horse-Drawn Vehicles in America* (Baltimore: John Hopkins Univ. Press, 2004): 297.

41. "Wagon Makers Say It's a Fad," *The Hub* 52 (June 1910): 79.

42. "Vehicle Builders are Optimistic," *The Hub* 51 (Nov. 1909): 289.

43. C. D. Crain, Jr., "Getting Automobile Trimming Business," *The Spokesman* 32 (Sept. 1916): 462.

44. C. D. Crain, Jr., "Blaze the Trail for the Trailers," *The Spokesman*, 29 (Sept 1913): 609.

45. "Carriage Dealers to be Guests at Auto Show," *The Hub* 51 (Nov. 1909): 303.

46. "Some Vermont Garages," *Horseless Age* 25 (Feb. 2, 1910): 199.

47. "Bicycle Business Booms; 1935 Second Biggest Year," *Motor* 66 (Oct. 1936): 78.

48. For an overview of bicycle and automobile manufacture early in the twentieth century, see Carl B. Glasscock, *The Gasoline Age: The Story of the Men Who Made It* (Indianapolis: Bobbs-Merrill, 1937).

49. Kinney, *Carriage Trade*, 286–87.

50. "Bicycle and Motor," *Horseless Age* 5 (Jan. 31, 1900): 10.

2. Garage Layout, 1900–1920s

1. "Department Store Remodeled as Automobile Salesroom," *Horseless Age* 25 (May 4, 1910): 668–69.

2. "The Garage Situation in Trenton, NJ," *Horseless Age* 27 (May 3, 1911): 758.

3. "The Old Post Road Garage, Tarrytown, NY," *Horseless Age* 24 (Nov. 3, 1909): 507.

4. "Zell Motor Car Company's Garage, Baltimore," *Horseless Age* 25 (May 4, 1910): 654.

5. Miller, Woolley, and Evans, Architects, "The New Automobile Center, Social Hall Avenue, Salt Lake City," *American Architect* 115 (Mar. 6, 1918): 281, 284–85.

6. "McCurdy-May Salesroom and Garage, Pittsburgh, Pa." *Horseless Age* 31 (May 7, 1913): 799.

7. "Is the Garage Business in New York a Paying Proposition?" *Horseless Age* 29 (Feb. 14, 1912): 365.

8. "Premier Garage, Los Angeles," *Horseless Age* 25 (May 4, 1910): 678.

9. "Make Utility the Keynote of Your Truck Sales," *Motor World* 63 (June 30, 1920): 11.

10. Corliss H. Topping, "Business in the Earthquake," *Automobile Topics* 109 (Apr. 1, 1933): 398.

11. "Get Ready for the Touring Season," *Motor Age* 35 (May 15, 1919): 7–9.

12. "No. 69, Space More Than Ample," *Motor Age* 35 (June 19, 1919): 27.

13. "Fit Your Building to Your Business," *Motor World* 63 (June 2, 1920): 30.

14. See Stephen L. McIntyre, "'The Repair Man Will Gyp You': Mechanics, Managers, and Customers in the Automobile Repair Industry, 1896–1940" (PhD diss., Univ. of Missouri, 1995), 268–270.

15. B. M. Ikert, "Departments Essential to Transportation Store," *Motor Age* 46 (Dec. 4, 1924): 9.

16. Tom Wilder, "Laying Out the Dealer Building for Economy and Efficiency," *Motor Age* 41 (July 20, 1922): 9–14.

17. For example, see Joseph E. Mills, *Garage Management and Control* (Chicago: A. W. Shaw, 1928).

18. Betsy Hunter Bradley, *The Works: The Industrial Architecture of the United States* (New York: Oxford Univ. Press, 1999), 226.

19. See Stephen L. McIntyre, "The Failure of Fordism: Reform of the Automobile Repair Industry, 1913–1940," *Technology and Culture* 41 (Apr. 2000): 269–99.

20. David Gartman, *From Autos to Architecture: Fordism and Architectural Aesthetics in the Twentieth Century* (New York: Princeton Architectural Press, 2009), 12.

21. For example, see Donald D. Blanchard, "Good Lighting is Good Salesmanship," *Motor World* 65 (May 14, 1922): 16–17; and S. H. Graf, "It Can't Be Seen or Felt," *Automobile Topics* 104 (Nov. 28, 1931): 242–44.

22. "A Real Service Plant," *Ohio Motorist* 13 (Nov. 1921): 12.

23. Frank H. Williams, "Why They Never Come Back," *American Garage and Auto Dealer* 27 (Sept. 1927): 19.

24. For an introduction to place-product-packaging in the gasoline trade, see John A. Jakle and Keith A. Sculle, *The Gas Station in America* (Baltimore: Johns Hopkins Univ. Press, 1994), 18–47.

25. Richard L. Mattson and John A. Jakle, "Good-Bye to the Horse: The Transition from Horse-Related to Automobile-Related Businesses in an Urban Landscape," *Pioneer America Society Transactions* 2 (1979): 31–51.

26. "Some Philadelphia Garages," *Horseless Age* 27 (May 3, 1911): 740.

27. "Automobile Storage and Repair Facilities," *Scientific American* 86 (Mar. 29, 1902): 226.

28. "The Garage Situation in Buffalo, New York," *Horseless Age* 23 (Apr. 21, 1909): 524.

29. "Curtain Raised on Chicago's 'Row'," *The Automobile* 24 (Apr. 20, 1911): 933–34.

30. Ibid., 935.

31. "How New York Supports the Automobile Industry," *The Automobile* 24 (Mar. 30, 1911): 809–11,

3. Garage Layout, 1930–1950s

1. See Gabrielle Esperdy, *Modernizing Main Street: Architecture and Consumer Culture in the New Deal* (Chicago: Univ. of Chicago Press, 2008).

2. See John A. Jakle and Keith A. Sculle, *The Gas Station in America* (Baltimore: Johns Hopkins Univ. Press, 1994).

3. "A Modern Gasoline Station," *Horseless Age* 34 (Nov. 18, 1919): 744.

4. George A. Kaiser, "Curbside Pumps a Nuisance," *Motor World* 76 (Aug. 15, 1923): 29.

5. V. B. Guthrie, "'Super' Stations and Oil Companies Compete for Gasoline Business," *National Petroleum News* 18 (Mar. 10, 1926): 64.

6. "Poor Garage Credit Starts Big Station Plan," *National Petroleum News* 5 (Oct. 1913): 1.

7. Warren C. Platt, "The Service Station," *National Petroleum News* 17 (May 13, 1925): 71.

8. "More and More Service Business," *Accessory and Garage Journal* 28 (June 1929): 9.

9. See "The One-Stop Station: Is It the Station of the Future?" *National Petroleum News* 21 (Oct. 2, 1929): 111; and "Automotive Servicing Goes One-Stop," *National Petroleum News* 23 (Feb. 18, 1931): 79–81.

10. "The 'Complete Service Station' Arrives," *Motor World* 74 (Mar. 28, 1922): 16.

11. E. L. Berringer, "One-Stop Servicing Is Function for Oil Industry," *National Petroleum News* 22 (Sept. 17, 1930): 67.

12. William E. Green, "Super Service Stations Thrive Best Operated by Individual Owner," *National Petroleum News* 20 (Mar. 14, 1928): 97.

13. "Beauty Shop in Super Station to Draw Women," *National Petroleum News* 22 (Aug. 14, 1930): 106.

14. For a history of Pure Oil's English Cottage designs, see Jakle and Sculle, *Gas Station*, 163–82.

15. Ward K. Halbert, "Super Service Stations Under One Roof," *National Petroleum News* 25 (June 22, 1927): 81.

16. Ibid., 82.

17. "Super Service," *Automotive Abstracts* 7 (Apr. 20, 1927): 128.

18. E. L. Berringer, "Ford Only Car Manufacturer Supporting Dealer Neighborhood Stations," *National Petroleum News* 27 (Jan. 9, 1935): 30.

19. "Motor Service," *Business Week*, May 24, 1933, 10.

20. "Knowledge of Products and Equipment Key to Success in 1931 for Station Men," *National Petroleum News* 23 (Mar. 4, 1931): 152.

21. "A Byzantine Service Station," *National Builder* 67 (Apr. 1924): 99. See also "Super Station Designed as Mosque," *National Petroleum News* 20 (Apr. 18, 1928): 93.

22. C. L. Buehl, "What About Super-Service Stations?" *Accessory and Garage Journal* 19 (Aug. 1929): 16.

23. See Gartman, *From Autos to Architecture*.

24. "We Look Pretty Good," *Motor* 46 (Oct. 1936): 59.

25. For an excellent pictorial history of auto dealerships in the United States, see Robert Genat, *The American Car Dealership* (Osceola, WI: MBI Publishing Co., 1999).

26. Richard L. Reddy, "Planning Building Plans," *Motor* 66 (Jan. 1947): 49.

27. "In Modernizing Your Business, Glass Adds Class," *Motor Age* 68 (Dec. 1948): 126.

28. For treatment of the parking lot as a land-use dominant in American cities, see John A. Jakle and Keith A. Sculle, *Lots of Parking: Land Use in a Car Culture* (Charlottesville: Univ. of Virginia Press, 2004).

29. John A. Jakle and Keith A. Sculle, *Motoring: The Highway Experience in America* (Athens: Univ. of Georgia Press), 13.

30. "Planning to Move?" *Automobile Topics* 132 (Dec. 12, 1938): 279.

4. Dealerships

1. "G.M. III: How to Sell Automobiles," *Fortune*, Feb. 1939, 71.

2. Ralph C. Epstein, *The Automobile Industry: Its Economic and Commercial Development* (Chicago: A. W. Shaw Co., 1928), 152, 160–61.

3. "Brief History of the New York Shows," *Motor Age* 43 (Jan. 4, 1923): 32.

4. James J. Flink, *The Automobile Age* (Cambridge, MA: MIT Press, 1988), 25, 145.

5. "Brief History of New York Motor Shows."

6. James J. Flink, *America Adopts the Automobile, 1895–1910* (Cambridge, MA: MIT Press, 1970), 47.

7. Dorothy Weinz Jerse, *New Automobile Dealers, 1900–1999: Vigo County, Indiana* (Terre Haute, IN: Esten Fusen, c. 2000), 11.

8. "The Madison Square Garden Show," *Horseless Age* 15 (Jan. 18, 1905): 70.

9. "Seattle Automobile Show," *Western Motor*, May 1916, 11–12.

10. For example, see "G.M. III: How to Sell Automobiles," *Fortune*, Feb. 1939, 71–73.

11. Harry Tipper, "Distributors or Factory Branches?" pt. 1, *Automotive Industries* 46 (Jan. 19, 1922): 140–41; and Tipper, "Distributors or Factory Branches?" pt. 2, *Automotive Industries* 46 (Mar. 2, 1922): 17. Harry Tipper deserves a biography; for a short summary of his accomplishments, see his obituary, "Harry Tipper, 61, Rubber Firm Aide," *New York Times*, May 8, 1941, 23.

12. Tipper (Mar. 2, 1922), 16.

13. Tipper (Jan. 19, 1922): 140.

14. James M. Rubenstein, *Making and Selling Cars: Innovation and Change in the U. S. Automotive Industry* (Baltimore: Johns Hopkins Univ. Press, 2001), 252–53.

15. Robert Genat, *The American Car Dealership* (Osceola, WI: MBI Publishing Co., 1999), 17; Donald Finlay Davis, *Conspicuous Production: Automobiles and Elites in Detroit, 1899–1933* (Philadelphia: Temple Univ. Press, 1988), 17; Flink, *Automobile Age*, 18–19, 40; "The Dealer No Longer An Agent," *Automobile Topics* 47 (Sept. 29, 1917): 853; Lawrence H. Seltzer, *A Financial History of the American Automobile Industry* (New York: Houghton Mifflin Company, 1928), 19–21; and Epstein, *Automobile Industry*, 136, 138–39.

16. "Ford Service and Assembling Plants," *Ford Times* 8 (June 1915): 430; "Four Assembling Plants Open," *Ford Times* 8 (Apr. 1915): 296, 298–99; Elgin Six advertisement, *Wisconsin Motorist* 8 (Feb. 1917): 14.

17. "Distributor or Branch House?" *Horseless Age* 38 (Dec. 15, 1916): 413.

18. Ibid., 414.

19. "A Monument to Service," *Ohio Motorist* 8 (Mar. 1916): 22–24.

20. "Home of White Motor Car Co., Portland, Ore.," *Horseless Age* 27 (May 2, 1911): 755–56.

21. "Agency Wanted," *Horseless Age* 4 (June 21, 1898): 24.

22. "Some Considerations in Selecting a Car Agency," *Horseless Age* 34 (Aug. 5, 1919): 199–200.

23. "These Factors Help Build One of the Largest Distributor Organizations in Northwest," *Motor World Wholesale* 84 (May 6, 1926): 12–13.

24. Joseph E. Mills, *Garage Management and Control* (Chicago: A. W. Shaw Co., 1928), 5–6.

25. John B. Rae, *The American Automobile: A Brief History* (Chicago: Univ. of Chicago Press, 1965), 20; "New Merchandising Plan," *Ohio Motorist* 8 (Apr. 1916): 19–20; Joe Kelly, "Making Sales Through Service," *Hoosier Motorist* 9 (Mar. 1921): 41; "When Organization Serves," *Automobile Topics* 49 (Apr. 6, 1918): 895.

26. "Durant Motor Company of Michigan Appoints the Oldest Automobile Dealer in the United States as Indiana Distributor," *Hoosier Motorist* 10 (Jan. 1922): 29–30.

27. Seltzer, *Financial History*, 60; "The Subdealer Problem," *Automotive Industries* 50 (June 19, 1924), 1340; "Sub-Dealers," *Automotive Abstracts* 3 (Sept. 19, 1925), 292; and "Sub-Dealers in Cleveland," *Automotive Abstracts* 2 (Oct. 1924): 37.

28. Rae, *American Automobile*, 100; "G.M. III: How to Sell Automobiles," 77; Homer H. Gruenther, "Block Men as Business Builders," *Motor World Wholesale* 89 (Sept. 10, 1928): 16–17, 41–42.

29. Ralph Shrenkeisan, "Who Benefits *from your* Sub Dealers?" *Motor World Wholesale* 53 (July 30, 1928): 28–29, 72; "The Subdealer Problem," *Automotive Industries* 50 (June 19, 1924): 1340.

30. The husband-and-wife sociologist team of Robert Staughton Lynd and Helen Merrell Lynd made clear the automobile's importance in American life in their famous work *Middletown: A Study in Modern American Culture* (New York: Harcourt, Brace, 1929), but several decades would have to pass before scholars—most notably historian Thomas Dicke and political economist Sally H. Clarke—would effectively penetrate the obscure realm of automobile sales during the 1920s and 1930s. New business fields are typically forged in practice, not by broad theoretical constructs. At the dawn of the automobile industry, truly exploratory entrepreneurs such as Henry Ford and Alfred Sloan Jr., to name but two widely known ones, definitely operated within broad paradigms; but nothing like broad generalizations over long periods of time, searching analysis, and conscientious re-examination akin to academic scholarship occurred on the subject of dealerships

until a third of a century after the first car was sold in America. First, there was the doctoral dissertation of Lawrence Seltzer, "A Financial History of the American Automobile Industry," about the industry's financing, which he completed in 1925 at the University of Michigan (and published in book form three years later). Shortly thereafter came Ralph Epstein's *The Automobile Industry*, the work of a businessman turned academic. Harry Tipper was alone among businessmen during Seltzer's and Epstein's time in addressing the subject and, then, only in the two brief articles cited in note 11 for this chapter. Work was added only sporadically over the next eighty years, and then it was never wholly focused in a monograph about the history of dealerships but only in portions of other monographs.

Seven years before Dicke's *Franchising in America: The Development of a Business Method, 1840–1980* (Chapel Hill: Univ. of North Carolina Press, 1992), Thomas G. Marx, a planning director at GMC, produced a brief article (or "note," as he called it) in which he attempted to launch a theoretical exchange about franchising rooted in the automobile industry; see Marx, "The Development of the Franchise Distribution System in the U.S. Automobile Industry," *Business History Review* 59 (Autumn 1985): 465–74. It lacked Dicke's historical depth. In her *Trust and Power: Consumers, the Modern Corporation, and the Making of the United States Automobile Market* (New York: Cambridge Univ. Press, 2007), 65–81, Sally Clarke has explained franchising's origins in terms of legal theory.

31. Dicke, *Franchising in America*, 54. For the case of Cooperstown, New York, see John M. Emery, "For Prosperity's Sake, Buy An Automobile: Car Dealers and Consumer Demand in Depression Era Cooperstown," *New York History* 88 (Winter 2007): 97–117.

32. Rae, *American Automobile*, 97; Dicke, *Franchising in America*, 97.

33. Seltzer, *Financial History*, 85.

34. Dicke, *Franchising in America*, 64–65.

35. Ibid., 72.

36. Ibid., 83–84; Rubenstein, *Making and Selling Cars*, 267; Flink, *Automobile Age*, 217; Rae, *American Automobile*, 98; Clarke, *Trust and Power*, 213.

37. "Car Dealers' Profits," *Business Week*, Sept. 28, 1935, 16; "How Are Car Dealers Doing?" *Business Week*, May 23, 1936, 31; "Auto Dealers' Income," *Business Week* Aug. 8, 1936, 27; "Auto Dealers Seek a New Deal," *Business Week*, Jan. 1, 1938, 22, 27; Rae, *American Automobile*, 124–25.

38. For a personable dealer's narrative including this quotation (p. 27) of how Ford's pressure drove him out of Ford sales, see Jesse Rainsford Sprague, "Confessions of a Ford Dealer," *Harper's Monthly Magazine* 155 (June 1927): 26–35.

39. Dicke, *Franchising in America*, 72.

40. Ibid., 74–75, 77.

41. Flink, *Automobile Age*, 230.

42. Dicke, *Franchising in America*, 78–82.

43. "Automobile Dealer on His Way Toward Becoming a Business Man," *Business Week*, Apr. 29, 1931, 9; "Auto Dealers Seek a New Deal," *Business Week*, Jan. 1, 1938, 28; Ruth Brindze, "Automobile Dealers Can't Win," *The Nation*, Apr. 27, 1940, 539.

44. "Hudson to Drop Middlemen," *Business Week*, May 22, 1948, 70–71; "Flare-Up in the Auto Dealer War," *Business Week*, Nov. 26, 1955, 54.

45. Dicke, *Franchising in America*, 82; Flink, *Automobile Age*, 283.

46. Flink, *Automobile Age*, 281

47. Milan V. Ayars, "Financing—Rise and Problems," *Automobile Topics* 135 (Aug. 7, 1939): 51.

48. Flink, *Automobile Age*, 281–82.

49. Ibid., 282; Rubenstein, *Making and Selling Cars*, 286; John A. Jakle and Keith A. Sculle, *Motoring: The Highway Experience in America* (Athens, GA: Univ. of Georgia Press, 2008), 92; John Heitmann, *The Automobile and American Life* (Jefferson, NC: McFarland and Co., 2009), 146; Steven M. Gelber, *Horse Trading in the Age of Cars: Men in the Marketplace* (Baltimore: Johns Hopkins Univ. Press, 2008), 108.

50. Marc Braun, "Shipping 2000 Cars a Day," *The Automobile* 33 (Oct. 7, 1915): 646, 648; "Entraining Ford Cars," *Ford Times* 8 (June 1915): 423.

51. "Carbo Steel Deck for Loading Automobiles," *Automotive Industries* 39 (Nov. 7, 1918): 783; "Novel Hook-Up of 60 Foot Truck Trailer," *Accessory and Garage Journal* 18 (Dec. 1928): 54.

52. "4 Out of Every 10 Cars Are Delivered Over Highways," *Automobile Topics* 101 (Mar. 7, 1931): 334–35, 338.

53. C. B. Glasscock, *The Gasoline Age: The Story of the Men Who Made It* (Indianapolis: Bobbs-Merrill Co., 1937), 42; Rubenstein, *Making and Selling Cars*, 274; Sprague, "Confessions of A Ford Dealer," 26; Elmer W. Stout, "A Properly Financed Business," *Motor World* 64 (Aug. 11, 1920): 11; "Bankers Discourage Automotive Buying," *Motor World* 63 (June 30, 1920): 34.

54. Ayres, "Financing—Rise and Problems," *Automobile Topics* 135 (Aug. 7, 1939): 50; Genat, *American Car Dealership*, 9; Clarence J. Landen, "Finance Companies Strike Back at Insurance Propaganda," *Automotive Topics* 121 (Mar. 23, 1931): 305;

"Finance," *Automotive Abstracts* 4 (Oct. 20, 1926): 324; "Car Finance System Approved by Banker," *Automotive Industries* 44 (Apr. 14, 1921): 8; Seltzer, *Financial History*, 54–56.

55. Ayres, "Financing—Rise and Problems," 50.

56. A. R. Erskine, "How Dealers' Stocks of Cars Are Financed," *Motor Age* 46 (July 3, 1924): 25.

57. Rubenstein, *Making and Selling Cars*, 275.

58. "Time Sales of Automobiles Have Reached Enormous Proportions," *Automotive Industries* 49 (July 26, 1923): 160.

59. Ibid., 161–62.

60. C. E. Gambill, "Why Dealers Want Sound Financing," *Motor Age* 48 (Dec. 3, 1925): 10; "Financing Car Dealers," *Business Week*, Jan 19, 1935, 24; "Ford Tries New Purchase Plan," *Automotive Industries* 52 (Apr. 16, 1925): 715; "Ford Purchase Plan Creates Sensation," *Automotive Industries* 52 (Apr. 23, 1925), 760; "G.M. III: How to Sell Automobiles," *Fortune*, Feb. 1939, 106; Ayres, "Financing—Rise and Problems," 51. For an example of an advertisement to draw dealers to finance companies, see "Good for You—C. I. T. Corporation Sales Financing," *Automobile Topics* 137 (Feb. 5, 1940): 52.

61. "But Can the Dealers Sell 'Em?" *Business Week*, Aug. 13, 1955, 25–26; "No More Automobiles?" *Fortune*, Nov. 1941, 79.

62. James Parker, "Fifteen Years of Selling Automobiles," *Motor Age* 46 (Aug. 21, 1924): 10.

63. J. H. Newmark, "Exit—Pleasure Car[,] Enter—Quick Transportation," *Automobile Topics* 47 (Oct. 13, 1917): 1080.

64. Parker, "Fifteen Years," 10.

65. "Automobiles Bought Largely by Wage Earners and Lower Salaried Group," *Accessory and Garage Journal* 19 (Aug. 1929): 34.

66. Parker, "Fifteen Years," 11.

67. Ibid., 10.

68. Roy Alden, "They Sell to Farmers," *Motor Age* 48 (Aug. 20, 1925): 10.

69. Ibid., 19.

70. H. H. Batcheller, "Training Automobile Salesmen," *Accessory and Garage Journal* 19 (Dec. 1929): 14–15.

71. K. H. Burroughs, "Ask for Burroughs," *American Garage and Auto Dealer* 27 (May 1927): 7, 10.

72. Parker, "Fifteen Years," 12.

73. Batcheller, "Training Automobile Salesmen," 14.

74. Ibid., 15.

75. "Your Salesmanship," *Motor World* 63, Summer Merchandising Number (Apr. 14, 1920): 17.

76. Ibid.

77. M. L. Clayton, "'Smiling Service,'" *System, the Management of Business* 57 (May 1927): 629–30; B. E. Hutchinson, "Selling Automobiles in 1931," *Review of Reviews* 84 (Aug. 1931): 59.

78. "How Much Should Salesmen Earn?" *Motor World* 67 (May 11, 1921): 27; Genat, *American Car Dealership*, 88, 90.

79. Clarke, *Trust and Power*, 237.

80. Gelber, *Horse Trading*, 2.

81. For the broader issue, see Virginia Scharff, *Taking the Wheel: Women and the Coming of the Motor Age* (Albuquerque: Univ. of New Mexico Press, 1992); Rubenstein, *Making and Selling Cars*, 293–94; Charles L. Sanford, "Women's Place In American Car Culture," in David L. Lewis and Laurence Goldstein, eds., *The Automobile and American Culture* (Ann Arbor: Univ. of Michigan Press, 1980), 137–52.

82. Scharff, *Taking the Wheel*, 37.

83. "The Woman's Influence," *Electric Vehicles* 9 (Sept. 1916): 98.

84. Seltzer, *Financial History*, 60–61.

85. Ibid., 123. Not only women in the family helped decide on the car purchased but "the twelve-year-old boy who has carefully read the catalogues dealing with engine specifications" (Epstein, *Automobile Industry*, 59).

86. Rubenstein, *Making and Selling Cars*, 294.

87. De Sault B. Kirk, "Sell the Woman—Sell the Car," *Motor World* 67 (Apr. 6, 1921): 15.

88. Gelber, *Horse Trading*, 159.

89. Alle Mac, "If You Would Sell Women Cars—Read This Story of How They Buy," *Motor World* 75 (Oct. 5, 1923): 14.

90. "'Takes a Woman to Sell to a Woman,'" *Motor World* 63 (June 23, 1920): 21.

91. Scharff, *Taking the Wheel*, 83–84.

92. Luke Hayes, "Selling Cars is a Sex Problem," *Motor Age* 53 (May 31, 1928): 25.

93. Epstein, *Automobile Industry*, 61.

94. Hayes, "Selling Cars Is a Sex Problem," 36.

95. Alle Mac, "How Women Buy Accessories—" *Motor World* 75 (May 2, 1923): 12.

96. "Same Appeal That Sells Hats Sells Tires, Woman Dealer Finds," *Motor World* 72 (Sept. 20, 1923): 20.

97. "Replacement Parts: How A Woman 'Keeps House' in Her Own Replacement Parts Business," *Motor World Wholesale* 83 (Sept. 17, 1925): 44–45.

98. "Dealers' Buildings Reflect Merits of Buick," *Buick Bulletin* 7 (Mar. 1924): 14; Rubenstein, *Making and Selling Cars*, 253.

99. Pete Philipps, "Walking In and Driving Out: A Brief Architectural History of Automobile Dealerships," *SCA Journal* 12 (Spring–Summer 1993): 2; Chester H. Liebs, *Main Street to Miracle Mile: American Roadside Architecture* (Boston: Little, Brown, and Company, 1985), 75–76; Genat, *American Car Dealership*, 40; "The Boston Closed Car Week," *Marmon News* 12 (Apr.–May 1918): 8.

100. Joe Kelly, "Selling Automobiles by Artistic Display," *Hoosier Motorist* 7 (Mar. 1919): 51.

101. "Demand for Beauty in Sales Room," *Accessory and Garage Journal* 28 (Apr. 1929): 14.

102. "No Place for Used Cars," *Motor World* 75 (June 13, 1925): 39.

103. For example, see "McDermott Motor Company Housewarming Monday," *Waco-Times Herald*, Dec. 16, 1928, 12.

104. "Morriss Motor Company Show Room Crowded by More Than 1,000 Visitors To See Pictures of New Ford Car," *Corpus Christi Times*, Dec. 2, 1927, 5.

105. Liebs, *Main Street to Miracle Mile*, 79; "Marmon Has Beautiful House in Pasadena," *Marmon News* 1 (July 1917): 8.

106. "Distinctive Decorations Make Salesroom Attractive," *Motor World* 14 (Mar. 28, 1923): 18.

107. "Seventh Floor, Center Drive Right," *Motor Age* 47 (Feb. 12, 1925): 1, 10, 17.

108. Clyde Jennings, "Pass the Word Down to the Dealer—It's Slick-Up Time," *Automotive Industries*, Sept. 10, 1925, 414; Genat, *American Car Dealership*, 43–44, 56–63; Liebs, *Main Street to Miracle Mile*, 86–93; Phillips, "Walking In and Driving Out," 4–7.

109. Rae, *American Automobile*, 79–80.

110. For the REO Motor Car Company sales manager's stern talk to his peers about the self-defeating nature of over-production and the voluminous used car inventory, see Flink, *Automobile Age*, 193, 212.

111. Lowell K. Butcher, "Keeping the Confidence of the Public," *American Garage & Auto Dealer* 23: 9 (Sept. 1924): 18; "Dealer Losses on Used Cars," *Automotive Industries* 50 (Jan. 24, 1924), 197; "Depreciation," *Automotive Abstracts* 4 (Oct. 20, 1926): 325.

112. "Dealers Decided Against Taking in Second Hand Cars," *Horseless Age* 31 (Jan. 8, 1913): 43.

113. "Corporation Formed to Sell Used Cars," *Motor World* 67 (Apr. 6, 1917): 7.

114. "Dealers Decided Against Taking in Second Hand Cars," 43.

115. "Philadelphia's Plan to Solve Used Car Problem," *Horseless Age* 31 (May 7, 1913): 844.

116. "No Place for Used Cars," *Motor World* 75 (June 13, 1925): 39.

117. Lowell R. Butcher, "Keeping the Confidence of the Public," *American Garage & Auto Dealer* 23 (Sept. 1924): 16–17, 23; Fred M. Loomis, "Breaking Even on Used Cars," *Motor Age* 35 (Apr. 17, 1919): 20–21; J. A. Tanney, "Stauffer Sells Seventy-Five Cars Monthly in a Small Town," *Accessory and Garage Journal* 28 (Apr. 1929): 12–13; "Making Money In Automobiles," *Automobile Topics* 139 (Oct. 7, 1940): 339.

118. J. A. Webb, "Texas Dealer Sells Unused Transportation Through Specialized Stores," *Sales and Service Reference Number* 51 (May 5, 1927): 12–13.

119. "Advertising the Used Car," *Automobile Topics* 103 (Aug. 22, 1931): 166.

120. "Making Money in Automobiles," *Automobile Topics* (Apr. 25, 1938): 489, 492; "Outdoor Plan Sells Used Cars," *Motor Age* 47 (Apr. 23, 1925): 14.

121. "Outdoor Plan," 14.

122. Seltzer, *Financial History*, 62.

123. "Used Car Salesroom a Feature of Dealer Building," *Motor World* 74 (Mar. 28, 1923): 31; "Sales, Service and Storage in Two-Story Building,") *Motor World* 75 (Apr. 11, 1923): 30.

124. "Something New in Selling Used Cars," *Accessory and Garage Journal* 19 (Aug. 1929): 39.

125. "California to Bar the Used Car Lot," *Motor Age* 52 (Nov. 10, 1927): 16.

126. Charles B. Hanaran, "Can the Dealer Make Independent Salvaging Pay?" *Motor Age* 54 (Aug. 30, 1928): 20–21, 34.

127. A. V. Cummings, "Used Car Stocks Must Be Considered in Future Production Programs," *Used Car Stocks* 52 (May 21, 1925): 896–98; "Studebaker Offers to Back Dealers in Pledging Honest Resale Values," *Motor Age* 47 (June 25, 1925): 14; "Ford Launches Used Car Policy," *Automotive Industries* 52 (Apr. 2, 1925): 637, 645; D. M. McDonald, "Ford Launches National Used Car Sales Plan for Dealers," *Motor World* (Apr. 2, 1925): 13, 42; "New Ford Plan Creates Sensation," *Motor World* 82 (Apr. 23, 1925): 1, 38; Harold E. McClelland, "Cooperative Junking," *Automobile Trade Journal* 34 (July 1929): 50–51, 106; Don Blanchard, "Who Shall Scrap Them," *Automotive Trade Journal* 34 (July 1929): 32–33, 81; "Famous Junking Fund to be Used as Needed by Manufacturers," *Automobile Topics*, Apr. 25, 1938, 492.

128. "No More Automobiles?" *Fortune*, Nov. 1941, 196; Genat, *American Car Dealership*, 107–8; "Why People Aren't Buying Cars," *U.S. News & World Report*, May 2, 1958, 36.

129. Genat, *American Car Dealership*, 115–16, 118.

130. "Trouble in Automobile Row," *Fortune*, Nov. 1941, 128.

5. The Domestic Garage

1. John Heitmann, *The Automobile and American Life* (Jefferson, NC: McFarland and Co., 2009), 23; Kevin L. Borg, *Auto Mechanics: Technology and Expertise in Twentieth-Century America* (Baltimore: Johns Hopkins Univ. Press, 2007), 13–14; "Garage of the Ex-Mayor of Cincinnati," *Horseless Age* 27 (May 3, 1911): 781; "Private Garage of Adrian Riker, Newark, N.J.," *Horseless Age* 25 (May 4, 1910); "In the Building of a Private Garage," *The Automobile* 22 (May 5, 1910): 850.

2. Borg, *Auto Mechanics*, 24–25; "A Word For Chauffeurs And Garages," *Literary Digest* 44 (June 8, 1912): 1214, 1216.

3. Borg, *Auto Mechanics*, 29; Stephen L. McIntyre, "'The Repair Man Will Gyp You': Mechanics, Managers, and Customers in the Automoble Repair Industry, 1896–1940" (PhD diss., Univ. of Missouri, Columbia, 1995), 42.

4. W. V. Woehlke, "The Private Garage in the West," *Horseless Age* 23 (Apr. 21, 1909): 587; Dorothy and Julian Olney, *The American Home Book of Garages* (Garden City, NY: Doubleday, Doran, and Co., 1931).

5. A. Raymond Ellis, "A Stable Converted to a Garage," *House and Garden* 13 (June 1908): 209–10.

6. William A. Radford, *Radford's Garages and How to Build Them* (Chicago: Radford Architectural Co., 1910), 62–63; Jan Jennings, "Housing the Automobile," in Jan Jennings, ed., *Roadside America: The Automobile in Design and Culture* (Ames: Iowa State Univ. Press, 1990), 101; Floyd R. Mansberger, "A Tale of a Great Chicago

Rivalry: Radford Architectural Company Versus Fred Hodgson and the Frederick J. Drake Company," unpublished paper in authors' possession; Harry B. Haines, "Housing the Automobile," *House and Garden* 13 (May 1908): 173.

7. James F. Harbeson, "The Automobile and the 'Home' of the Future," *Annals of the American Academy of Political and Social Science* 116 (1924): 59.

8. Carleton Monroe Winslow, "The Garage for the Country or Suburban House," *House and Garden* 17 (Mar. 1910): 92.

9. Regarding women and the early automobile mechanic, see Virginia Scharff, *Taking the Wheel: Women and the Coming of the Motor Age* (Albuquerque: Univ. of New Mexico Press, 1992), 7–13.

10. C. H. Claudy, "Taking Care of Her Own Car," *The World To-day: A Monthly Record of Human Progress* 21 (Aug. 1911): 965. For historical reflections on female mechanical aptitudes with automobile, see Scharff, *Taking the Wheel*, 26–27.

11. "A Portland Garage and Its Double Driveway," *Horseless Age* 25 (May 1, 1912): 798.

12. Alexander Johnson, "Equipping the Garage," *House and Garden* 46 (Aug. 1924): 74; Morris A. Hall, "Constructing the Private Garage," *House and Garden* 30 (Aug. 1916): 24.

13. James J. Flink, *America Adopts the Automobile, 1895–1910* (Cambridge: MIT Press, 1970), 23.

14. J. B. Jackson, "The Domestication of the Garage," *Landscape* 20 (Winter 1976): 11; "In the Building of a Private Garage," *The Automobile* 22 (May 5, 1910): 851.

15. "In the Building of a Private Garage," 851.

16. "In the Building of a Private Garage", 850–51; Herbert L. Towle, "Planning a Private Garage," *National Builder* 52 (May 1911): 41, reprinted from *Motor* (1911); Radford, *Radford's Garages*, 3, 12, 30–31, 50, 56; Winslow, "The Garage for the Country or Suburban Home," 93; Leslie G. Goat, "Housing the Horseless Carriage: America's Early Private Garages," in Thomas Carter and Bernard L. Herman, eds., *Perspectives in Vernacular Architecture*, III (Columbia: Univ. of Missouri Press, 1989), 64–65; A. Raymond Ellis, "Serviceable Garages of Good Design," *House and Garden* 23 (Feb. 1913): 134; B. F. Geyer, "Private Garage Equipment," *Horseless Age* 25 (May 1, 1912): 791.

17. "A Portland Garage and Its Double Driveway," *Horseless Age* 25 (May 1, 1912): 799.

18. Geyer, "Private Garage Equipment," 792; Winslow, "Garage for the Country or Suburban House," 93.

19. Geyer, "Private Garage Equipment and Arrangement," 792.

20. Winslow, "Garage for the Country or Suburban House," 112.

21. Ibid. Also see "Tools for the Private Garage," *The Automobile* 24 (Apr. 27, 1911), 1000; "The Garage in Relation to the House," *House and Garden* 34 (July 1918), 42; and "A Private Garage for Every Need," *American Carpenter and Builder* 70 (Mar. 1916): 48.

22. Radford, *Radford's Garages*, 4.

23. Jennings, "Housing the Automobile," 98.

24. "Private Garages, Portland," *Horseless Age* 27 (May 7, 1913): 850.

25. For example, see Winslow, "Garage for the Country or Suburban House," 94.

26. "Portable Private Garages," *Horseless Age* 25 (May 1, 1912): 804.

27. J. C. Campbell, "Garages, Sites, and Entrance Drives," *House and Garden* 40 (Nov. 1921): 46–47; "How to Plan a Garage and Garden," *Building Age and National Contractor* 48 (Apr. 1926): 272; A. Raymond Ellis, "Serviceable Garages of Good Design," *House and Garden* 23 (Feb. 1913): 112.

28. "Why Is [sic] a Garage?" *Automotive Industries*, Aug. 30, 1923, 427.

29. "A Portland Garage and Its Double Driveway," 799; advertisement, *House and Garden* 30 (Dec. 1916): 55.

30. Jennings, "Housing the Automobile," 95.

31. Alexander Johnson, "Equipping the Garage," *House and Garden* 46 (Aug. 1924): 74.

32. "Making the Most of the Garage," *House and Garden* 48 (Nov. 1925): 79; A. Smith, "Automobile Buildings: Service and Storage," *Building Age and National Builder* 49 (Apr. 1927): 186; Olney, *American Home Book of Garages*, 10; Folke T. Kihlstedt, "The Automobile and the Transformation of the American House," *Michigan Quarterly Review* 19 and 20, combined issue (Fall 1980, Winter 1981): 559; Jennings, "Housing the Automobile," 103; Drummond Buckley, "A Garage in the House," in Martin Wachs and Margaret Crawford, eds., *The Car and the City: The Automobile, the Built Environment, and Daily Life* (Ann Arbor: Univ. of Michigan Press, 1992), 138–39; Goat, "Housing the Horseless Carriage," 70.

33. Goat, "Housing the Horseless Carriage," 68; Jennings, "Housing the Automobile," 99–100.

34. "Garage Modernizing Increases," *America Builder and Building Age* 53 (June 1932): 29.

35. "Safe Construction for Built-In Garages," *National Builder* 66 (May 1923): 57; Radford, *Radford's Garages and How to Build Them*, 69.

36. Regarding concrete in the United States, see Carl W. Condit, *American Building: Materials and Techniques from the First Colonial Settlements to the Present* (Chicago: Univ. of Chicago Press, 1968), 155–67.

37. Gerald K. Geerlings, "Courtyards and Garages," *House and Garden* 69 (Jan. 1936): 55.

38. "A Cement Driveway," *House and Garden* 23 (Feb. 1913): 146.

39. "The Garage Approach," *House and Garden* 38 (Apr. 1928): 162.

40. Jennings, "Housing the Automobile," 100.

41. "Frozen Radiators Sell Garages," *American Builder and Building Age* 52 (Oct. 1931): 46.

42. "Opportunities in Garage Modernizing," *American Builder* 55 (Sept. 1933): 20.

43. Jennings, "Housing the Automobile," 102.

44. "The Garage Court," *National Builder* 62 (1920): 37–39.

45. "Garage Flats," *Horseless Age* 31 (1913): 852.

46. Thomas Adams, *The Design of Residential Areas: Basic Considerations, Principles, and Methods* (Cambridge: Harvard Univ. Press, 1934), 170.

47. "A Program for Community Conservation in Chicago and an Example: The Woodlawn Plan" (Chicago Plan Commission and Woodlawn Planning Committee, July 1946), 49. For rooming houses, see Paul Groth, *Living Downtown: A History of Residential Hotels in the United States* (Berkley: Univ. of California Press, 1994), 269–71.

48. Alton H. Skinner, "Parking Lots—and 3-Minute Meters to Encourage Their Use," *American City* 56 (Nov. 1940): 52; "Keeping Today's Traffic Moving," *Traffic Engineering* 11 (Nov. 1940): 134.

49. "The Garage: Part of the Home Today," *American Builder* 72 (Aug. 1950): 74.

50. "The Garage," *American Builder* 72 (Aug. 1950): 75.

51. Kenneth T. Jackson, *Crabgrass Frontier: The Suburbanization of the United States* (New York: Oxford Univ. Press, 1985), 252–53.

52. "House of Ideas," *House and Garden* 106 (July 1954): 95.

53. Larry R. Ford, *Cities and Buildings: Skyscrapers, Skid Rows, and Suburbs* (Baltimore: Johns Hopkins Univ. Press, 1994), 167–68.

54. For example, see "The Garage Has Become the Front Entrance," *House and Garden* 101 (Feb. 1952): 92–95.

55. For example, see "Your Garage: Asset or Afterthought?" *House and Garden* 98 (Dec. 1950): 134; "Six Ideas For Planning a Garage," *House and Garden* 108 (Nov. 1955): 252–53.

56. "How to Build Your Private Parking Space," *House and Garden* 115 (Mar. 1959): 87–91.

57. Chritopher Tunnard and Boris Pushkarev, *Man-Made America: Chaos or Control?* (New Haven: Yale Univ. Press, 1963), 110, 112.

58. For example, see advertisement, U.S.S. American Welded Wire Fabric, *American Builder* 74 (Nov. 1952): 181.

59. Gary Dayness, "Cars, Carports, and Suburban Values in Brookside, Delaware," *Material Culture* 29, no. 1 (1997): 1–11. For an editorial with the same thrust, see James Crockett, "The Great American Garage," *Landscape* 18: 3 (Fall 1969): 34–35.

60. "Remodel Your Garage to Gain an EXTRA ROOM," *House and Garden* 106 (Aug. 1954): 57.

61. "Garage into Entertainment Center," *House and Garden* 135 (May 1969): 122.

62. Deanne Raffel, "Unclutter the Garage," *House and Garden* 150 (June 1978): 62; Gerry Lofland, "Garage Shelf System," *Family Handyman* 42 (Feb. 1992): 80–81; "A Place for Everything—Even Boats!" *House and Garden* 150 (Apr. 1978): 154–55; "The Great Space Chase: Building a Garage Apartment," *Mechanix Illustrated*, Sept. 1980, 50–53; Constance N. Swenson, "Converting Your Garage into a Studio," *American Artist* 59 (Mar. 1995): 54.

63. Jackson, *Crabgrass Frontier*, 252; "Garages and Carports," *Changing Times* 18 (Feb. 1964): 13.

64. Hubbard H. Cobb, "Versatile Carport Converts to Summer Fun House," *American Home*, Apr. 1959, 41. For another example, see "A Well-Designed Carport Can Enhance Your House As Well As Shelter Your Car," *House and Garden* 121 (Mar. 1962): 234–35.

65. "Carport Plus," *Mechanix Illustrated* 68 (May 1972): 91–92.

66. Matthew S. Robinson, "Taj Mahal on a Cul de Sac: Concrete Blocks, Carports and Architectural Appropriation," *Arris: Journal of the Southeast Chapter of the Society of Architectural Historians* 11 (2000): 80.

67. Regarding men, see, for example, "Expanded Garage Houses Second Car and Boat," *Popular Mechanix* 112 (Sept. 1959): 180; "Success Formula for Do-It-Your-

selfers," *House and Garden* 120 (July 1961): 92; Thomas H. Jones, "Storm Windows for Your Garage," *Mechanix Illustrated* 78 (Jan. 1982): 92; and "Side Glances," *Road and Track* 42 (Dec. 1990): 24–26. Regarding women, see, for example, Swenson, "Converting Your Garage into a Studio," 54–56; Elizabeth Jager Thompson, "The Ultimate Garage," *Workbench* 52 (Aug.–Sept. 1996): 28–31; and Linda Hallam, "Garage to Gorgeous," *Southern Living,* Dec. 1996, 120–21.

68. "Carport Plus," 91.

69. "Have You Given up on the Garage, Men? *House and Garden* 113 (Apr. 1958): 105.

70. "How to Build Your Private Parking Space," *House and Garden* 115 (Mar. 1959): 132.

71. Anthony Downs, "Some Answers to the Parking Puzzle," *Journal of Property Management* 19 (Mar. 1954): 173–75, 179; Robert D. Katz, *Design of the Housing Site: A Critique of American practice* (n.p.: Small Homes Council–Building Research Council, Univ. of Illinois, 1966), 127. Regarding the tendency to shift parking to residences' back side, see, for example, Detroit City Plan Commission, "Rear Lot Parking: Neighborhood Conservation Information Bulletin" (Detroit Committee for Neighborhood Conservation and Improved Housing, n. d.).

72. "New Ordinance Prevents 'Asphalt Lawns,'" *American City* 79 (Jan. 1964): 98.

73. For example, see James Smiechen, *Raising the Roof: A History of the Buildings and Architecture in the Saugatuck and Douglas Area* (n.p.: Saugatuck-Douglas Historical Society, 1999), 130; and Marsh Davis, "Indiana Observed," *Indiana Preservationist,* May/June 1998, 21.

74. Timothy Eagan, "In Portland, Houses Are Friendly Or Else," *New York Times,* Apr. 20, 2000, B13.

75. Ibid., B12–B13.

76. Donald Appleyard, *Liveable Street* (Berkeley: Univ. of California Press, 1981); Walter Kulash, "The Third Motor Age," *Places* 10 (Winter 1996): 42–49; Mark C. Childs, *Parking Spaces: A Design, Implementation, and Use Manual for Architects, Planners, and Engineers* (New York: McGraw-Hill, 1999).

77. Childs, *Parking Spaces,* 78.

6. Garage Evolution

1. James J. Flink, *America Adopts the Automobile, 1895–1910* (Baltimore: Johns Hopkins Univ. Press, 1970), 223.

2. Kevin L. Borg, *Auto Mechanics: Technology and Expertise in Twentieth-Century America* (Baltimore: Johns Hopkins Univ. Press, 2007), 31–32.

3. Flink, *America Adopts the Automobile*, 226.

4. John A. Jakle and Keith A. Sculle, *Lots of Parking: Land Use in a Car Culture* (Charlottesville: Univ. of Virginia Press, 2004), 115.

5. Flink, *America Adopts the Automobile*, 226.

6. "The Chain Store Idea for Repair Shops," *American Blacksmith and Motor Shop* 23 (Feb. 1924): 19.

7. See, for example, "Winter Overhaul Chart," *American Garage and Auto Dealer* 24 (Dec. 1925): 20.

8. M. H. George, "Getting the Car Ready for Spring," *American Blacksmith*, Mar. 1919, 137, 141; "Overhauling Time Here," *Wisconsin Motorist* 9 (May 1918): 25–26.

9. "Winter Overhaul Chart," 20.

10. "Where Shall We Draw the Line on Free Service?" *Motor Age* 39 (Apr. 28, 1921): 7–9.

11. *Official Automobile Blue Book* (Chicago: Automobile Blue Books, 1923), 10–15.

12. Fred Mason, "Ali Baba and His Forty Thieves," *Illustrated World* 32 (Feb. 1920): 977.

13. B. M. Ikert, "Correct Diagnosis Big Factor in Making Maintenance Pay," *Motor Age* 42 (Nov. 16, 1922): 9.

14. "Before a Buick Dealer Can Put Up This Sign," *Buick Bulletin* 33 (Jan. 1923): 13.

15. J. C. Andrews, "And Now the Star-Durant Maintenance Service Plan," *American Garage and Auto Dealer* 24 (Apr. 1925): 16–17, 34.

16. "The Franklin Monthly," *Motor Age* 47 (Mar. 3, 1927): 14–15.

17. See Stephen L. McIntyre, "'The Repair Man Will Gyp You': Mechanics, Managers, and Customers in the Automobile Repair Industry, 1896–1940 (PhD diss., Univ. of Missouri, Columbia, 1995).

18. B. M. Ikert, "*Motor Age*'s Flat Rate Forum," *Motor Age* 48 (Oct. 1, 1925): 28.

19. "Service Station Groups Customers for Better Personal Contact," *Motor Age* 46 (Dec. 11, 1924): 16.

20. Ikert, "*Motor Age*'s Flat Rate Forum," 9.

21. "Ultra-Modern Service," *Automobile Dealer and Repairer* 36 (Feb. 1924): 18.

22. D. O. Blanchard, "Universal Flat Rate Plan Pays Mechanics on a Job Basis," *Motor World* 72 (Aug. 23, 1922): p.14.

23. "The Service Manager Speaks," *Motor Age* 40 (Aug. 18, 1921): 12.

24. R. C. Reper, "Flat Rates and a Service System Bring 'Em Back," *American Garage and Auto Dealer* 24 (Aug. 1925): 16.

25. Lowell R. Butcher, "How Service Built the Business," *American Garage and Auto Dealer* 23 (July 1924): 19.

26. McIntyre, "Repair Man"; Steven L. McIntyre, "The Failure of Fordism: The Reform of the Automobile Repair Industry, 1913–1940," *Technology and Culture* 41 (Apr. 2000): 269–99; Borg, *Auto Mechanics*.

27. Douglas Harper, *Working Knowledge: Skill and Community in a Small Shop* (Chicago: Univ. of Chicago Press, 1987), 111.

28. Borg, *Auto Mechanics*, 111–13.

29. Harper, *Working Knowledge*, 111.

30. McIntyre, "Repair Man," 173.

31. *Fifteenth Census of the United States: 1930 Population*, vol. 5, *General Report on Occupations* (Washington, DC: United States Printing Office, 1933), 126.

32. Mrs. Matilda Black, "Maintenance Woman," *Motor Age* 32 (Sept. 1936): 41.

33. E. L. Barringer, "One Stop Service? Yes, if You Have the Personnel, and Right Market," *National Petroleum News* 24 (Jan. 13, 1932): 37.

34. "Auto Laundries for the Gasoline Stations: What the Middle West Is Doing with This Service to Motorists," *National Petroleum News* 19 (Dec. 28, 1927): 25.

35. McIntyre, "Repair Man," 258.

36. "Teaching by Example," *Automobile Topics* 135 (Sept. 18, 1939): 244.

37. "Fire Destroys Lancaster, O. Garage," *Horseless Age* 35 (Jan. 6, 1915): 6.

38. Fred E. Kunkel, "Sperry Goes Over the Top," *Accessory and Garage Journal* 19 (Nov. 1929): 10.

39. See John A. Jakle and Keith A. Sculle, *The Gas Station in America* (Baltimore: Johns Hopkins Univ. Press, 1994), 36–47.

40. "First Lubritorium Station Built by L. V. Nicholas," *National Petroleum News* 28 (Mar. 4, 1936): 50.

41. "New Lubrication Station Presents Unique Appearance," *Hoosier Motorist* 11 (Feb. 1923): 25.

42. Ward K. Halbert, "Standard of Indiana Is Experimenting in Chassis Lubrication," *National Petroleum News* 29 (July 18, 1928): 21

43. E. L. Barringer, "Oil Men Warned of Competition from Automobile Dealer," *National Petroleum News* 23 (Mar. 18, 1921): 33.

44. Terence McCabe and William Wolfe, "Digest of Modern Equipment and Tools," *Chilton's Motor Age* 79 (Dec. 1959): 37.

45. Abner Doble, "Steam Cars, Past and Present," *The Automobile* 35 (Nov. 2, 1919): 272.

46. Fred B. Schaeffer, "Chicago's Latest Exclusively Electric Garage," *Electric Vehicles* 7 (Nov. 1915): 163.

47. F. E. McCall, "A Study of Electric Vehicle Garaging," *Electric Vehicles*, Vol.6 (Jan. 1915): 9.

48. "Exide's 50 Years of Growth," *Motor Age* 57 (June 1938): 639.

49. "Auto-Lite Doubles Factory Facilities," *The Automobile* 32 (Apr. 8, 1915): 639.

50. Donald D. Blanchard, "Modern Methods of Storage Battery Service," *Motor World* 63 (June 22, 1920): 24.

51. "Eight-Hour Battery Charge Possible," *Hoosier Motorist* 11 (Feb. 1923): 22.

52. "How the Elite Garage Cuts Down Its Rent," *Accessories and Garage Journal* 18 (Aug. 1, 1928): 31.

53. Jack Montgomery, "Everybody Benefits from Preventive Maintenance," *Chilton's Motor Age* 73 (Sept. 1954): 43.

54. R. C. McWane, "The How, Why, and Wherefore of Engine Reconditioning," *American Garage and Auto Dealer* 24 (July 1925): 30.

55. "The Automobile's Foot-Wear," *The Automobile* 24 (Jan. 26, 1911): 331.

56. "Profits in Replacement Spring Service," *American Garage and Auto Dealer* 23 (June 1924): 25.

57. "There's Profit in Brake Service," *Motor Age* 59 (Jan. 1940): 14.

58. Advertisement for the Briskin Manufacturing Company, *Hoosier Motorist* 9 (Jan. 1921): inside front cover.

59. C. T. Schaefer, "Taking the Dents Out," *American Garage and Auto Dealer* 24 (Jan. 1925): 20

60. Earle Eldridge, "Some Dealerships Shutting down Auto Body Shops," *USA Today*, Oct. 11, 2004, 7B.

61. J. M. Shearer, "Raising Tide of Profits by Using Water," *Automobile Trade Journal* 33 (Sept. 1, 1928): 32.

62. Ibid., 34.

63. Frank L. Drinkwater, " A Car Wash in 25 Minutes," *Automobile Trade Journal* 33 (July 1, 1928): 37–38.

64. "Cars are Washed in 12 Minutes," *Motor Age* 47 (June 11, 1925): 13.

65. Donald H. Blanchard, "Storekeeper—Or Main Street Merchant?" *Motor World* 75 (May 9, 1923): 9.

66. See Leon F. Banigan, "Voluntary Chain!" *Motor World Wholesale* 96 (June 1932): 11.

67. "Selling Ford Accessories," *Automobile Dealer and Repairer* 31 (May 1921): 31.

68. "Motor Service," *Business Week*, May 24, 1933, 10.

69. "45 Percent of Car Dealers Handle Automotive Supplies," *Automobile Industries* 49 (Sept. 20, 1923): 58.

70. See "Put an Accessory Store in Your Garage," *Motor World* 68 (Aug. 17, 1921): 27.

71. "Minor Mention," *Horseless Age* 6 (Jan. 1901): 24.

72. "Trade Buying Habits Create Necessity for Distributorships in 'Main Street,'" *Automotive Industries* 57 (July 30, 1927): 156–60.

73. David Beecroft, "Study of Trade Buying Habits in Seven Ohio Counties," *Automotive Industries* 57 (July 23, 1927): 123.

74. "Jobbers and the Jobbing Trade," *Horseless Age* 38 (Oct. 1, 1916): 229.

75. "Gigantic Jobber Covers Middle West Area," *Motor Age* 64 (Nov. 1945): 30–31, 75.

76. Anthony J. Yanik, "Alfred Owen Dunk: Owner of Almost 800 Automobile Companies" *Chronicle* 26 (Jan. 1997): 9.

7. A Landscape Legacy?

1. "Paving the Road to Service Profits," *Motor Age* 39 (Apr. 7, 1921): 13.

2. J. Howard Pile, "How to Make Service an Asset to Your Business," *Motor World*, Summer Merchandising World, Apr. 27, 1921, 54; "Does Money Talk?" *Motor Age* 24 (June 19, 1919): 7–9. Regarding the flat rate, see chap. 6, p. 145–147, 189, and

194. 3. H. R. Dorman, "What Does It Cost to Do Business?" *American Garage and Auto Dealer* 23 (Nov. 19, 1924): 24; Fred A. Oberheu, "The Truth About Your Shop Labor Cost," *Automobile Dealer and Repairer* 37 (Apr. 1924): 18; Joseph E. Mills, *Garage Management and Control* (Chicago: A. W. Shaw Co., 1928): 86–87.

4. Mills, *Garage Management and Control*, 79; Stephen L. McIntyre, "'The Repair Man Will Gyp You': Mechanics, Managers, and Customers in the Automobile Repair Industry, 1896–1940" (PhD diss., Univ. of Missouri, Columbia, 1995), 145–47.

5. George H. Jones, "How to Pay Your People," *Chilton's Motor Age* 70 (Apr. 1951): 38–39, 94, 96–100.

6. Kenneth M. Thompson, "Democratic Profit Sharing Works," *Chilton's Motor Age* 70 (Mar. 1951): 120; "Employee Policy Pays Off," *Chilton's Motor Age* 71 (Aug. 1952): 59; "Mechanics' Earnings Studied in 21 Areas," *Chilton's Motor Age* 73 (Jan. 1954): 82–83, 106.

7. McIntyre, "Repair Man," 139–40, 182, 197, 225–27, 310; Kevin L. Borg, *Auto Mechanics: Technology and Expertise in Twentieth-Century America* (Baltimore: Johns Hopkins Univ. Press, 2007): 105–6.

8. "Activities of the New York Garage Association" *Horseless Age* 31 (May 7, 1913): 843–44.

9. "Garage and Salesroom: The Illinois Garage Association," *Horseless Age* 24 (Nov. 10, 1909): 545; "Philadelphia Garage Owners Organize," *Horseless Age* 24: 12 (Sept. 22, 1909): 326.

10. "Dealers Now Organized," *Motor Age* 32: 3 (July 19, 1917): 24; "Dealers Now Have A National Body," *Automobile Topics* 46 (July 14, 1917): 1127; Robert Genat, *The American Car Dealership* (Osceola, WI: MBI Publishing Co., 1999), 25; Borg, *Auto Mechanics*, 143–44; "Dealer Gatherings To Be Big," *Automobile Topics* 49 (Jan. 11, 1919), 981; "38 Highway Bodies Form A Federation," *Automobile Topics* 49 (Jan. 25, 1919): 1203.

11. Ralph James, "Progress Report on IGO of America," *Chiton's Motor Age* 75 (Jan. 1956): 42–43.

12. "Dealers May Be Without Cars," *Automobile* 36 (Feb. 22, 1927): 399; "Quartermaster To Buy 5000 Class A Trucks," *Automotive Industries* 38 (Jan. 24, 1918): 207; "Passenger Car Market Practically Drained at End of 1918," *Automotive Industries* 40 (Jan. 30, 1919): 270; "Ford Releases 25,000 Cars," *Automotive Industries* 39 (Nov. 21, 1918): 893.

13. John B. Rae, *The American Automobile: A Brief History* (Chicago: Univ. of Chicago Press, 1965), 109, 114–15; James J. Flink, *The Automobile Age* (Cambridge, MA.: MIT Press, 1988), 189–93, 212–20; Genat, *The American Car Dealership*, 9;

John A. Heitmann, *The Automobile and American Life* (Jefferson, NC: McFarland and Company, 2009), 102.

14. "War Influence in Industries," *Automotive Industries* 37 (Dec. 27, 1917): 1125–26.

15. Harry L. Spooner, "Wartime Super Service," *Motor Age* 63 (Dec. 1943): 23, 50.

16. "Dealers Convert," *Business Week* (Oct. 17, 1942), 58, 60. Also, see "A Car Dealer In Arms Production," *Motor Age* 62 (Dec. 1942): 26–27, 64.

17. "Dealers Survive," *Business Week*, Apr. 24, 1943, 88, 90.

18. Bill Toboldt, "Victory Demands Automobiles," *Motor Age* 61 (Feb. 1942): 19, 70–71.

19. "Small Shops May Raise Wages and Prices," *Motor Age* 62 (Mar. 1943): 18.

20. "Car Dealers Weep," *Business Week*, Jan. 24, 1942, 14–15.

21. Borg, *Auto Mechanics*, 116. See also "Repair Shops Lose 112,000 Mechanics," *Motor Age* 62 (Feb. 1943): 18–19.

22. "Girl Mechanics Make Good," *Motor Age* 62 (Feb. 1943): 26–27.

23. Rose Lu Goldman," Women and Victory," *Motor Age* 61 (Feb. 1942): 34, 49.

24. "Woman Dealer Carries On," *Motor Age* 64 (Sept. 1944): 30–31, 60.

25. Victor Pope, "A Dealer Who Met and Licked the Problem of Declining Profits," *Automobile Topics* 101 (Feb. 21, 1931): 180, 184; "Dealers' Code Works—So Far," *Business Week*, Apr. 29, 1934, 18–20.

26. David E. Castles, "Post-War Dealer Picture," *Motor Age* 63 (June 1944): 20–21, 82.

27. "Car Dealers Ready," *Business Week*, Apr. 21, 1945, 19.

28. Ibid., 20.

29. Ibid.

30. "Competition for Vast Post-War Market to be Keen," *Motor Age* 63 (July 1944): 20.

31. "Number of Mechanics Increasing," *Motor Age* 65 (Dec. 1945): 20–21, 46, 50.

32. "Great Day for the Dealer," *Fortune*, Nov. 1950, 90–92, 171–72, 174.

33. Ibid., 171.

34. "From 425 to $60,000 in Three Years," *American Garage & Auto Dealer* 11 (Mar. 1920): 11–13, 50, 52.

35. "Success Story of a Country Garage," *Automobile Topics* 38 (Aug. 7, 1915): 1105–6.

36. Ibid., 1106.

37. "Seven Brothers Success," *Horseless Age* 40 (May 15, 1917): 22–24.

38. Bill Balkema, telephone interview with Keith A. Sculle, Nov. 21, 1999.

39. Keith A. Sculle, "He Kept 'Em Up & Running," *Historic Illinois* 23: 1 (June 2000): 8–10. For other examples of garages in small-town Illinois, see Sculle, "Just a Garage," *Historic Illinois* 1 (Dec. 1978): 9; Sculle, *Timepiece* 22 (Dec. 1999): 2; and Sculle, "Making a Place: The Country Corners at Withrow's Garage in Sherman," *Historic Illinois* 24 (Oct. 2001): 12–14; Sculle, "Highway Heritage: The Hookers and Sidell's Longest Lived Automotive Services," *Illinois Heritage* 12 (January–February 2009): 27–28.

40. William A. Moffett, "Henry T. Ewald[,] Automobile Dealer," *Automobile Topics* 103 (Aug. 15, 1931): 96, 98.

41. James M. Rubenstein, *Making and Selling Cars: Innovation an Change in the U.S. Automotive Industry* (Baltimore: Johns Hopkins Univ. Press, 2001), 283; Mark Lacter, "Big Lots," *Los Angeles Magazine* 54 (Aug. 2009): 82–86; John A. Jakle and Keith A. Sculle, *Motoring: The Highway Experience in America* (Athens: Univ. of Georgia Press, 2008), 93; Jonathan Fahey, "Used Cars, New Software," *Forbes*, Mar. 27, 2006, 98, 100.

42. Bond Mejeh, "Car Dealerships Closing," *Ezine9.com* website, Jan. 10, 2010, http://vehicle.ezine9.com/car-dealerships-closing-14724ec1e6.html (accessed Dec. 13, 2012).

43. Lacter, "Big Lots."

44. Keith Schneider, "Last Year's Auto Dealership May Be This Year's Grocery," *New York Times*, June 30, 2010, B6.

45. Ibid.

46. Ronald E. Schmitt, "The Ubiquitous Parking Garage: Worthy of Preservation?" in Deborah Slaton and William G. Foulks, eds. *Preserving the Recent Past* (Washington, DC: Historic Preservation Education Foundation, National Park Service, Association for Preservation Technology, 2000), 2-193. It should be noted that parking garages, because of their prime locations, can be especially vulnerable to redevelopment; such was the case of New York City's Tunnel Garage, which was razed in 2006 for a residential building. See "End of the Tunnel Garage," *Forgotten New York* website, Mar. 26, 2006, http://forgotten-ny.com/2006/03/end-of-the-tunnel-garage (accessed Nov. 14, 2012).

For an example of an automobile dealership deserving historic preservation statues, see Amy Bennett, "Griffin Auto Company Building, El Dorado, Arkansas," sec. 8, p. 1, National Register of Historic Places nomination, signed by Arkansas SHPO, Apr. 4, 2001).

47. John A. Jakle and Keith A. Sculle, *Remembering Roadside America: Preserving the Recent Past as Landscape and Place* (Knoxville: Univ. of Tennessee Press, 2011).

48. See especially John A. Jakle, "Landscapes Redesigned for the Automobile," in Michael Conzen, ed., *The Making of the American Landscape* (Boston: Unwin Hyman, 1990), 293–310; John A. Jakle and Keith A. Sculle, *Lots of Parking: Land Use in a Car Culture* (Charlottesville: Univ. of Virginia Press, 2004); Jakle and Sculle, *Signs in America's Auto Age: Signatures of Landscape and Place* (Iowa City: Univ. of Iowa Press, 2004), Jakle and Sculle, *Motoring: The Highway Experience in America* (Athens: Univ. of Georgia Press, 2008); and Keith A. Sculle, "Anchor Travel Village and Branson's Evolving Tourist Accommodations," *Missouri Historical Review* 105 (Oct. 2010): 1–13.

49. For example, see Richard B. Carson, *The Olympian Cars: The Great American Luxury Automobiles of the Twenties and Thirties* (New York: Knopf, 1976); Helen Frye, "The Automobile and American Fashion, 1900–1930," in David L. Lewis and Laurence Goldstein, eds., *The Automobile and American Culture* (Ann Arbor: Univ. of Michigan Press, 1980), 48–58; Karla Ann Marling, *As Seen on TV: The Visual Culture of Everyday Life in the 1950s* (Cambridge: Harvard Univ. Press, 1994), 136–38; and Susan Sessions Rugh, *Are We There Yet? The Golden Age of American Family Vacations* (Lawrence: Univ. of Kansas Press, 2008).

50. Kaisa Barthuli, program manager, Route 66 Corridor Preservation Program, emails to Keith A. Sculle, Aug. 17 and 18, 2011.

Epilogue

1. Pete Wagoner, email exchange with Keith A. Sculle, Mar. 8, 2012.

2. Lee Appleton, *This Was Camden: A History of Camden, Indiana* (Bloomington, IL: Heartland Printing, 2007), 84.

3. Wagoner, email exchange with Sculle, Mar. 8, 2012.

4. Ibid.

5. Ibid.

6. Ibid.

7. Gary Robey, email exchange with Keith A. Sculle, Mar. 16, 2012.

8. Information on file at Tennessee State Historic Preservation Office, Nashville, and at the Robertson County, Tennessee, Archives, Springfield.

9. Molly Myers Naumann, "Courthouse Square Historic District," National Register of Historic Places Nomination Form, Amended May 2003, sec. 8, p. 34.

10. Ibid., section 7, p.19.

11. *Centerville Daily Iowegian*, Oct. 3l, 1919, 1.

12. *Centerville Daily Iowegian*, Nov. 3, 1919, 1, and Nov. 4, 1919, 6.

13. John Linn Hopkins, "Collierville Historic District, National Register of Historic Places Nomination Form," Nov. 1989, sec. 8, p. 5.

14. Ibid., sec. 8, p. 6.

15. McGinnis Oil Company website, http://www.mcginnisoilcompany.com (accessed Feb. 24, 2012).

16. Bill Cox, telephone interview with Keith A. Sculle, Feb. 25, 2012.

17. Thomas L. Knous, telephone interview with Keith A. Sculle, Feb. 4, 2012.

18. Ibid.

INDEX

Pages numbered in **boldface** refer to topically-relevant illustrations.

Aamco, 151
Akron, OH, 199
Alexandria, NY: Thomson & Britton Garage, 49
Allied Independent Dealers (AID), 179
Alva, OK: Bill's Auto Supply, 202
American Automobile Club, 142
American Automobile Assoc., 95
American Motor Car Manufacturers Assoc., 21
American Society of Planning Officials: Clearing House, 130
Appleyard, Donald, 138
architectural engineering, 28, 40
architectural styling, xii, 26–29, 32, 40, 50, 56, 64–66, **67**, 69, 106–7, 114, 118, 123; in International Style, 65, 67; in Prairie Style, 127; in Streamline Modern Style, 53, 66
Associated Highways of America, 195
Astoria, OR, 114
Atlanta, GA, 78
Auburn Automobile Co. 70
automobile accessories and parts, xi–xii, 7, 21, 34, 41, 51, 55–56, 58, 60, 62, 64, 89, 104, 149, 178–86, **182**, 183; standardization of, 40, 142, 145, 148
Automobile Club of America, 93
automobile clubs, 3, 13, 15, 93, 95; garages operated by, 3, 13
Automobile Dealer's Assoc. of New York, 109
Automobile Dealer's Franchise Act of 1956, 89
automobile dealerships, xi–xii, xvi, 6–7, 10, **12**, **23**, 25–26, 38, 48–50, 64, 68–75, 77–115, 145, 178, 190–91, 195–96, 198–206, 210; layout of, 26–27, 30, 34, **35**, **36**, 37–39, **42**, **44**, 63, **71**, 82–83; location of, 70–71, **72**, **73**, 85; number of in U.S., 7–9, 14, 68, 200, 205; ownership of, 83–85, 95, 105, 148–49, 198–99; auto repair floors in, 25–26, 28, 32, 34, 38–39, 50, 69, **71**, 83, 90–92, 144–47, 186–87, 201; auto sales floors in, 26, 29–30, **31**, 34–41, 60–69, 74, 77, 81–82, 105–8, 186; show windows on, 26, 29, 50, **68**, 70, 72, 74, 95, 105–9, **108**, 115; stock rooms in, 34–35, 42, 50–51, 201;
automobile factories: assembly lines in, 40–41; factory floor organization in, 40, 147
Automobile Information Disclosure Act of 1958, 89
automobile manufacturers, xvi, 7, 14–15, 22, 69, 78–80, 82, 85–86, 114, 142–45, 148, 186; dealer networks of, xvi, 26, 80, 83, 86–88; factory branches of, xvi, 14, 29, **30**, 45, 48–49, 69, 77, 80–81, **82**, 83, **84**, 86; autos sold annually by, 87; number of workers employed by, 9
automobile mechanics, xi, 10–11, 16, 21, 37, 39, 51, 86, 142–44, 147–49, 191–94; trade schools for, 98–99, 109, 142, 144–49, 203

automobile name-plates (brands), 3, 48, 69, 78, 136; customer loyalty to, 149

automobile-related industries: numbers employed in, 7, 9

Automobile Rotary Lift Co., **158**

automobile rows, xvi, 69, 105, 114: at Champaign, IL, 45; at Chicago, IL, 48–49; **106**; at Cleveland, OH 47; at Indianapolis, IN,47; at Kansas City, MO, 48–49; at New York City, NY, 48–49; at Omaha, NE,48

automobiles, xiv–xvi, 1–2, **13**, **16**, **27**, **29**, **33**, 40–41, **45**, 64, **70**,73–74, 93, 100,**106**, **108**, **111**, **113**, 121, 132–33, **158**, **166**, **169**, **174**, **177**, **179**; ownership of, xv, xvii, 43, **6**, 9, 49, 93, 114, 143–45, 159, 181, 196; repair and maintenance of, xi, xiii–xvi, 1–3, 5, 10–11, 17–19, 21, 24–26, 33, 51, 54–55, 58, 63–64, 98, 141–51, 154–78, 189; sale of, xi, xiii, xvi, 3–5, 7, 9–11, 13–14, 21, 24, 26, 35, 37–40, 49, 55, 72–115, 189; storage of, xi, xvi, 5, 10–15, 26, 38, 49, 51, 55, 68–69, 72–73, 79, 118–19

automobile sales, 79–96, 141, 145, 186, 189, 199–200, 205–6; by mail order, 81, 86; on commission, 97–98, 100; with installment buying, 93, 95; through distributors and sub-dealers, 80–88; with rebates and discounts, 87, 89; with trade-in allowances, 90, 109–10, with warranties, 143–45

automobile shows: at Atlanta, GA, 78; at Chicago, IL, 78; at Detroit, MI, **78**; at New York City, NY, 21, 49, 79–79; at Seattle, WA, 79; at Terre Haute, IN, 78

automobile supply stores, 1, 7–9, 38, 41, 49, 64, 178–79, **180**, **181**, 182–84, **185**, 186, 201

automobility, xv, 1, **2**, 4, 12, 100, 121, 131, 139, 145, 196, 198–99, 208–10, 221

axle repair, 3, 173

Babcock Electric Carriage Co., 26

Baltimore, MD: Zell Motor Car Co., 28

Batcheller, H.H., 98–99

Baton Rouge, La: Capitol City Auto Co., 112

Balkema, William, 202–3

Battery charging, repair, and sales, xvi, 1, 8–12, 16, 26, 38, 55, 60–75, 150, 158–59, **161**, **162**, **163**, **164**, 165, 186, 201–2

Bear Manufacturing Co., 172, **173**

Beaver Falls, PA: Sahli Motors, Inc., **75**

Bel Geddes, Norman, 66

Bendix Stromberg Carburetor Co., **166**

B.F. Goodrich Co, 151, 202

bicycles and bicycle shops, xvi, 3, 10–11, 21–23, 80, 84–85

bicycle mechanics, 22

Black, Matilda, 148–49

blacksmiths and blacksmith shops, xvi, 3–4, 10,17, **18**, **19**, 20, 24–25, 44, 54, 174, **187**, 189

Blanchard, Donald, 179

Bloomfield Hills, MI, 205

Bloomington, IL: C.U. Williams & Sons Garage, 191

body, paint, and fabric shops, xvi, 10, 21, 35, 84, 174–76, 187; number of in U.S, 9–10

Boozer-Test Management Service, 185

Borg, Kevin L., 147–48

Boston, Ma, 124, 141, 180

Bowen Products Co., 156

Bradfordton, IL: John H. Teufel Horse Shoeing, **19**

Brakes and brake repair, 10, 169, 193

Brookline, Ma: L.A. Morgan Dodge, 200–201

Brookston, IN, 202–3

Bridgman, M.L., 84

Briskin Manufacturing Co., 174

Brookside, DE, 133

Buehl, C. L., 65

Buffalo, NY, 3, 55–56, 125; garage locations in, 46, **47**

building materials in commercial garages, 27, 31–32, 41, 53, 65–69; brick masonry and brick veneer, xiii, 21, 28, 30, 50; cinder block and cement block, xiii, 63; clay tile and glass tile, 28,30, **67**, 68; metal (including frames), xiii, 29; plate glass and window casement, **xiv**, 30, 40, **60**, 107; concrete (including reinforced concrete), 28–29, 50; stone masonry and

INDEX

stone veneer, 28; terra cotta, 28, 30; wood (including frames), xiii, 50
building materials in domestic garages: brick, 129; cinder block and cement block, 121; clay tile, **128**,121; concrete, 123, 127; wood frame, 127
Burroughs, E. A., 98

Camden, IN: Wyatt Auto Co., xii, **xiii**, 214–16
Carbo Steel Co., 90–91
"car kits," 11, 90, **91**
CarMax, Inc., 203–6
car washing and car washes, 35, 58, 60, 63, 66, 82, **177**, 178, **179**, 187
carports, 135, **136**
carriage and wagon shops, xvi, 3–4, 10, 20–21, 24–25, 44, 186, 189
Castles, David E., 199
Cedar Rapids, IA, 152
Centerville, IA: Fisher Garage, 217, **218**
central business districts, xi, xiv, 1, 5, 11, **14**, 23, 25, 27, 44–45, 53, 60, 68–69, 72, 105, 137
Chalmers Motor Car Co., xii, 13, 96
Champaign, IL, 45
Champion, Albert, 180
Champion Ignition Co., 180
Champion Spark Plug Co., 180, **181**
Chapin, Roy, 81
chauffeurs, xvi, 1, 11, 82, 112–13, 120, 177, 186
Chicago, IL, 48–49, 78, 93–94, 98, 106, 119, 130, 137, 145, 159, **162**, 195–96; A-B-C Auto Radiator Works, **175**; Cunningham Car Wash, 178; Tudor Garage, 13
Chicago Automobile Trade Assoc., 85
Chicago Heights, IL, 90–91
Chrysler Corp., 66, **69**, 100, 151, 196, 198; Dodge Division, **70**, 110, 112; De Soto Division, 198–99; Jeep Division, 220; Plymouth Division, 198–99
Chrysler, Walter, 66
Childs, Mark, 138
Cincinnati, OH, 98, 103–4, 112
Clarinda, IA, 146

Clarke, Sally H., 233n30
Cleveland, OH, 47, 81, 85, 178, 184, 203; Euclid Square Garage, 11, **14**; Ohio Buick Co., 146; Willis-Overland Agency, 84; Moyer Car Wash, 178
Collierville, TN: McGinnis Oil Co., 218, **219**, 220
Columbus, OH, 184: Early Motor Car Co., 26
commercial garages, xi–xvi, 1, 3–6, 10–11, 23, 25–31, 61–67, 73–74, 84, 112–13, 141–87, 189–90, 198–99; car maintenance and repair in, xii, xv, 7, 10–11, 17, **19**, 21, 24, 32–33, 37, **38**, 41, 63–65, 141–51; geographical distribution in U.S.,6–8; layout of, xii–xiv, 5, 24, 51, 61–64, 69, 187; in buildings converted from other uses, xvi, 25–27, 44–45, location and siting of, xvi, 1,25, 27, 29, 34–36, 44–49, **50**, 51, 53–54, 63, 69, **72**, **73**, 207; management of, xviii, 13, 38, 41, 51, 145–48,189–94; multiple-story, **14**, **23**,27, **28**, 29–30, **42**, 51, 82, **132**, ,145–46, 201, **206**, **207**, **208**; number in U.S. 6–10, 150; single-story, **xiii**, **xvi**, 13, **16**, 31–33, **34**, **35**, **36**, **39**, **49**, **63**, **67**, **68**, **70**, **71**,201; workers employed in, 7, 148
commercial intrusions into residential neighborhoods, 46, **47**,48, 54, 56
Commercial Investment Trust Corp. (CIT), 94
Commonwealth Edison Co., 159, **162**
corner lots, 47, 49, **50**, 61, 63, 72, **73**, 74
Corpus Christi, TX: George H. Jones Ford, 192–93
Cox, William and James, 219
"curb appeal," 43, **44**, **45**, **46**, 56
Curtis Publishing Co., 80

Daimler-Benz AG, 78
Dallas, TX, 111
Davis, Donald Finlay, 80
Dayton Engineering Laboratory (Delco), 182
Dayton, OH, 184: Buick Building, 82
Denver, Co: Gray Automobile Co., **22**
department stores, 60–61
Detroit Electric Car Co., 159

Detroit, MI, 22, 54, **55**, **78**, 80, 91, 102, 112, 145, 185–86, 204; Grand Circus Garage, 13; Mack-Gratiot Chevrolet, **113**, 203
DeVilbiss Co., 175
Dicke, Thomas, 88
Dodge Brothers Co., 86, 110
Dodge, John and Horace, 22
domestic garages, xi, xvi, 5–6, 12, 112–139, 189–90; attached to houses, **124**, 125–26, **133**, **134**; battery rechargers in, **122**; converted stables as, 118–19, **124**, 125; driveways for, 127; for apartment dwellers, 129, **130**, **131**, **134**; freestanding, **120**, **121**, 125–26, **128**; plan books for, 119, **120**, **121**, remodeling of, 134; turntables in, 122
Durant Motors, Inc., 85, 145

Economic Depression of the 1930s, 53, 64, 69, 88, 114, 181, 196, 199, 203–4, 210; "New Deal" programs during, 53, 66
Electric Auto-Lite Co., 162, 186
electric automobiles, 12, 17, 26, 101, **122**, 159–62, **163**, 164; ownership of, 159; recharging stations for, 7–8, 11, 21, 159–60, **161**, **163**
Electric Storage Battery Co. (Excide), 162, **163**, 186
Elgin, IL, 81
Elgin Motor Car Co., 81
Ellis, A. Raymond, 119
Emmittsburg, MD, 154
Equal Credit Opportunity Act of 1974, 100
Erskine, A. R., 93
Evanston, IL, **60**, **62**
Ewald, Henry T., 203–4

Fairfield, CT, 135
fast food restaurants, xi, xv, 13; in gasoline stations, 60
Finley-Wheeler, Inc., 125
finance companies, 92–93, **94**, 115
financing: of dealer auto purchases, 80, 82–87; of customer auto purchases, 86–87, 93–95, 115

fire hazards and fire codes, 11, 35, 127, 151–52
Firestone Tire & Rubber Co., 55, 61, 151, 167
Fisk Rubber Co., 168–69, **171**
Flat-rate repair charges, 145–147, 189, 194
Flink, James, 89–90, 141–42
Flint, MI, 144
"Fordism," 40–41, 66
Ford, Henry, 22, 40, 87–88, 233n30
Ford Motor Co., 13, 27, 40–41, 70, 87, 90–91, 93–94, 99, 113, 146, 150–51, 157, 163, **183**, 192–93, 196, 203, 206; branch factories, 80–81; dealer network, 87–89; Model A, 107, 182; Model T, 40, 64, 80, 96, 181; River Rouge Plant, 87
Fort Worth, TX, 105
Foster, Charles Evans, 40
franchising, 13, 26, 33, 85, 87–89, 151, 166, 168, 181–82, 198; territorial rights in, 26, 80–81, 85
Franklin Automobile Co., 21, 26, 145
"front and back regions," 29–30, 37–39, 42, 50–51, 121, 145

garage preservation and adaptive reuse, iv, xii, **xiii**, xviii, **xv**, xvii–xviii, 67–69, 205–6, 206, **207**, 208–11, 213–17, **218**, **219**, 220–23, 252n46
garages: as distinctive places, xii, xvii, 5, 24, 35, 43–45, 49, 213–14, 223; defined, xi, 7, 24, 77; origin of word, xi, 10; *See* commercial garages and domestic garages
Garage Owner's Association (New York), 194
garage (exterior) signage, **13**, **15**, **18**, 24, **26**, **28**, **29**, **33**, **34**, 43, **44**, **45**, **46**,**49**, 56, **58**, 65–67, **70**, **73**, **163**, **164**, **165**, **166**, **206**, **221**
garage trade associations, 194–96
Gartman, David, 40
gasoline retailing at garages, xi–xv, 4, 7, 9, 11–13, 15, 18, 26, 34, 35, 54–66, 72, 151, **152**, 153–54, 198, 211
gasoline pumps, 18, 34, **46**, 63, 65, 151–52, **153**
gasoline stations, xi–xii, 1, 9, 15, 43, 45, 47, 53, **55**, 56, **57**, 64–65, **66**, 67, **153**, 154, 178, 189,

208, 210; number of in U.S., 9; as "super service stations," 58, **59**, 60, **61**
Gelber, Steven, 101
gender issue: men, 138; demonstrating mechanical skill as, 119–20
gender issues: women, 138: as business owners, 105, 148–49, 198–99; as customers, **37**, **38**, 60, 66, 12, 100–102, **103**; as employees, 103–5,147, 198–99; as motorists, 102, 120, **122**; through impacting car styling, 101–2
General Electric Co., **122**
General Motors Corp., 14, 66, **68**, **72**, **73**, 87–88, 92–93, 103, 115, 144, 151, 157–58, 162, 180, 196, 206, 218; Buick Division, 87–88; Cadillac Division, 84; Chevrolet Division, **75**, 88, 110–12, 186, 198; GMC Division, 89; Oakland and Pontiac Division, 72, 146, **160**, 204–5, Oldsmobile Division, 193
glass repair, 10, 176
Glendale Co.: Glendale Auto Laundry, 178
Good Roads Movement, 22, 85, 195
Goodyear Tire & Rubber Co., 61, 82,151, 167, 169, 180
Graham-Paige Motors Corp., 70
Grant Motor Co., 81
Guarantee Liquid Measure Co., 153
Gulf Oil Co., **55**, 151, 154
Guthrie, V.B., 56

Harlan, IA: Hulsebus Motor Co., 200
Harper, Douglas, 147–48
Harrison Radiator Corp., 182
Hartford, CT, 118
Harvey Spring Co., 172, **174**
Hawkins, Norval, 87
heating and ventilation in garages, 41
Henry's Cars of Yesteryear, **208**
Highland Park, MI, 137
Hoosier Motor Club, 13, **15**
Hopkins, John Lewis, 218–19
horsedrawn transport, 1, 3–5, 8, 10, 15–19, 44–45, 54, 121, 143

hotels, 45, 48
Houston, TX, 134
Huddle, L. E., 151
Hudson Motor Car Co., 60, 70, 81
Hupp Motor Car Co., 70, 93
Hyatt Roller Bearing Co., 182
Hyde, J. Grant, 199

Illinois Garage Assoc., 195
Independent Garage Owners of America, 195–96
Indianapolis, IN, 13, 47, 156, **159**, 174, 185; American National Bank, 92; Grant Motor Co., 84
Iowa City, IA, 193
Ithaca, NY, 124

Jacobs, Jane, 138
Jenkins, Madella, 198–99
Jenny Manufacturing Co., **56**
Jewell, Eva, 104
Jones, Dean, 193
Jones, George H., 192–93

Kansas City, MO, 7, 47–49, 164, 185; Willys-Overland Garage, 29, **30**
Kingsbury, IN, 203
Klaxon Company, 182
Knox, John B., 118
Knous, Thomas, 220, 223
Kokomo, IN: Jenkins De Soto-Plymouth, 198–99
Kramer, Stephen, 91
Kulash, Walter, 138

labor/management relations in the garage industry, xi, xvii, 38–39, 147, 191, **192**, 193–94; profit sharing in, 193
Lancaster, OH, 151

landscape as built environment, 189, 211, 213–14, 221–22; preservation of, 189, 213–14
landscaping, 127–28, 132
Larned, KS, **16**
Lansing, MI, **160**
League of American Wheelmen, 3, 22, 38
Lee, Don, 84
Liebs, Cheser, 167
lighting in garages, 41, **42**
Lincoln, NE, 86
livery stables, xvi, 10, 13–17, 25, 44, 54, 121
Loewy, Raymond, 66
Long Beach, CA, earthquake of 1933, **33**
Los Angeles, CA, 32–33, 58, 65, 84, 107, 13l: Manchester & Alameda Garage, **53**
Louisville, Ky, 111: Cooke Pontiac Co., **111**; Leyman Motor Co., 107, **108**; O.K. Motors, 146
lubrication, xii, 7–8, 13, 35, 38, 56, 58, 60, 66, 82, 141, 154, **155, 156, 157, 158**, 160, 164–65,198, 211; by "grease monkeys," 38, **157**
lubritoriums, 156–57, **159**
Lynd, Robert Staughton and Helen Merell Lynd, 233n30

Mac, Alle, 102–4
machine shops, xvi, 10, 21, **22**, 186
Manchester, NH: Jenny Service Station, **57**
Marmon Motor Co., 106–7
Marr, Elsie D., 105
Maxwell Motor Co., 96, 104
Mc Claren Tires, **168**
Mc Intyre, Stephen L., 147
Melvin, J. B., 84
Memphis, TN, 158
Mersohn and Morley Co., 124
Metal Shelter Co., 124
Midas, Inc., 151
Milwaukee, WI: Storage Battery Service Co., **165**; Philip Gross Hardware Co., 183–84, **185**
Minneapolis, Mn, 207
modernity and modernization, 43, 51, 54, 64–69, 121; "machine aesthetic" as, 40

Morfitt, Neil Lewis, 114
Montgomery Ward & Co., 61
Moroney, A.S., 90
Morrison, L., 217–18
motels, xi, xv, 208
motor cycles, 23
motoring, 2, 10, 20, 24, 43, 54, 102, 139, 208; annual cost of, 7, 9–10, **44**, 58, 64; mechanical problems in, 3, 11, 142; preparations for, 143
Motor World: Department of Better Business Buildings, 36
Morgan, L.A., 200–201
Moyer, W.A., 178
Muffler and tailpipe repair and sales, 173

Nash, C.W., 4–6
Nash-Kelvinator Corp., 70
Nashville, TN, xiv
National Assoc. of Automobile Manufacturers, 78
National Automobile Dealers Assoc. (NADA), 88–89, 93, 109,195, 199
National Automotive Parts Assoc. (NAPA), 185
National Register of Historic Preservation, 217–18
Nebraska Buick Co., 86
Newark, NJ, 179
New Departure Manufacturing Co., 182
New Urbanism, 138–39
New York City, NY, 11, 21, 31, 48–49, 83–84, 93, 95, **96**, 130, 137, 142, 150, 159, 164, 181, 194–95; Automobile Exchange & Supply Co., **12**; Bank Brothers Garage, 142; Holman & Schulz Garage, 11; Times Square Automobile Co., 186, **187**; Tunnel Garage, 252n46
New York Garage Association, 194
New York World's Fair, 1939, 150, 157

INDEX

Olds, Ransom, 22, 85
Omaha, NE, 48, 156, 176; Farnam Ford Repair Garage, **164**; Wm. Pfeiffer Auto & Carriage Works, 176
"one-stop service," 58, 73
Opitz, John and Paul, 146–47
Oshkosh, WI, 81
Oxnard, CA, 97

Packard Motor Car Co., 70, 145
Parker, James, 95–97, 99
parking lots and garages, xi–xii, 9–12, **13**, 14–15, 26, 49, 51, 68–69, 72–73, 79, 131, 133, 137, 146
Parry Auto Co., 26
Pasadena, CA, 107
Patterson Automobile Co., 26
Patterson, NJ: City Hall Garage, **33**
Pawnee County, KS, 7
Peckham, G.G.C., 81–82
Pella, IA: Pella Motor Co., 110
Penske Automotive Group, 205
Peoria, IL, 63; Auto Parts Service Station, 198; Crown Garage, 202
Perlman Rim Corp., 182
Petersburg, IL: Knous Garage, 219–20, **221**
petroleum industry, 17, 45, 54, 55–58, 60, 64, 66, 211
Philadelphia Automobile Trade Assoc., 109
Philadelphia Garage Owners Assoc., 195
Philadelphia, PA, 45, 109–10, 142, 159, 162, 195–96; American Garage & Machine Shop, 45; Lacy L. Redd & Co. Garage, **165**; Progressive Tire & Rubber Store, **168**
Phillips Petroleum Co., 218
Pierce-Arrow Motor Car Co., 30, **31**, **32**
Pittsburgh, PA, 198; McGurdy-May Pierce-Arrow, 30, **31**, **32**
place-product-packaging, 43–44, 56, 65, 211
Platt, Warren C., 57–58
Pompano Beach, Fl: Pompano Ford, 206
Pope, Albert, 22, 84
Portland, Me, 138

Poughkeepsie, NY: John King Auto Supply, 178–79
Powhatan, Va, 207
prefabrication in garage construction, xii, 31, 40 123–24, **125**
programming garage space, 27, 36, **37**, 38, **39**, 40–41
Pure Oil Co., 60, **61**, 64
Puritan Auto Parts Co., 186

Racine, WI, 172
Radford Architectural Co., 119, **120**, **121**, 122–23, 127
Radford, William, A., 119
radiator repair, 173, **175**
radiator repair and radiator shops, 9–10
railroads, 1, 3, 16, 90, 91, 196
Remy Electric Co., 182
Reo Motor Co., 21
Riceville, PA: Riceville Ford Garage, 35
Richfield Company, 56, 60
Richmond, VA, 205
Roadside America, xi, 189, 208–11
Roberts, Elmer, 17
Robey, Gary, 216
Rochester, NY, 153
roof truses in garage construction, xiii, **xiv**, 11, **13**, 31–32, 50
Rock Island, IL, 172
Route 66, 209
Rutland, VT, 21: Rutland Carriage Co./ Rutland Machine and Automobile Co., 21, **23**

Saginaw, MI, 124
St. Charles, MO: Travis GMC, 89
St. Louis, M., 3; St. Louis Automobile & Supply Co., 183
St. Paul, MN, 124
Salesmanship, 77, 95–100; deal closing in, 99–100

Salt Lake City, UT: White Garage, 82
San Antonio, TX: Wroten-Hundley Motor Co., 112–13
San Diego, CA, 184
San Francisco, CA, 137, 164
Santa Monica, CA, 131
Sarasota, FL, 208
Savannah, GA: Jacob's Detroit Electric Service Station, 159, **163**
Sears, Roebuck & Co., 60–61
Seattle, WA, 83, 105
Selzer, Lawrence, 234n30
Shelbyville, TN: Hotel Dixie, **48**; Smith Garage, **48**
shock absorber and spring repair, 3, 17, 169, 172, **174**
shopping center and shopping malls, xv
Simmons-Boardman Co., **124**
Sinclair Refining Co., 157
Sloan, Alfred P., Jr., 66, 87–88, 233n30
small-town "Main Streets," xiv, ii, **16**, 23, 25, 47, 53
South Bend, IN, 20, 166, 220
specialization and departmentalization, xvi, 37, **38**, 149–87
Spencer, IA, 116
Sperry, R. S., 154
Springfield, TN: 638 Garage, xiv, **xv**, 217
Spokane, WA: Eldridge Buick Co., 83, **84**
standardized garage plans, 31–32, **34**, **35**, **36**, 39, 74
Standard Oil Co. of California, 58, 60
Standard Oil Co. of Indiana, **15**, 55, 58, **66**, **155**, 157
Standard Oil Co. of New York, 55, **57**, 194
Standard Oil Co. of Ohio, 57
Stanley Motor Carriage Co., 4, 15, 48
steam automobiles, 4, 12, 15, 17, 112, 159
"sticker prices," 90
Studebaker Corp., 20, 93, 113–14, 220
Suburbs and suburbanization, xv, 4, 45, 69–70, 132, 138, 209, 219
Superior Lamp Co., 181

Table Grove, IL: Ulmer;s Garage, 203, **204**
Tarrytown, NY: Old Post Road Garage, 27–28, **29**
Taylor, W. H., 97–99
Temple, Ralph, 85
Terre Haute, IN, 78
Teufel, John, 18
Teutopolis, IL: Thoele's Garage, **193**, 194
Texas Company, 151
Thoele, Albert and Mort, 193
Tipper, Harry, 79, 234n30
tires, batteries and acessories (TBA), xii, xvi, 7–9, 58, 66
tire repairs and sales, xvi, 3, 9–10, 38, 56, 58, 63, 75, 105, 150, 167–73, 186–87, 198, 201, 215
tire stores, xii, xiv, **xv**, 9, 35, 61, 82, **168**, **169**, **170**, **171**, **172**
Toledo, OH, 22, 100, 162, 175
trade journals, 13, 24, 28, 34–36, 38, 41, 82, 110, 133, 135, 143, 192, 194, 200
trailers, 21, 91
Travis, J. E., Jr., 89
Trenton, IL, **xiv**
Trenton, NJ: Brock's Garage, 26, **28**
trucks and truck dealers, xi, 9, 17, 32, **33**, 41, 68, 91–92, 260, 196, 198, 215
tune-ups and light engine repairs, xiii, xvi, 60, 65, **165**, **166**, 167

Ulmer, Duane, 203, **204**
Underwriters Laboratory, 127
Union Oil Co., 58, 60
United Motors Co. (United Motors Service), 182, **184**
United States Rubber Co., 167, 169, **170**
used car lots and showrooms, 9, 36, 85, 98, 108–10, **111**, 112, **113**, 114, 143, 181, 199
U.S Bureau of the Census, 9–10, 24
U.S. Department of Commerce: Building Code Committee, 127
U.S. Federal Housing Administration (FHA), 67, 131–32
U.S. Office of Price Administration, 198

Vac Liquid Equipment Co, **152**
vulcanizing, 5, 7, 21, 63

Wagoner, Peter, 214
Warren-Detroit Motor Co., 26
Washington, DC, 195
West Allis, WI, 193
West Chester, PA: William Wood's Garage, 26, **27**
Western Auto Supply Co., 185
Western Oil Refining Co., 156
wheel, axle, and spring repair shops, 10
Whitehall, MI, 207
White Motor Car Co., 35, **82**
Whiting Motor Co., 26
Wilder, Thomas, 38

Williams, W. E., 7
Willys, John N., 22
Willy-Overland Motor Car Co., 29, **30**, 70, 84, 162, 164, 186
Winton Motor Carriage Co., 15, 142
Woolson, Ira H., 127
World War I, 5, 53m 81, 85, 88, 95, 101–2, 111, 118, 141, 143, 158, 185, 196, 202, 215
World War II, xii, 67, 70, 89, 95, **101**, 114, 126, 131–32, 185, 195–96, **197**, 198–200, 203, 215
WSIX, xiv
Wyatt, Olpha and family, **xii**, 214–16
Wycoff Lumber & Manufacturing Co., 124
Wyoming, PA, 110–11

Young Men's Christian Assoc., 142

www.ingramcontent.com/pod-product-compliance
Lightning Source LLC
Chambersburg PA
CBHW030309080526
44584CB00012B/504